Lincoln
of
Kentucky

Lincoln
of *Kentucky*

Lowell H. Harrison

THE UNIVERSITY PRESS OF KENTUCKY

Publication of this volume was made possible in part by
a grant from the National Endowment for the Humanities.

Scholarly publisher for the Commonwealth,
serving Bellarmine College, Berea College, Centre
College of Kentucky, Eastern Kentucky University,
The Filson Club Historical Society, Georgetown College,
Kentucky Historical Society, Kentucky State University,
Morehead State University, Murray State University,
Northern Kentucky University, Transylvania University,
University of Kentucky, University of Louisville,
and Western Kentucky University.

Editorial and Sales Offices: The University Press of Kentucky
663 South Limestone Street, Lexington, Kentucky 40508–4008

04 03 02 01 00   5 4 3 2 1

Library of Congress Cataloging-in-Publication Data

Harrison, Lowell Hayes, 1922-
    Lincoln of Kentucky / Lowell H. Harrison
        p. cm.
    Includes bibliographical references and index.
    ISBN 0-8131-2156-6 (cloth : alk. paper)
        1. Lincoln, Abraham, 1809-1865—Miscellanea. 2. Kentucky—
History—19th century—Miscellanea. 3. Lincoln, Abraham,
1809-1865—Views on slavery. 4. Slavery—Kentucky—History—
19th century. 5. Kentucky—History—Civil War, 1861-1865.
I. Title.
E457.2.H34   2000
973.7'092—dc21   99-048123

This book is printed on acid-free recycled paper
meeting the requirements of the American National Standard
for Permanence of Paper for Printed Library Materials.

Manufactured in the United States of America

Contents

Illustrations follow page 150

Preface

Although Abraham Lincoln left his native Kentucky before his eighth birthday and returned for only a few visits during the rest of his life, he had numerous ties with the state. Thousands of Kentuckians other than the Lincolns had crossed the Ohio River by the early nineteenth century, and in Indiana and Illinois Lincoln had frequent contacts with many of them. His three law partners were all Kentuckians, and so were the three women with whom he had more or less romantic attachments, including Mary Todd, whom he married. Henry Clay was his political idol; George Prentice's *Louisville Journal* was one of his favorite newspapers; Joshua Speed of Farmington was his best friend.

The Kentucky connections were especially important during the Civil War. Kentucky was often seen as the bellwether of the four slave states that remained in the Union. When Kentucky, divided in sentiment over the crisis, declared neutrality in the spring of 1861, the president accepted that unique status until the Unionists were able to secure firm control of the state. Two major Confederate invasions of the state in 1861 and 1862 focused military attention on the commonwealth, and during the rest of the war occasional Confederate raids and frequent clashes between civilian and military authorities created problems that were referred to President Lincoln.

Lincoln thought it essential that the four slave states in the Union adopt some scheme of compensated emancipation, and he made repeated but futile efforts to persuade his native state to lead the way. His relationship with Kentucky during the war years was important for him, the state, and the nation. A Kentuckian could be loyal to the Union but bitterly opposed to many of Lincoln's policies, and that stance helps explain why after the war Kentucky became a part of the Solid South for many years. When the president was assassinated on April 14, 1865, the Civil War was coming to an end, and the Thirteenth Amendment, which ended slavery, was in the process of ratification. Lincoln knew that he had been successful in preserving the Union and ending slavery.

This study is neither a biography of Abraham Lincoln nor a history of the Civil War in Kentucky. It describes the interrelationship between Lincoln and Kentucky throughout his life, with emphasis on the Civil War years, particularly the skill with which he dealt with problems encountered in a loyal slave state in which a sizable minority of the people were pro-Confederate. With his understanding of Kentucky and Kentuckians, President Lincoln kept the state of his birth in the Union. Although more than four thousand books have been written about Lincoln, only two deal specifically with the general Lincoln-Kentucky connections: William H. Townsend, *Lincoln and His Wife's Home Town* (1930) and its revised version, *Lincoln and the Bluegrass: Slavery and the Civil War in Kentucky* (1955, 1989). Mr. Townsend was an attorney who loved history, and much of his life was spent collecting, studying, and writing. A great raconteur, he would sometimes sacrifice a little historical accuracy in favor of a good story. My study is broader in scope than his books, and I have had the advantage of access to much research on both the man and the war that was not available to Mr. Townsend.

The studies of Abraham Lincoln are so voluminous that simply listing their bibliographical details would fill several volumes. I have tried to remain focused on the topic "Lincoln of Kentucky," without straying off onto interesting bypaths. And I have endeavored to avoid the fascinating but often inaccurate legends that have become associated with this son of Kentucky who overcame many handicaps to become the nation's greatest president. Some Kentuckians who objected to his policies were slow to admit his greatness, but now there are few who contest it.

Prior to this study, suggested to me by Kenneth Cherry, director of the University Press of Kentucky, I had published a few articles dealing with Lincoln. Much of my research and writing on Kentucky subjects provided invaluable background for this undertaking. In particular, *The Civil War in Kentucky* (1975, 1988), *The Antislavery Movement in Kentucky* (1978), and my portion of *A New History of Kentucky* (1997), with James C. Klotter, helped prepare me for this project.

I owe grateful thanks to the librarians and archivists in many locations who have assisted my research during the last half century. Especially helpful during my recent search for Kentucky reactions to Lincoln were James J. Holmberg and James T. Kirkwood of the Filson Club, James M. Prichard of the Kentucky Department for Libraries and Archives in Frankfort, Lynne Hollingsworth of the Kentucky Historical Society, and William J. Marshall, Claire McCann, and Lisa Carter of Special Collections, University of Kentucky. The Library Special Collections, Western Kentucky University, has a good basic collection of Lincoln materials and Civil War sources, and much of my research for this book was done there. Nancy D. Baird, Patricia M. Hodges, Jonathan D. Jeffrey, Constance Ann Mills, and Sue Lynn Stone have once again gone far beyond just being helpful. They, Carol Crowe-Carraco, Marion B. Lucas, and the anonymous readers for the University Press of Kentucky, gave the manuscript critical readings. I am grateful for their help. Debra Gale Day and Alan Scott Logsdon of the Helms-Cravens Library at Western Kentucky University gave every assistance in finding needed sources.

Once again, my wife, Elaine "Penny" Harrison, has endured the agonies that go with my writing a manuscript. Her careful reading has saved me from many errors. And again, Elizabeth Jensen, once an incomparable departmental secretary, found time from her teaching to shift the manuscript from my type-script to the computer.

Lincoln in
Kentucky's Memory

President Abraham Lincoln spent part of April 14, 1865, consulting with his cabinet on ways to restore the Southern states to their rightful place in the Union as quickly as possible. Although only Robert E. Lee's Army of Northern Virginia had surrendered by then, the long war was practically over. Lincoln remarked that it would be good "to reanimate the States and get their governments in successful operation, before Congress came together in December." Some members of Congress had "feelings of hate and vindictiveness," which he could not agree with or accept.[1]

Most of the day was filled with the routine tasks that had taken so much of his time since 1861: appointments, petitions, papers to be signed, patronage requests to be considered. Those who saw him that day commented that though he had been exhausted by the long travail of the war, his mood and appearance had been greatly improved by the welcome news from Virginia. He quit work about three o'clock to take a carriage ride with Mary around the city and out to the Naval Yard, where he visited the *Montaur* and talked with some of the crew. When his wife commented on his unusual cheerfulness, he replied that he considered the war as having ended that day. Then in a mild rebuke to Mary, Lincoln added, "We must *both*, be more cheerful in the future—between the war and the loss of our darling Willie—we have both been very miserable." They discussed a trip to Europe after his term ended; he suggested that they might consider a move to California.

When they returned to the White House, Lincoln had a lengthy visit with Illinois governor Richard J. Oglesby and Gen. Isham N. Haynie. Because he read them four chapters of Petroleum V. Nasby's *Nasby Papers,* the president was late to dinner; it was served early because the Lincolns had promised to attend the performance of the comedy *Our American Cousin.* Mary, saying that she had a headache, suggested that they not go to the theater, but Lincoln overruled her. The papers had announced their intent to attend, and tickets had been sold on that basis. Besides, he added, if he remained in the White House, he would be besieged by visitors all evening. As they started to enter the carriage, Congressman Isaac N. Arnold approached, but the president waved him off: "I am going to the theatre. Come and see me in the morning."[2]

The faithful Ward Hill Lamon, who had appointed himself as the bodyguard of the president-elect, had gone to Richmond on a presidential mission. Before leaving he begged Lincoln not to go out at night while he was gone, especially not to a crowded theater. Secretary of War Edwin M. Stanton had often warned the president of the danger of attending the theater. When Lincoln invited the Stantons to join them that evening, Stanton repeated his warning as he declined the invitation. Gen. U.S. Grant accepted an invitation to attend the play but then asked to be excused so that he and Mrs. Grant could visit their children in New Jersey. Both Mrs. Stanton and Mrs. Grant disliked Mary Todd Lincoln. Mrs. Grant remembered vividly the hysterical scene Mrs. Lincoln had created a few days earlier at City Point when she had publicly accused Mrs. Ord of flirting with the president and demanded that Gen. O.C. Ord be removed from his command. Neither lady had any desire to be in the presidential box with a person of such uncertain temperament. Governor Oglesby and General Haynie had a previous engagement, and, for various reasons, several others also declined an invitation. In the end, the Lincolns were accompanied by a young couple, Maj. Henry R. Rathbone and his stepsister (also his fiancée), Clara Harris, daughter of New York senator Ira Harris.[3]

The party arrived after the play had started, but the audience rose and cheered as the orchestra played "Hail to the Chief." Lincoln stepped to the front of the box and bowed to the audience, then sat in the rocking chair that the management had thoughtfully provided. Once they were seated, the members of the presidential party were almost invisible to the audience except when they leaned forward. Mary was nestled close to Lincoln, and she whispered, "What will Miss Harris think of my hanging on to you so?" Lincoln smiled: "She won't think anything about it."[4] No one noticed that a small hole had been bored in the door to the box and that some plaster had been chipped away so that a prop could be used to block the door to the box. Police officer John F. Parker, who had been assigned to guard the president, went off to find a spot from which he could watch the play.

John Wilkes Booth, a twenty-six-year-old Marylander, was a handsome member of a notable family of actors. He had gained public acclaim from Southern audiences, and he held strong proslavery views. Booth saw the South as being destroyed by radical Republicans, and he was openly contemptuous of President Lincoln. By the late summer of 1864, Booth had become convinced that he must rid the nation of Lincoln in order to save the South. After consulting with some Confederate agents in the North (there is no proof that Confederate leaders were aware of his scheme), Booth plotted to kidnap Lincoln, carry him behind Confederate lines, and hold him hostage for the release of Confederate prisoners of war. Booth enlisted several associates in his plan, and he left with a brother-in-law a long letter explaining his reasons for taking action. When the kidnaping plot was abandoned, the actor turned to assassination. As the Confederacy collapsed in the spring of 1865, Booth was left on his own except for a few recruits. On April 11, listening to Lincoln speak outside the White House,

Booth swore, "That is the last speech he will ever make."[5] Somehow, he convinced himself that the Confederacy could yet be saved if Lincoln, Vice President Andrew Johnson, and Secretary of State William H. Seward were all killed. Some of Booth's followers deserted him at that point, but when he learned that Lincoln was expected to attend Ford's Theatre on April 14, he decided to carry out the assassination at 10:15 that evening. In his diary Booth wrote that Lincoln was responsible for all the nation's troubles: "God simply made me the instrument of his punishment."[6]

Familiar with Ford Theatre, Booth slipped upstairs behind the dress circle. Charles Forbes, a White House footman, admitted the assassin to the presidential box when Booth showed him a calling card. Moving quietly, Booth barred the door with a piece of a music stand. Drawing a six-inch single-shot derringer and a 7¼-inch knife from his coat, he stepped up behind the president, who was intent on the play. At about 10:13 Booth shot Lincoln behind the left ear.

Major Rathbone turned at the sound and, although unarmed, attempted to seize Booth. The actor broke free and slashed the major's left arm with a wound several inches deep and an inch and a half long. Then Booth vaulted over the railing onto the stage as Rathbone again failed to hold him. "Stop that man!" Rathbone shouted. Booth's spur caught in the flags decorating the box, and he fell awkwardly, breaking a bone in his left leg just above the ankle. Waving his knife, he shouted "*Sic semper Tyrannis!*" (Thus always to tyrants) and limped off the stage.

The audience, at first stunned and puzzled, began to realize what had happened, cued by Mrs. Lincoln's screams: "They have shot the President! They have shot the President!" Some apprehensive playgoers began to leave the auditorium. Others rushed to the presidential box, only to find the door wedged shut. Bleeding profusely from his wound, Major Rathbone managed to dislodge the piece of wood with which Booth had blocked the entrance. Dr. Charles A. Leale, a twenty-three-year-old army surgeon, was the first person to enter the box. He was closely followed by Dr. Albert F.A. King, a local physician, and William Kent, a government employee. Rathbone saw Lt. Alexander M. Crawford in the crowd and asked him to prevent others from entering the packed box. But William H. Flood, acting ensign of the steamer *Primrose*, who as a boy had known Lincoln in Illinois and who had talked with him that afternoon, scrambled up into the box from the stage with the help of Miss Harris. He was soon followed by Dr. Charles Sabin Taft, an army surgeon in Georgetown, who responded to the cries for a doctor and was lifted from the stage by members of the audience.

Leale thought that the president had been stabbed; but after Lincoln was stretched out on the floor, he saw evidence of brain damage by examining the eyes. Finding only a faint pulse, Leale and others applied artificial respiration and stimulated the heart. The heart action improved and the president breathed independently. But Leale saw that recovery was impossible. "His wound is mortal," the young doctor said. "It is impossible for him to recover." Miss Laura Keene, one of the leads in *Our American Cousin*, appeared with a pitcher of water. According to some reports, she sat on the floor and cradled Lincoln's head in her lap.

Agreeing that the dying man could not survive a rough ride back to the White House, the doctors decided to have him carried across the street to a house owned by William Petersen, a merchant-tailor. With considerable difficulty, a way was cleared through the large crowd, and four soldiers from the audience carried their commander-in-chief carefully to a room rented by an army clerk who was away at the time. The room was only nine and a half by seventeen feet, and the bed was so short that the president had to be placed diagonally across it. His head rested on extra pillows, and he was covered by an army blanket and a wool coverlet. Hot water bottles were applied as his hands and feet became cold.

The Lincoln family physician, Dr. Robert K. Stone, became

the doctor in charge after he arrived about eleven o'clock. He consulted with Surgeon General Joseph K. Barnes, and Drs. Leale and Taft remained in the room. Many offers of help came from other medical men in the city. All of them who saw the president agreed that recovery was impossible; an ordinary man without Lincoln's great strength would have died sometime earlier.[7]

Mary Lincoln came across the street with Miss Harris and Major Rathbone, whose severe wound had been bleeding profusely for some twenty minutes. When he fainted in the hallway of the Petersen house, Miss Harris probably saved his life by tying a handkerchief tightly over the wound and stanching the flow of blood. The doctor who examined him after he was carried to the Harris home said that if the wound had been one-third of an inch to the side, Rathbone would have bled to death in five minutes.[8]

Mrs. Lincoln rushed into the room where her husband lay and fell to her knees by his bedside, sobbing and pleading with him to speak to her. The doctors persuaded her to go to the parlor so they could examine the president to see if there were any other wounds. There her son Robert, Mrs. Elizabeth Dixon, and the Reverend Phineas D. Gurley attempted to soothe and comfort her. From time to time she would become alarmed and rush into the bedroom.

Stanton and Secretary of the Navy Gideon Welles were the first cabinet members to arrive, shortly after eleven. They had been at the home of Secretary Seward, who had been attacked by Lewis Paine, one of Booth's accomplices. The powerful Paine had stabbed Seward, who was in bed because of a serious carriage accident, three times before being driven off. Paine also wounded four others, including Seward's son, who tried to apprehend him. Alarmed by the assassination attempts and uncertain of just what was happening, Stanton sat at a table in the back parlor of the Petersen house and calmly issued orders to deal with the crisis. Vice President Johnson was informed that the president was dying; Chief Justice Salmon P. Chase was alerted to be ready to administer the oath of office to Johnson; a search was begun for the assassins; and civil and military authorities were alerted to deal with any emergencies that might develop. Roads and bridges were closed, and testimony was taken from witnesses who had seen the attacks. By noon several of the coconspirators had been arrested. Booth had fled from Washington before the dragnet was in place, eluding capture until April 26, when he was found and killed on a farm in northern Virginia.[9]

By six o'clock on the morning of April 15, Lincoln's pulse was fading and his respiration was becoming more difficult. Mrs. Lincoln was called back into the room before seven o'clock. Alarmed by his deteriorating condition, she fainted. Revived, she kissed him, called him endearing names, implored him to speak to her once more, to live for the children. Alarmed by his labored breathing, she "sprang up suddenly with a piercing cry and fell fainting to the floor." Stanton came in from an adjoining room, surveyed the situation, and commanded: "Take that woman out, and do not let her in again!"

Lincoln's death struggle began soon after seven o'clock. Son Robert stood by the head of the bed, weeping on the shoulder of Sen. Charles Sumner. Dr. Leake continued to hold Lincoln's hand, his finger on the fading pulse; Dr. Barnes had a finger on the carotid artery. Abraham Lincoln drew his last breath at 7:21:55; his heart ceased beating at 7:22:10.[10]

After several moments of hushed silence, Stanton asked the Reverend Dr. Gurley, "Doctor, will you say anything?" And Gurley prayed that the whole nation would become more united in their devotion to the cause of their beloved, imperiled country. When he closed, there was a spontaneous "Amen" from those in the crowded room. Then Stanton, who had often disagreed with Lincoln but had served him and the country well, said as tears coursed down his cheeks, "Now he belongs to the ages."[11]

As the image of Lincoln was enhanced during the years following his death, many places sought to claim at least a part of him as a vital component of their and the nation's heritage. Washington was an obvious claimant, for it was there that Lincoln had achieved greatness as he guided the United States through its greatest crisis and directed an end to the national disgrace of human slavery. There he had lived during the shortened term of his presidency, and there he had died a tragic death. After the great Lincoln Memorial was dedicated in 1922, the Lincoln statue by Daniel Chester French became one of the most beloved likenesses of Lincoln. Seated on a chair, looking out over a part of the city, Lincoln seemed an integral part of the nation's capital.

But the people in Springfield, Illinois, pointed to the longer years that he had lived among them and the work that he had done to transfer the state capitol there. The president-elect had not planned to say anything on the morning of February 11, 1861, when he began the circuitous trip that took him to Washington and his inauguration as president. But a thousand people had gathered at the Great Western depot to bid him farewell, and when he left the waiting room to board the train, he could not deny their request.

> My friends—No one, not in my situation, can appreciate my feeling of sadness at this parting. To this place, and the kindness of these people, I owe every thing. Here I have lived a quarter of a century, and have passed from a young to an old man. Here my children have been born, and one is buried. I now leave, not knowing when, or whether ever, I may return, with a task before me greater than that which rested upon Washington. Without the assistance of that Divine Being, who ever attended him, I cannot succeed. With that assistance I cannot fail. Trusting in Him, who can go with me and remain with you and be every where for good, let us confidently hope that all will yet be well. To His care commending you, as I hope in your prayers you will commend me, I bid you an affectionate farewell.[12]

On Sunday, the day before his departure, Lincoln had paid a final visit to his law office, where he reminisced with Billy Herndon about the sixteen years during which they had been partners. As they left the office, Lincoln looked back at the "Lincoln and Herndon" sign that hung outside the building. Leave it as it is, Lincoln insisted; the partnership was not ending just because he had been elected president. "If I live, I'm coming back some time, and then we'll go right on practicing law as if nothing had ever happened."[13] Mary insisted that he be buried in Springfield, and her will prevailed.

The few people in the New Salem, Illinois, area pushed their claims to Lincoln, for he had lived there from 1831 to the spring of 1837, a gangling youth maturing into a man who had earned the respect of the community. With the assistance of friends, he had embarked upon the program of self-improvement that had made possible his later successes. There he had become enthralled with politics and had become a Whig as that national party emerged. There he had lost his first bid for political office, and there a failing store had left him with what he called a "national debt," which in time he paid off. There he had been elected captain of a militia company during the Black Hawk War, an indication of respect and affection that was one of his proudest achievements. There with intense study he had mastered enough law to secure his license in 1836 to practice in that profession. Surely, New Salem and its people had some claim to Lincoln.[14]

Southern Indiana also had a claim to him, for his home had been there from December 1816, when Thomas Lincoln moved his family from Kentucky to the Pigeon Creek community, until the family migrated to Illinois in 1830. During those years the youth had attained most of his growth and had become a strong man. There he had completed the last of his meager formal education, and there he had become aware of what could be accomplished with reading and individual study.[15]

Many Kentuckians who were loyal to the Union opposed

President Lincoln and his administration during the Civil War. Even in 1864, when he was elected to a second term, a large majority of Kentuckians voted for his opponent, former general George B. McClellan. Nonetheless, most Kentuckians were shocked by the death of the president to whom they had refused full support.

The Reverend William M. Pratt of Lexington wrote in his diary on April 17, 1865: "Never was my moral sense so shocked nor did greater gloom fill my mind. Lizzie, only 10 years old went out by herself & cried as if her heart was broke. . . . Like Moses he caught a glorious glimpse of a restored country & was taken away."[16] Gen. John M. Palmer, the military commander in the state, called for calm on April 15. "Let the people of Kentucky disappoint the miscreants who would involve them in bloodshed and strife, by conducting themselves with calmness and moderation. Avoid all heated conversations and imprudent expressions. Let all unite in every means for preserving order. The wicked need not rejoice nor the patriotic despond. The Government will still go on, and as great as the calamity is, the country will accomplish its high destiny."[17] The *Frankfort Commonwealth* carried Palmer's message on April 18 and added, "His counsels to moderation and forbearance in view of the terrible wrong inflicted upon our land will commend themselves to every loyal man."

Gov. Thomas E. Bramlette had often disagreed with the president on policy matters, but he paid Lincoln a gracious tribute in a proclamation issued on April 17. "He has fallen at a time when his great qualities of humanity were so hopefully invoked for the healing of our National woes! With no stain of vindictive nature upon his soul—with a great heart of generous sympathies and broad humanities—his untimely fall has bowed a Nation's head in mourning." At noon on Wednesday, April 19, Bramlette continued, "Let every church bell be tolled throughout the Commonwealth; and on that day let all business be suspended and all business houses be closed, the public offices closed, and draped in mourning." He invited

Kentuckians "to pay that homage to the National grief which such a great calamity inspires."[18]

When Bramlette spoke at a Louisville mass meeting on April 18, he made a handsome apology for his and Kentucky's frequent disagreements with President Lincoln. "We may differ with him, and have differed with him, but when the judgment of future events has come, we found we were differing blindly; that he was right and we were wrong. Standing as we did in local positions, surrounded as we were by local prejudices, he occupied an elevated stand-point and viewed the whole political surroundings of the country." Looking toward the future, Bramlette predicted accurately that "the name and cause of Mr. Lincoln will go down to future ages as part of the record of our country. . . . His course has been marked by the honest purposes of preserving the institutions of our country—to preserve all that is worth preserving and that could possibly be preserved from the wreck of this revolution. We cannot deny, fellow citizens, that a revolution has swept over our country. . . . [E]xperience and time has demonstrated that his was the only line of salvation for our country."[19]

Louisville mayor William Kaye asked citizens to put aside partisan feelings and consider "this event in its true light as a great national calamity." He called for a great public meeting on the evening of April 18 to express grief. The Committee on Resolutions told the large audience that day, "We have seen a man born in the lowliest, rise and grow in the affections of the people, and finally called by them to the loftiest position in human affairs. . . . The people soon learned to trust him with a boundless confidence, and as the map of grand, startling events gradually unrolled, the popular mind felt that 'the pilot who could weather the storm' was at the helm." His administration during the past four years had given people confidence "in that which constitutes the corner-stone of representative institutions—the capacity of the people to govern themselves." Lincoln's purpose had been unselfish, and he had brought the nation to the heights of relief and joy that the war was won.[20]

In its April 18 issue the *Frankfort Commonwealth* declared that "a good man has fallen, a true and pure patriot; a President who has done his duty well, with a conscience void of offense toward God and man, and who had ruled his people as a loving father, always tempering justice with mercy and always ready to succor and forgive." He had no hatred of the rebellious states, no desire for revenge; he simply wanted to draw them back to the old allegiances. "When Abraham Lincoln died, the South lost its best and truest friend."

"Mr. Lincoln, according to the estimate of all who knew him, and especially of those who have ever had occasion to appeal to his clemency, was an amiable, genial, kind-hearted man," the *Lexington Observer and Reporter* commented in its April 19 issue. "If he had personal enemies we were not aware of it; and however much men may have differed with him in regard to the policy pursued during his eventful administration, no one felt toward him the slightest animosity." Because of war issues, this paper had often been critical of this "man of remarkable mental endowments" who "possessed many excellencies of character." It was a sad day when he fell by the hands of an assassin.

The Kentucky General Assembly, called into a special session, created a joint committee on May 20 to draft appropriate resolutions. Presented on May 26, the resolutions noted the difficult times in which Lincoln had served and said that he had "exhibited high qualities of honesty, clemency, patriotism, and ability." But Kentucky, historian Willard R. Jillson wrote many years later,

> was slow, very slow, to accept Lincoln, her greatest son. She was reluctant and unwilling to appreciate, to understand him while he lived. The profound contradictions of his personality and his career were large enigmic [*sic*] to his own people during his brief life span. Only when the Angel of Death, holding the assassins's hand had taken him suddenly, his life work

ended— . . . were the bandages of sectional prejudice and misunderstanding torn from the eyes of the people of Kentucky to reveal Lincoln towering in simple greatness above the strife of the battlefield and forum, the man of men, America's supreme gift to the unfolding, liberty-loving civilization of the world.[21]

Lincoln's tragic end accounted for some of the belated praise bestowed upon him in his native state, but his death seems to have made many of his political opponents reconsider their opposition to him and the odious insults that some of them had lavished upon the late president. It was the beginning of a reevaluation of Lincoln by Kentuckians; they would finally pay thankful homage to their native son.

At first, however, not all Kentuckians shared the sorrow and the belated recognition of Lincoln's contributions that were expressed in newspapers and civic resolutions. Negative feelings and comments were best concealed from the public during the period of mourning, but it was observed that some businesses did not close in respect of the late president, and some buildings were not shrouded in mourning colors.[22]

Wartime animosities died slowly, but gradually Kentuckians began to take pride in the native son who had gained recognition as one of the nation's greatest presidents. It was true that Lincoln had lived in the commonwealth for less than eight years, but did he not carry that Kentucky influence throughout his life? The Jesuits were reputed to claim that if they had a child for the first seven years, he was always theirs; if that was so, then a part of Lincoln was always Kentucky.[23] In time Kentucky would raise monuments to the man who left the state as a lad, then married a Kentucky girl and achieved national and international fame and honor. The most significant of the tributes was the memorial established at the Sinking Spring site of Lincoln's birth.

In 1894 New Yorker Alfred W. Dennett purchased the 110-acre Sinking Spring farm with the intent of making it into a memorial park. He also purchased from Jack A. Davenport, a local man, a log cabin that, according to oral tradition, was the one in which Lincoln had been born; it had been removed in 1861. Reassembled on the original site, the cabin was soon disassembled and sent to Nashville for an exhibition. Nine years later the logs were returned to the farm. Dennett's dreams were not realized, and in 1905 the farm was advertised to be sold for taxes. Richard Lloyd Jones, a young journalist who became interested in the historical worth of the farm, persuaded his father, Jenkin Lloyd Jones, to visit the site. The senior Jones had already founded the Abraham Lincoln Center in Chicago, and upon his return from Hodgenville he wrote "The Neglected Shrine" for his Unitarian paper, *Unity.* Young Jones also interested Robert J. Collier, editor of *Collier's Weekly,* in the homesite, and Collier agreed to bid for the property. Jones later claimed that the night before the auction, he spent the evening in Elizabethtown getting two other serious rivals drunk. Jones, acting for Collier, had no serious opposition at the sale, and for $3,600 he purchased the property. Collier announced that ultimately he would give the property to the nation as a Lincoln memorial. He and others formed the Lincoln Farm Association, and Joseph W. Folk, a former governor of Missouri, headed a fund-raising drive. Some seventy thousand persons, most of them from out of state, became members by contributing as little as twenty-five cents. The only large gift was $25,000, donated by Mrs. Russell Sage. *Collier's Weekly* continued to provide valuable support for the project.[24]

John Russell Pope won the design competition for the memorial. Instead of trying to depict aspects of Lincoln's career, Pope decided to enclose the birth cabin in a replica of a Greek temple. Fifty-six steps, one for each year of Lincoln's life, would lead to the entrance of the temple. Inside was the cabin, slightly reduced in size from the original sixteen by eighteen feet. It was built from the oak logs located on Long Island, New York, that were said to be from the cabin in which Lincoln was born. It is believed that at least some of the logs had been in the original structure. Congress appropriated $50,000 in 1908, and President Theodore Roosevelt spoke at the laying of the cornerstone on the rainy February 12, 1909. In November 1911 President William Howard Taft dedicated the birthplace memorial for the nation. In 1916 the Lincoln Farm Association relinquished custody of the property, and President Woodrow Wilson dedicated the memorial as a shrine to democracy. Now some three hundred thousand visitors a year climb the steps to view the log cabin and honor the man born there in such a humble structure.

The Lincoln Farm Association wisely decided not to erect a statue of Lincoln; nothing should detract from the shrine's stark simplicity. A large statue by Adolph Weinman was placed in the town square at Hodgenville by the state of Kentucky and was dedicated on Memorial Day 1909. Another statue by Weinman was placed in the rotunda of the state capitol at Frankfort in November 1911. A Lincoln museum was later opened in Hodgenville.[25] In 1997 a bust of Lincoln by sculptor Robert Berks was acquired by the state for placement in the Kentucky History Center in Frankfort.[26] By the twentieth century, most Kentuckians had accepted Abraham Lincoln as a native son in whom they could take great pride.

2

A Kentucky Boyhood

Abraham Lincoln never knew much about the history of his family, and he did not try very hard to learn about it. He was a self-made man in the truest sense of the term; his record could speak for him with little reference to ancestors. Lincoln once dismissed questions about his ancestry by saying, "I don't know who my grandfather was, and I am much more concerned to know what his grandson would be." He may have feared being embarrassed by what might be found by any detailed search into the family tree. In 1860 when he was receiving serious consideration as the Republican presidential candidate, the public knew very little about him. The editor of the *Chicago Press and Tribune* sent John Locke Scripps to Springfield to gather information for a short campaign biography. Scripps encountered some difficulty when he informed Lincoln of his mission. "Why, Scripps, it is a great piece of folly to attempt to make anything out of my early life. It can all be condensed into a simple sentence, and that sentence you will find in Gray's Elegy, 'The short and simple annals of the poor.' That's my life, and that's all you or any one else can make of it."[1]

But as an ambitious politician, Lincoln recognized the need to give the public some knowledge about himself, and he agreed to write out a brief account of his career. Scripps began work in Chicago on what he thought would be about a ninety-six-page campaign biography, but when party leaders decided that it should be limited to thirty-two pages and published in New York, the unhappy newspaperman had to rewrite and condense his manuscript. In his haste to get it into print, Scripps had no time to send it to Lincoln for his approval. The somewhat apprehensive author wrote Lincoln on July 11, 1860, to explain what he had done. "I think you will find nothing in the biography which will in any respect annoy you or give you pain. Having failed to submit it to you, I was the more careful, and struck out several matters for that reason which probably you would have allowed. Of course I have been compelled to omit much that I would have got in had we published a large pamphlet."[2]

Lincoln had also responded to a similar request the previous year. In December 1859 Jesse W. Fell, a Bloomington politician, had forwarded a request for biographical information from the *Chester County (Pa.) Times*. Pennsylvania was a key state in national elections, and Lincoln prepared a short, factual account of his life, with the disclaimer, "There is not much of it, for the reason, I suppose, that there is not much of me. If anything is to be made out of it, I wish it to be modest, and not to go beyond the material." He dismissed his family background with a terse statement: "My parents were both born in Virginia, of undistinguished families—second families, perhaps I should say."[3]

Lincoln's mother was Nancy Hanks, who was born in 1783 or 1784 to Lucy Hanks. According to William Herndon, Lincoln's longtime law partner, Lincoln believed that his mother was illegitimate, "the daughter of Lucy Hanks and a well-bred Virginia farmer or planter."[4] From that unknown father, Lincoln believed he had inherited the traits of intellect and ambition that set him apart from the other members of his family. Those who believed in this theory speculated endlessly as to the identity of the maternal grandfather. Some of the possibilities mentioned included George Washington and John C. Calhoun. Others decided that Lucy Hanks had fallen in love with a young planter of good family and had given birth to Nancy, probably on February 5, 1784, in the Patterson Creek area of Virginia. In the spring of that year the family passed through the Cumberland Gap and settled near the Rolling Fork of the Salt River in Kentucky. Lucy Hanks married Henry

Sparrow at Harrodsburg in 1790. In 1796 twelve-year-old Nancy went to live with an aunt and her husband, Elizabeth and Thomas Sparrow. Herndon reported Lincoln's saying to him with deep feeling: "God bless my mother; all that I am or ever hope to be, I owe to her." If he said that, he must have been thinking of the genes she allegedly transmitted from his unknown grandfather.[5]

Nancy Hanks Lincoln died in 1818 when Lincoln was nine years old, and his memories of her were vague. Persons who had known her gave widely variant descriptions. She could read, although she signed her name with an X, but she was said to possess an excellent memory and could recite long prayers and Bible passages to her children. She was described as being kindly and affectionate and deeply religious with an inclination toward a doctrine of fatalism. Personal descriptions, recalled many years later, varied widely.[6]

Much more is known about Lincoln's paternal heritage. He lacked specific knowledge beyond his grandfather, but genealogists have traced his lineage to Samuel Lincoln, a weaver who migrated from Norfolk County, England, to Hingham, Massachusetts, in 1637. He prospered there, both as a businessman and as the father of eleven children. Descendants spread into other regions, one of the most successful being grandson Mordecai Lincoln; he became a wealthy landowner and ironmaster in Pennsylvania, where he was a member of the social and economic elite of the Quaker colony. Abraham Lincoln, the grandfather of the president, was born there in Berks County in 1744 to John and Rebecca Lincoln. The Lincolns became associated with the Boone family in Pennsylvania, and at least five intermarriages are known to have occurred between the families. Before 1768 John Lincoln moved his family southward to Rockingham County, Virginia, to a 210-acre farm his father had purchased for him. More land was acquired, and the family prospered in the lovely Shenandoah Valley.[7] During this period in Virginia some of the Lincolns who had been Quakers became Baptists.

The president's grandfather Abraham was a militia captain during the American Revolution. He married on June 9, 1770, in Augusta County, but the records do not give the name of the bride. By 1780 he was married to Bersheba Herring, who was his wife until his death. She may have married him in 1770, or there could have been a first wife before her.

The Kentucky region beyond the mountains was touted as a veritable "Eden of the west," and as early as 1780, perhaps influenced by Daniel and other members of the Boone clan, Abraham was disposing of his land holdings in the eastern part of the Commonwealth of Virginia. In March 1780 he secured two land warrants, each allowing him 300 acres in any county of Virginia where unclaimed land was available. Kentucky County had been created in 1776, and in late 1780 it was divided into Jefferson, Lincoln, and Fayette Counties. Abraham Lincoln probably moved westward in the fall of 1782 with his family, then including three sons, Mordecai, Josiah, and Thomas, and two daughters, Mary and Ann. They settled near Hughes Station in Jefferson County, about twenty miles east of the Louisville settlement. After acquiring more land, in March 1783 Abraham had 2,268½ acres surveyed on the Green River. The following year he had another Green River tract of 800 acres surveyed. The Floyd's Fork land, where the family lived, was not surveyed until 1785. It was still largely wild country. Despite the end of the American Revolution, Indian raids continued, and most settlers lived in small stations for mutual protection.

On a May day in 1786, Abraham and his three sons were putting in a corn crop in a field about half a mile from the Hughes Station. At the end of the day they had started for home when they were fired on by a small band of Indians. Abraham was killed instantly. Fifteen-year-old Mordecai ordered thirteen-year-old Josiah to run to the station for help. Mordecai rushed into a new, unoccupied cabin nearby, while ten-year-old Thomas remained by the side of his father. When an Indian approached the body to scalp it or perhaps to seize or kill the boy, Mordecai shot him. Men from the station soon appeared to chase away the other Indians. Mordecai inherited his father's estate and became a wealthy citizen of Washington County.[8] His reputation as a humorist was shared by his brother Thomas and his nephew Abraham. Well after Thomas Lincoln moved his family north of the Ohio River, both Mordecai and Josiah also went to Indiana.

The Virginia law of primogeniture left young Thomas almost destitute, with little opportunity to secure an education. President Lincoln knew little in detail about his father, and what he said about Thomas Lincoln contributed to the derogatory accounts of the man displayed in most of the early biographies of the president. In 1848, when Congressman Abraham Lincoln responded to a query of Solomon Lincoln of Massachusetts about his father, he wrote, "Owing to my father being left an orphan at the age of six years, in poverty, and in a new country, he became a wholly uneducated man; which I suppose is the reason why I know so little of our family history." When he was asked for campaign biographical material in 1859 and 1860, Lincoln continued to depict his father as a functional illiterate: "He never did more in the way of writing than to bunglingly sign his own name." Lincoln did not mention that his father could at least read some simple materials.[9] It was easy for such writers as Woodrow Wilson to conclude that Abraham Lincoln "came from the most unpromising stock on the continent, the 'poor white trash' of the South,"[10] and other biographers and historians reached much the same conclusion.

The truth was somewhat different. Thomas managed to make a living by hard labor, some of it perhaps on the farm of his uncle Isaac Lincoln in Tennessee. Somewhere along the way he acquired the skills of carpentry and cabinetmaking. Three years before marrying Nancy Hanks in 1806, he was able to buy a 238-acre farm on Mill Creek in Hardin County for $574.07, cash in hand. Before the birth of Abraham in 1809, Thomas purchased, again for cash, the 348½-acre birthplace farm, and he owned the lots in Elizabethtown where he and

Nancy lived before moving to the Sinking Spring farm. Then he was able to buy the better Knob Creek farm to which the family moved in 1811. Thomas Lincoln was a respected member of each community in which he lived in Kentucky. Honest and hardworking, a good storyteller, he paid taxes, served on juries and in the militia, and was active in his Baptist church. Although he was certainly never well-to-do, the 1814 tax roll listed him in fifteenth place among ninety-one payees in the county.[11]

On June 12, 1806, Thomas Lincoln and Nancy Hanks were married by Jesse Head, a Methodist minister, at Beechland, six miles north of Springfield in Washington County. Some early biographers of the late president who did not find a record of the marriage in Hardin County concluded that their union was a common law marriage. The record was easily found when research extended to Washington County.[12] The young couple moved to Elizabethtown almost immediately after the wedding, for two days later Thomas bought some knives and forks and skeins of silk at the Blearey & Montgomery store in that town.[13] They lived in a cabin Thomas built on one of the two town lots he owned. There Sarah Lincoln was born on February 10, 1807.

In the late fall of 1808 the family moved to the Sinking Spring farm that Thomas had purchased for $200. He also assumed a small debt of the previous owner. The land was located about three miles from Hodgen's Mill in Hardin County. It became part of Larue County when that county was formed in 1843. The soil was poor, and the farm's most attractive feature was the spring, which bubbled up from a deep cave. On a rise above the spring, Thomas Lincoln, no doubt aided by neighbors, built a log cabin, sixteen by eighteen feet. It had only a dirt floor, and it lacked glass windows, but it was typical of the cabins that were built in that area of Kentucky in that period. Abraham Lincoln was born there on February 12, 1809.[14]

By 1809 Kentucky was passing from its frontier stage of development except in some isolated areas. Harrodsburg was founded as Kentucky's first permanent settlement in 1775, and, despite the Indian problems, which were fostered by the British use of the Indians during the American Revolution, the Kentucky population had grown to 73,077 by 1790, when the first federal census was taken. By 1810, the year after Lincoln's birth, the population was listed at 406,509. Most of the settlers had come from Virginia, North Carolina, and Pennsylvania; in 1790 over 93 percent of them were descended from immigrants from the British Isles. Until about 1800 most Kentucky immigrants made their way through the difficult and dangerous Cumberland Gap, although wagons could not negotiate the route until 1796, when work was done on a rough road. After the turn of the century, the Ohio River became the favorite route, with Limestone (Maysville) and Louisville as the major ports of destination. Slaves had come to Kentucky from the first days of settlement, and by 1810 they numbered 80,561 and accounted for 19.8 percent of the population. The 1,711 free blacks in 1810 constituted less than 1 percent of the population. Opposition to slavery developed early, and an effort was made in the 1792 convention that drew up Kentucky's first state constitution to include a provision that would provide for emancipation at some future date. Instead, Article 9 of the constitution fixed slavery firmly in the legal framework of the new state. With slight modifications, it provided the legal basis for slavery in Kentucky for over seventy years. Some of the early opponents of slavery were in Baptist churches, and it has been suggested that one reason the Lincolns left Kentucky in 1816 was their opposition to that peculiar institution.[15]

Thomas Lincoln soon realized that making a living from the infertile acres of the Sinking Spring farm would be difficult if not impossible. In 1811 he moved again, about ten miles northeast of Sinking Spring to a Knob Creek farm of 238 acres that he purchased. Because of the steep, wooded hills that gave that area its name, the usable land was limited to about thirty acres along the creek. Nonetheless, those few acres were much more productive than the barren ones he had left.

Abraham Lincoln's first recollections were of the Knob Creek farm. In his autobiographical sketch for Scripps, Lincoln wrote that as a child he had lived "on Knob Creek, on the road from Bardstown, Kentucky to Nashville, Tennessee at a point three or three and one half miles south or southwest of Atherton's Ferry on the Rolling Fork of Salt River." The boundaries of the farm were irregular, as was true of many Kentucky properties. Virginia had never provided surveys of its public lands before settlement; and in staking out their claims, claimants naturally endeavored to avoid as many bad acres as possible. Conflicts were common, and the shingled claims provided a living for an ever-increasing flock of lawyers. An astute individual remarked, "Who buys land in Kentucky, buys a lawsuit"; the Knob Creek farm was no exception.

On January 1, 1815, a bill of ejection was filed against Thomas Lincoln and nine of his neighbors who occupied land lying within a ten-thousand-acre tract claimed by some Philadelphia investors. Thomas Lincoln was made the defendant in a test case. Apparently because he had not made full payment for his farm to George Lindsey, the latter was added to the case and described as "Landlord of said Lincoln." This suit was still undecided when Thomas Lincoln left Kentucky in late 1816. In June 1818 a jury rendered a verdict in favor of Lincoln and Lindsey and awarded them $17.89 ½, the costs of the case. Lincoln's Kentucky lawyer sued to secure payment, and in September 1820 he won another verdict, this time for $21.36. Since the ones who were to pay were out of state, it is doubtful that Thomas Lincoln ever collected what was due him.[16]

He had problems with titles to all three of the farms he had owned in Kentucky, and this uncertainty about titles was the major reason he decided to leave the state. Such moves were not unique with Thomas Lincoln, and they did not indicate a shiftless nature. Much of Kentucky's good land was claimed by speculators and individuals who had the means to secure their titles through the cumbersome Virginia land system, which allowed claims to be filed prior to actual survey. Many new

Kentuckians were disappointed by their inability to obtain good land in what was reputed to be the "Eden of the West." When Kentucky became a state in 1792, approximately two-thirds of the adult white males did not hold title to any land. They could become tenants, they could try squatters' rights without a legal claim—or they could go elsewhere. Thomas Lincoln's efforts to find good land on which he could support his family indicate that he was not a worthless failure as a frontiersman. But his failures to secure good Kentucky land with a clear title persuaded him to try in Indiana under more favorable conditions. Thanks to the Northwest Ordinance of 1785, the lands north of the Ohio River were to be surveyed into ranges of townships, each township having thirty-six sections, each containing 640 acres. Surely, such a system would eliminate the conflicting claims that threatened the titles to so many Kentucky lands.

Young Abe was probably not aware of the problems that concerned his father. The boy's few years on Knob Creek were filled with the details of growing up that were common to boys of his age in Kentucky in the early nineteenth century. Much of his time was spent playing, with the creek as a constant source of fun. Sister Sarah was his closest companion, but other families lived not too far away. Austin Gollaher, nearly four years older than Abe, is credited with saving him from drowning when he was about to be swept away by the flooded creek. A brother who was born there and named Thomas might have provided more companionship, but he died soon after his birth in 1811 or 1812. Even a small boy was expected to contribute what he could to the family's well-being, and as Abe increased in years and size, chores interfered with his play. He must have carried wood and brought water from the creek, but he also recalled helping his father plant corn in the "big field" of seven acres next to the stream. His job was to drop two pumpkin seeds in every other hill in alternate rows after his father had dropped the corn kernels. Lincoln remembered that after one planting a heavy rain up in the knobs had swollen the creek and washed away not only the corn but much of the topsoil as well.

The most significant event of Abe's few years at Knob Creek was his introduction to school. He and Sarah attended two ABC schools for brief periods. Each term probably ran only two or three months, for the mature Lincoln wrote that "the aggregate of all his schooling did not amount to one year," and he attended three terms in Indiana schools in 1820, 1823, and 1826. The two Kentucky terms were in 1815 and 1816, when Abe was six and seven years old. His first teacher was Zachariah Riney, who was born in Maryland in 1763. His Catholic family had moved to Kentucky before 1795 and, like so many other Catholic families, had settled in the Bardstown region—sometimes called "the Holy Land." The little log schoolhouse for the Knob Creek neighborhood was located about two miles from the Lincoln cabin. It was a subscription school, with parents paying small sums to the teacher. A "blab school," its students recited lessons aloud and in unison. Lincoln probably did little more than learn his ABCs, although he may have been able to do some simple reading when he left Kentucky. Much of the fun of attending school for Abe and Sarah must have been the companionship of the other children and the games that they played at recess.

Abe's second teacher was Caleb Hazel, a surveyor about fifty years old who lived on a farm adjacent to the Lincolns. Through marriage, he was related to the Hanks family. Hazel may have interested Abe in reading and possibly writing. Dilworth's *New Guide to the English Tongue* is usually cited as the first schoolbook that Abe used, but his introduction to it may not have come until he was in Indiana. The book was essentially a speller, but it also contained some rules of grammar and a collection of short statements in both prose and poetry. In one of the 1860 biographical sketches that Lincoln proofed before its publication, Lincoln let stand the statement that during his childhood in Kentucky he "acquired the alphabet and other rudiments of education."[17] By the time the Lincolns left Kentucky, Abe had enough education to be able to start learning largely on his own.

3

Kentuckians in Indiana

In the fall of 1816, Thomas Lincoln made a trip into Indiana to select a spot for their new home. He decided on a heavily wooded area on Pigeon Creek in Perry County. (It later became Spencer County.) Vines and underbrush were so heavy that a path had to be hacked through them to reach the site he had selected, about sixteen miles from the Ohio River. Thomas liked what he saw, and before leaving he blazed trees and piled up brush to indicate the boundaries of the parcel of land he intended to buy from the federal government. Either then, or as soon as he and his family reached the site, he built a half-faced camp, quickly constructed, with only three sides. A fire burning at the open side was expected to supply enough heat to make the fourth wall unnecessary. The mistake that Thomas made was neglecting to locate near a good water supply. The spring from which the family obtained its water was nearly a mile distant, and it can be assumed that carrying water was one of the chores assigned to Abe.[1]

The Lincoln family, probably using pack horses to carry their meager possessions, reached their new home site in December 1816, the same month in which Indiana achieved statehood. With an ample supply of timber at hand Thomas Lincoln soon built a more adequate cabin. If typical frontier practice was followed, the few neighbors in the thinly settled region came to help with the cabin raising. Like the cabins they had left behind in Kentucky, this one had a hard-packed dirt floor and lacked glass windows, but it had a stone chimney and a loft, in which Abe slept. Its dimensions were later recalled as being between fourteen and eighteen feet. The chinking between the logs had to wait until warmer weather when the clay and grass could be mixed.

Although he was only eight years old, Abe was tall for his age, and as he later recalled, he "had an axe put into his hands at once; and from that [time] till within his twenty third year, he was almost constantly handling that most useful instrument—less, of course, in plowing and harvesting seasons."[2] This extra axe was of great help to Thomas as he struggled to clear enough land to plant the essential corn and vegetable crops. The years of swinging an axe made Abraham Lincoln an unusually powerful man. In 1865, when he was visiting an Army of the Potomac camp, he stopped to chat with a detail of soldiers who were chopping wood. The president told them that he had spent many years working with an axe. Then he picked up an axe and, holding it by the heft, extended it at arm's length without a quiver in his arm. None of the soldiers could duplicate that feat. Such strength helped Lincoln survive the intolerable pressure of the war.

Until the crops came in, the family depended heavily upon game for food. The forest was teeming with game, but in this endeavor Abe was of little help. Not long after they moved into the cabin, however, he stood inside the door and with his father's rifle shot and killed a wild turkey that came into the clearing. In his 1860 autobiographical sketch for Scripps, Lincoln wrote, "He has never since pulled a trigger on any larger game." Thomas, who was hunting to feed his family, must have been puzzled by this strange quirk in his son.[3]

One of the boy's tasks was to carry a turn of corn to Gordon's Mill to be ground into cornmeal. On one trip he hitched the old mare he had ridden to the mill to the arm of the gristmill. In a hurry to get home before dark, Abe tried to increase her speed by applying the whip each time the mare passed him. The mare, resenting the attention, kicked him in the forehead, and he fell to the ground, bleeding from the wound and unconscious. He was thought to be dead, and Thomas Lincoln was summoned to the side of his son. Abe could not speak for several hours, but he recovered with no ill effects.[4]

The results of their hard labor convinced Thomas Lincoln that he had made a good selection of land, and on October 15, 1817, he entered his claim to the southwest quarter of section 32, in township 4, south of Range 5 West, lying in Spencer County, Indiana. He must have been pleased by the exactness of the surveyed boundaries of his property; it was so different from what he had had for each of his three Kentucky farms. Ten years later, in 1827, he gave up half of his quarter section. The money that he had paid the federal government completed the purchase of the other eighty acres, and he received a patent of ownership for it. Thomas also bought twenty acres of land from a settler whose land adjoined his, so that he had one hundred acres of land free of debt.[5]

The Lincolns began to feel less lonely as other settlers, many of them Kentuckians, moved into the area. Most important for Nancy Lincoln was the arrival of her aunt and uncle, Elizabeth (Hanks) and Thomas Sparrow, with whom she had lived for several years. They had lost their Kentucky land and had followed the Lincolns across the Ohio River. With them was Dennis Hanks, an illegitimate nephew of Elizabeth Sparrow. About eighteen years old and always in good spirits, he enlivened any group of which he was a part. Dennis became one of the main sources of information concerning Abraham Lincoln's early years. Indeed, Dennis claimed that he had been the second person to touch Abe after his birth. Unfortunately, Dennis was not always the most reliable of witnesses. Though he liked Nancy Lincoln, he had an aversion to Thomas, and Dennis was responsible for some of the stories that discredited Thomas. The Sparrows and Dennis lived in the abandoned half-faced camp until they could build a more substantial dwelling. Several other Kentucky families to whom the Lincolns were related or whom they knew also moved into the neighborhood.[6]

The Kentucky influence was so pervasive in southern Indiana that one could almost suggest that the youthful Lincoln had never left the farm at Knob Creek. These associations, and those developed during his Illinois years, contributed much to his understanding of Kentucky and that state's sometimes prickly people. Most of the youth's contacts in Indiana were with members of his family's social and economic class.

In 1818 tragedy struck the little community when several members were stricken by milk sickness. People realized that the illness was associated with milk, but it was years before it was discovered that the illness resulted from cows' eating the plentiful white snakeroot plant. Many victims died after a week of great pain. Elizabeth and Thomas Sparrow were the first victims who were closely associated with the Lincolns. Thomas sawed boards and made the coffins in which they were buried. Then Nancy was stricken; she died on October 5, 1818, after telling Sarah and Abe to be good to their father, to each other, and to everyone. The grief-stricken Thomas made another coffin and buried his wife on a knoll about half a mile from the cabin. Dennis Hanks moved in with the Lincolns and provided valuable help with the farming and hunting. Sarah, who became twelve in February 1819 did her best to assume the household tasks of her mother, but the job was too great for her. She was reported to have become so unhappy and discouraged that she would sit by the fireplace and cry, despite efforts of Abe and Dennis to cheer her up.[7]

After several months, Thomas Lincoln realized that the home needed a wife and mother. Frontier life was not well suited to the lives of a widow or a widower; a family unit was much better equipped to deal with the rigors of frontier life. In late 1819 Thomas returned to Kentucky to find a wife. In Elizabethtown he found widow Sarah Bush Johnston. A member of a fairly well-to-do Hardin County family, she had married David Johnston in 1806 when she was seventeen. Thomas was a friend of the family, and legend has it that he had courted Sarah but had lost. When Johnston died in 1816, he was the county jailor and she cooked for the prisoners. Sarah had three children, whom she tried to raise in a small house in town.

Although Thomas was some ten years her senior, they were friends and each of them needed a mate. Sarah owed some small debts, and she refused to leave until they were discharged. After Thomas paid them, they were married on December 2, 1819, by Methodist minister George L. Rogers in the home of Benjamin Chapeze near the town square. Sarah owned several pieces of good furniture that she insisted on taking to Indiana, so Thomas borrowed a wagon and horses to carry her possessions.

The arrival of his stepmother made a difference almost immediately in Abe's life. Her possessions were far superior to the crude furniture in the cabin, and she insisted that a floor, a door, and windows be added and that Thomas make more furniture. The children were cleaned up and better fed, and the loft was fixed for the boys to sleep in. Her children were John D., Elizabeth, and Matilda, and with Dennis the family had suddenly expanded to eight members. From the moment of her arrival Sarah (called Sally) accepted Sarah and Abe as if they were her own; it was a happy family, and she did much to make it so. Abe and John, close in age, became the best of friends for many years.[8]

Sally was intelligent although probably illiterate, and she soon recognized unusual talents in Abe, whom she was quick to praise and encourage. Lincoln wrote in 1861 that "she had been his best friend in the world and that no son could love a mother more than he loved her." Herndon reported that she had told him in 1865: "Abe was a good boy, and I can say what scarcely one woman, a mother, can say in a thousand . . . Abe never gave me a cross word or look and never refused in fact, or even in appearance, to do anything I requested him. I never gave him a cross word in all my life. . . . His mind and mine, what little I had, seemed to run together, more in the same channel." It would be difficult to overestimate the influence that she had on the development of a sensitive boy who was becoming more and more estranged from his father. Charles H. Coleman summed up the relationship: "Where she could have brought bitterness and futility into the life of Abraham Lincoln, she brought affection and inspiration."[9]

During the Indiana years an estrangement developed between father and son that affected their relationship for the rest of Thomas Lincoln's life. Abraham Lincoln was especially close to his stepbrother, John D. Johnston, who was a year younger, and after Abraham came of age and left the family, many of his infrequent contacts were through John. None of Abraham's family attended his wedding, and neither his father nor his stepmother ever met Mary Todd Lincoln or saw their grandchildren from that marriage. Harriet Hanks lived with the Lincolns in Springfield in 1844–1845 to attend school, but she and Mrs. Lincoln did not get along. The girl was said to have been treated as a servant, and she soon left. In 1851 John Johnston proposed to send a thirteen-year-old son to live with the Lincolns while he attended school, but Mrs. Lincoln objected to the proposal.[10]

Even though estranged, Abraham gave limited financial support to his father. In 1841 he purchased forty acres from his father for $200 and deeded it to him for his life. Abraham promised to sell it to John Johnston for the same price after Thomas Lincoln's death. In 1848 John asked Abraham for $20 to prevent the land from being sold for back taxes and an additional $80 for himself. Lincoln sent the $20 but scolded John for being an "idler" who seldom did "a good whole day's work, in any one day" and who had led Thomas Lincoln into unsuccessful land and business transactions that had cost him heavily. Abraham may have given other small sums to his father, but his financial support was limited. Abraham carried a heavy debt for a number of years, but by midcentury he was prospering as a lawyer, and he could have done more than he did. Lincoln loved his stepmother dearly, and after his father's death he provided some financial help for her; he visited her for the last time on January 31, 1861, before leaving for Washington. Lincoln turned over to John Johnston the eighty acres he had inherited from his father, apparently on John's promise to take care of Sarah Lincoln, who was, after all, John's mother. Lincoln intervened when John proposed to sell the land and retain $100 of the proceeds for himself. If all of it was devoted to Sarah Lincoln's upkeep, Lincoln pointed out, she would have an income of $30 a year, enough to meet her essential needs.[11]

In May 1849 Lincoln was told that his father, desperately ill, was "anxious to see you before he dies. . . . He craves to see you all the time. . . . his only child that is of his own flush [*sic*] & blood." Thomas soon recovered, although his son did not visit him, but in early 1851 he was ill again. Lincoln's reply to John's report of the illness was delayed, Lincoln wrote, not because he had forgotten them or was unconcerned, "but because it appeared to me I could write nothing which could do any good." His business would not allow him to visit then, and his wife was still abed after giving birth to a son. Then Lincoln added a passage that reflected the strange distance that separated him from his father. "I sincerely hope that Father may yet recover his health; but at all events tell him to remember to call upon, and confide in, our great, and good, and merciful Maker; who will not turn away from him in any extremity. He notes the fall of a sparrow, and remembers the hairs of our heads; and He will not forget the dying man, who puts his trust in Him. Say to him that if we could meet now, it is doubtful whether it would not be more painful than pleasant; but that if it be his lot to go now, he will soon have a joyous [meeting] with many loved ones gone before; and where [the rest] of us, through the help of God, hope ere-long to join them."[12]

Thomas died five days after Abraham wrote his letter, and Abraham did not attend the funeral. In late 1867 Mary Todd Lincoln wrote to Sarah Lincoln, "My husband a few weeks before his death mentioned to me, that he intended *that* summer, paying proper respect to his father's grave, by a head & foot stone, with his name, age & & and I propose very soon carrying out his intentions. It was not from want of affection for his father, as you are well aware, that it was not done, but *his* time was so greatly occupied always." Mary Lincoln did not, however, remedy the neglect. In 1880 when Robert Todd Lincoln learned that a local effort was under way to erect a suitable monument for his grandfather Thomas, he made a generous contribution to the undertaking. Robert also helped provide a tombstone to mark the grave of Nancy Hanks Lincoln.[13]

Historian John Y. Simon, after a careful study of this strange relationship, offers some explanations for it. Did Thomas, not understanding his son's desire for an education, fail to provide the support that Abraham needed and expected? Was Thomas puzzled and alienated by the boy's aversion to hunting and fishing, activities essential to family survival on the frontier? Was Thomas shocked by his son's mimicking the Baptist minister in the local church that meant so much to the parents? Did Thomas favor his more conventional stepson, John Johnston, over his son, whom he had trouble understanding? Simon concluded that "Abe's ambitions exceeded his father's expectations and could not be fulfilled under his father's roof. If young Abe had been neglected or mistreated by his father, the explanations might depend more upon Thomas' poverty than his ill-will. Far more important was the matter of Thomas's favoritism toward his stepson." Simon suggested that his own divided house may have influenced Lincoln in selecting that term for his famous "House Divided" 1858 speech. Time and again during the Civil War the president discussed the conflict in those terms. Lincoln's intense interest in Shakespeare's plays may have reflected his own "painful relationships with his own father and [step] brother, unresolved at the times of their deaths. . . . Family relationships so strongly shaped his life and thought that it is impossible to understand this melancholy man without knowing the unhappy boy." But, Simon warns, "The significance of metaphor should be kept within bounds."[14]

The years in Indiana allowed Lincoln to continue the limited education begun in Kentucky. In 1820 Abe and the other four children attended a blab school taught by Andrew Crawford, a local justice of the peace, in a cabin a mile from the Lincoln home. In later years Lincoln was critical of the schools he attended and the men who taught them. "No qualification was ever required of a teacher, beyond *'readin, writin, and cipherin,'* to the Rule of Three. If a straggler supposed to understand Latin, happened to sojourn in the neighborhood, he was looked upon as a wizzard."[15] None of the youth's teachers were trained pedagogues, even by the inadequate standards of that day, but they were able to impart enough knowledge to create the foundation that later enabled him to educate himself. In these schools Abe did not always impress others with his brilliance. Cousin John Hanks recalled him as a dull student who worked his way by toil; though learning was hard for him, he would advance slowly but surely. However, Sally Lincoln soon recognized the determination to learn that obsessed her stepson. "He must understand every thing—even to the smallest thing—minutely and exactly; he would then repeat it over to himself, again and again—some time in one form and then in an other and when it was fixed in his mind to suit him, he . . . never lost that fact or his understanding of it." One unusual aspect of Crawford's school was his effort to teach manners to his students as well as book learning. He had them practice introductions to each other as if they were strangers meeting for the first time.

When Crawford quit teaching his school, none was available for over a year until James Swaney opened one, about four miles from the Lincoln home. Because the time spent walking to and from it interfered seriously with the household chores assigned to Abe, he was able to attend only occasionally. His last school, probably the one that he attended longest of the five to which he was exposed, was taught by Azel W. Dorsey, the treasurer of Spencer County and a sometimes storekeeper. It met in the same cabin that Crawford had used, and Abe's attendance was more regular than it had been with Swaney. Dennis Hanks insisted that he had given Abe much of his early instruction in reading, spelling, and writing, but since Dennis was barely literate, his claim must be suspect. Abe became proud of his penmanship, often writing letters for other members of the family and for some of the neighbors. The earliest known specimen of his script was a piece of doggerel that he penned in a copybook. "Abraham Lincoln, his hand and pen, / He will be good but God knows when." He was at this school long enough to develop close relationships with other students, and he began to emerge as a leader among them.

During these years in intermittent study Abe developed an obsession with reading that extended beyond such texts as *Dilworth's Guide to the English Tongue,* Murray's *English Reader* (which was probably his favorite), and Pike's *Arithmetic.* He probably read the Bible thoroughly, and he devoured *The Pilgrim's Progress, Aesop's Fables,* and *Lessons in Elocution.* He was fascinated by Parson Mason Weems's *Life of George Washington* and other accounts of the American Revolution. *Robinson Crusoe* was one of his favorite novels. He enjoyed *The Kentucky Preceptor,* published in Lexington in 1812, which contained a number of useful articles on reading and speaking. The boy memorized a great deal of what he read, including poetry, for which he developed a fondness. John Hanks remembered the eagerness with which Abe resumed reading at the end of a day's work: "He would go to the cupboard, snatch a piece of corn bread, take down a book, set down in a chair, cock his legs up as high as his head, and read." An enduring legend is of the tall, awkward boy in ill-fitting clothes reading by the light of the fireplace.

At least one of the textbook legends seems to have been true. When he learned that Josiah Crawford (not his teacher, Andrew Crawford) had a copy of Ramsey's *Life of Washington* that contained more on the Revolution than the Weems biography, Abe hastened to borrow it. Somehow the book got water-damaged, and the contrite youth confessed the disaster to Crawford. He had no money to pay for the book, Abe admitted, but he would be glad to work out the book's value.

Crawford had a field of corn in which the tops of the stalks were to be cut off as fodder for his cattle. If Abe would do that job, it would square accounts and Abe could keep the damaged volume. After three days of hard work, the account was settled, and Abe returned home with a book to add to his small collection.

Abe's hard work to pay for the damaged book belied his reputation for being lazy. In part, that may have been caused by his spurt of adolescent growth. By the time he was sixteen, Abe was six feet two inches tall but weighed only some 160 pounds. His clothes were nearly always too small for him, and neighbors laughed at the several inches of shin extending below the legs of his buckskin britches. Because of this rapid growth, he was always tired; he conserved energy whenever he could by avoiding work. An even more compelling reason for his being called lazy was his growing interest in matters unrelated to the work he was supposed to do. When Dennis Hanks later recalled that Abe was lazy, he gave an explanation with which young Lincoln would have agreed: "He was always reading—scribbling—writing—ciphering—writing poetry." The hardworking father must have found it difficult to understand his son's aversion to hard labor. Contrary to legend, there is some evidence that Thomas Lincoln encouraged his son to attend school. Sally Lincoln once said that "Mr. Lincoln never made Abe quit reading to do any thing if he could avoid it. He would do it himself first." But father and son had quite different ideas as to how much education was enough, and in Thomas Lincoln's eyes, Abe had gone beyond the desirable limit.[16]

Father and son also differed over religion. After supervising the erection of the Pigeon Creek Baptist Church, Thomas joined it in 1823, along with his wife. Daughter Sarah became a member in 1826. Abe got the low-paying job as sexton of the church, but he never became a member. He attended the sermons, but afterward he would mount a stump and mimic the preacher's remarks to an audience of the other children.

Thomas disapproved of his mimicry and was said to have spoken harshly to Abe about it. The father-son rift was widening.[17]

The family began to break up as the children grew older. On January 9, 1821, Abe's stepsister Elizabeth Johnston married Dennis Hanks; on August 2, 1826, his sister Sarah married Aaron Grigsby; and on September 14, 1826, his stepsister Matilda Johnston married Squire Hall. Abe was desolated when Sarah Grigsby died in childbirth on January 20, 1828. Abe blamed the Grigsby family for not calling a doctor in time to attend her, and for one of the few times in his life Abraham Lincoln maintained a grudge against a family.

The breakup of the family, his own maturation, and his alienation from his father combined to make Abe anxious to leave home. He began to attend social events all over the county, where his ability to tell funny stories always attracted an audience. He also took on more jobs outside the farm, although he continued dutifully to turn his earnings over to his father. In the spring of 1828 he made his first important trip away from home when he helped take a flatboat of produce to New Orleans. Until then his longest trip had been from Knob Creek to Pigeon Creek. Storekeeper James Gentry had taken a large amount of produce in trade, and he decided that he might make more profit by sending it to New Orleans himself. His son Allan and Abe Lincoln agreed to make the trip. Abe was to receive $8 per month and his food.

They had a leisurely voyage, carried along by the current of the Ohio and then the Mississippi River, stopping frequently at plantations and towns to sell their cargo. One night, when they were tied up at a plantation south of Baton Rouge, they were attacked by a gang of seven slaves from another plantation whose intent apparently was to kill and rob the two youths. Lincoln's strength came into play, for they were able to drive the intruders off the boat, cut their tie to shore, and hastily resume their voyage. Both Allan and Abe suffered slight injuries in the encounter.

New Orleans was a revelation to the Indiana boys, who had

never seen a city comparable to it: why, other languages were spoken almost as frequently as English. They made part of the trip home by steamboat, and Abe turned over to his father the $25 that he had earned. This limited contact with a larger world whetted the youth's desire to break away from the home that he had outgrown.[18]

But he was still a little underage, and the family needed his help in making another move and establishing another home. Despite its early promise for a better life than he had found in Kentucky, Thomas Lincoln's economic condition declined after his move to Indiana in 1816. Illinois had become a state on December 3, 1818, and John Hanks, who had moved there, boasted of rich, fertile land, better than that in Indiana. Milk sickness was rumored to be epidemic again in southern Indiana, and wanderlust always drew some personalities. Dennis Hanks and Squire Hall were anxious to make the move, and Thomas Lincoln agreed to go. Thomas sold his farm, his corn, and his hogs, and in March 1830 the Lincoln, Hanks, and Hall families headed west with Abe driving one of the oxen-pulled wagons that carried all of their possessions. Winter was still hanging on, and most streams were flooded; it was a cold, miserable trip. The group passed through the village of Decatur to the tract on the north bank of the Sangamon River that John Hanks had marked for them. Abe's axe once again helped with the laborious work of building a cabin, clearing land for a crop, and splitting rails to fence in the expanding fields.[19]

During that summer young Lincoln made his first political speech. Two candidates for the state legislature had spoken in Decatur but then had failed to extend the customary invitation for members of the crowd to drink with them. Some annoyed listeners called upon Abe Lincoln, who had already earned attention in his new community for quick wit and a lively tongue, to ridicule the stingy candidates. Instead, Abe spoke about the need for improving navigation of the Sangamon River to promote the economic growth of the area. He had been reading newspapers whenever possible for several years, and he was familiar with the concepts of Henry Clay's "American Plan," which called for a protective tariff, a national bank, and internal improvements to benefit the nation's economy.[20] Abraham Lincoln was in the process of becoming a Whig while that political party was still in the process of being formed.

The 1830–1831 winter was one of the worst on record, with temperatures well below zero for several weeks. Cattle and wild animals perished in the bitter cold, and humans huddled in their cabins and longed for spring. During the winter Abe, John Johnston, and John Hanks explored possible ways of earning money—a commodity in short supply for all of them. The best that they could come up with was to take a flatboat of produce to New Orleans for Denton Offutt, a speculative businessman who was also from Kentucky, in the spring. Before they departed, Offutt hired Lincoln to work for him as a clerk in the store that he was opening in the village of New Salem. This trip to New Orleans was uneventful. When Abraham Lincoln returned to take up his clerkship, Thomas and Sally Lincoln had moved to Coles County.[21] At last, Abraham Lincoln was on his own.

4

Kentuckians
in Illinois

When Abraham Lincoln moved to New Salem in July 1831 after his second trip to New Orleans, he had no idea what line of work he would undertake, except that if at all possible it would not be farming. Denton Offutt had not yet built the store in which Lincoln was to clerk, so for a time he supported himself with any odd jobs that were available. New Salem had only a hundred or so inhabitants, a number of them former Kentuckians, but it was the center of a trade area, and it had a surprising number of business establishments. Lincoln soon became a popular figure with his endless store of jokes and stories and his athletic abilities, especially in wrestling. His strength and courage won the support of Jack Armstrong and other toughs from the Clary Grove district, but Lincoln also earned the respect and affection of a number of the towns-people, who helped him forward his education. Several of them were surprisingly well educated. Dr. John Allen was a Dartmouth College graduate, Jack Kelso was very knowledgeable on the works of Shakespeare and Burns, and teacher Mentor Graham was glad to share his knowledge. James Rutledge welcomed the newcomer into the debating society that he organized, and Justice of the Peace Bowling Green encouraged the young man to attend his court and to help people with simple legal problems. When he began his clerkship, Lincoln impressed customers with his honesty and willingness to be of service.

Lincoln became so popular that several friends encouraged him to seek election to the state legislature in 1832. If elected, he could work to improve river navigation for New Salem, whose future was threatened by a proposed railroad that would bypass the town. He announced his candidacy and outlined his platform in the *Sangamo Journal* of March 15, 1832. In it he advocated the ideas in Henry Clay's American Plan, soon to become the principles of the Whig party as it organized to oppose the party of President Andrew Jackson. The new candidate admitted that he might be wrong on some issues, "but holding it a sound maxim, that it is better to be only sometimes right, than at all times wrong, so soon as I discover my opinions to be erroneous, I shall be ready to renounce them." His ambition, he asserted, was to become worthy of the esteem of his fellow man. "I am young and unknown to many of you," he concluded. "I was born and have ever remained in the most humble walks of life. I have no wealthy or popular relatives to recommend me. My case is thrown exclusively upon the independent voters of this county, and if elected they will have conferred a favor upon me, for which I shall be unremitting in my labors to compensate. But if the good people in their wisdom shall see fit to keep me in the background, I have been too familiar with disappointments to be very much chagrined." Lincoln lost his election, the only time in his career he was defeated by a direct vote of the people. Little known outside the New Salem community, he was eighth among thirteen candidates, with the top four being elected. But in his New Salem precinct, he received 277 of the 300 votes cast. Even his losing candidacy showed the amazing progress that the young man was making.[1]

The failure of Offutt's store left Lincoln without a job. But on April 21, 1832, he and other volunteers were sworn into military service for the Black Hawk War as some Fox and Sauk Indians made a futile attempt to recover their tribal lands. Lincoln experienced one of the proudest moments of his life when he was elected captain of the company. He made fun later of his military exploits, for he saw no fighting, but he gained some acquaintance with military life, and he gained valuable experience as a leader of men. He also learned something of the value of seeking pragmatic solutions to problems. Once as he marched his company toward a fence, he could not think of an order that would get it through a gate. His solution was to call a halt, tell the men to fall out, and to reassemble on the other side of the fence. It was a solution that worked. Still unemployed, Lincoln reenlisted twice for short terms, now as a private. The $124 and the land warrant he received were most welcome, and he also became acquainted with several men who would later influence his career.[2]

Lincoln considered studying law but was sidetracked when he and William F. Berry went heavily into debt to buy one of the three general stores in New Salem. Lincoln had time to do considerable reading while waiting for customers to come in. Deciding that he would need better grammar, whatever his long-term plans might be, he borrowed a couple of books and embarked upon intensive individual study. He also read such works as Thomas Paine's *Age of Reason,* and he acquired somewhat the reputation of a freethinker. In 1846 he would find it necessary to deny that he was an enemy of the Christian religion.

The Berry-Lincoln store failed, and Lincoln was again in need of employment. He might have left New Salem, but friends persuaded postmaster Samuel Hill to resign that position and got Lincoln appointed to what was usually a Democratic patronage position. Lincoln speculated that the post was "too insignificant to make his politics an objection," and he may have been right. The person receiving a letter had to pay postage, the rate depending upon the weight and the distance traveled. Mail was supposed to be delivered to New Salem twice a week, but it was often delayed. The postmaster received a percentage of what he collected; Lincoln's average for his three years in the office was probably close to $50 per year.

He had ample time to read as well as to visit with customers, and he was allowed to send and receive personal mail without charge. Now he could indulge his fondness for reading newspapers for political news. Most of the papers that came to the post office in Sam Hill's store were read thoroughly before being passed on to the subscribers, unless the subscribers insisted upon picking them up sooner. Lincoln embarked upon a sort of reading course in American politics. One of his favorite papers was the *Louisville Journal*, ably edited by George D. Prentice, a New Englander who had come to Kentucky in 1830 to write a biography of Henry Clay. He remained to edit the *Journal*, which appeared as a daily on November 24, 1830. Blessed with a vivid imagination, a sharp wit, an excellent command of the English language, and an exceptional memory, Prentice was soon producing one of the finest newspapers in western America. His short, pithy paragraphs were copied in papers across the country, especially in Whig papers, and were published in *Prenticeana: Or Wit and Humor in Paragraphs* (1860). The *Louisville Journal* became one of the top Whig newspapers, and Prentice became a leader in that party. Lincoln's careful reading of the *Journal* enhanced his admiration for and support of Henry Clay. Prentice was a frequent participant in Whig party conventions, and he often visited Washington and other eastern cities to forge union with the eastern members of his party. He was also a poet, publishing in the *Journal* a considerable amount of his own verses and the works of others. This may have been another reason why Lincoln was so fond of the *Louisville Journal;* on occasion Lincoln tried his hand at writing verse.

The post office income was not adequate to live on, and concerned friends suggested to Lincoln that John Calhoun, the county surveyor, needed an assistant. Knowing arithmetic to the rule of three did not meet the requirements of surveying, so Lincoln embarked upon another rigorous course of study to teach himself trigonometry and its application to surveying. Then, borrowing enough to purchase the necessary equipment and a horse and bridle, Lincoln started surveying in the county.

His work was careful and accurate, and soon he was being given more demanding (and better-paid) assignments. He often carried letters that he delivered while on a surveying job.

Lincoln was embarrassed in 1834 when his equipment, horse, and bridle were seized for nonpayment of debts. Again, friends came to his aid, and some of the auctioned equipment was purchased and returned to him so that he could resume work. But his financial situation became even more muddled after Berry died in January 1835. The partnership owed $1,100, a sum so great that Lincoln called it "the National Debt." He swore that in time he would pay all of it, and he finally managed to do so after years of effort. With these financial problems, he welcomed another chance to run for a legislative seat. He was approached by Democratic leaders who wanted to defeat John Todd Stuart, a Whig leader and a future law partner of Lincoln. They would support Lincoln instead of a Democratic candidate if he would run. Their hope was that Lincoln would take enough votes from Stuart to defeat him. Lincoln told Stuart of the offer, and Stuart, who was confident of winning, told him to accept the offer. Much to the surprise of the Democrats, both Stuart and Lincoln won. Lincoln borrowed $200 from Coleman Smoot in New Salem, and with $60 purchased his first suit; he was determined "to make a decent appearance in the legislature."[3]

At this time Lincoln made one of the most important decisions of his career; he decided to become a lawyer. He had been attracted to courts, and after watching some of the rough-and-tumble cases, he had become convinced that it was a profession in which he could compete successfully. It would also allow easy access into politics, an area with which he was becoming increasingly fascinated. He was encouraged by Stuart, whom he had met during the Black Hawk War, who loaned him law books to study. A cousin of Mary Todd of Lexington, Stuart was a Kentuckian whose father, a Presbyterian minister, taught classical languages at Transylvania University. Stuart graduated from Centre College, studied law, then moved to

Springfield, Illinois, in 1828. He developed a successful practice and in 1832 was elected to the state legislature, where he became a leader of the Whig party in the House. With Stuart's encouragement, Lincoln turned to the study of law with the intellectual intensity of which he was capable. He did not "read law" with a mentor; he studied it on his own until he understood the principles behind it. Sometimes he was so absorbed in his studies that he read as he walked around town.[4]

In the Illinois House of Representatives Lincoln developed skill in drafting legislation and a reputation of wit and clear thinking. The $258 he received for his labors allowed him to pay off a few of his smaller debts. While he studied, he continued with his postmaster duties and did some surveying to supplement his income. Seeing the decline in the New Salem population, he realized that the time was near when he would have to move elsewhere.

Lincoln won reelection to the legislature in 1836 in a spirited campaign in which he received the most votes of the seventeen candidates. He had a key role in the successful effort to move the state capital from Vandalia to Springfield. On September 9, 1836, two judges of the Illinois Supreme Court granted him his law license, and the following spring his name was added to the roll of attorneys in the office of the clerk of the state Supreme Court. Stuart invited him to join his law firm, and to that end on April 15, 1837, Abraham Lincoln rode into Springfield on a borrowed horse, all of his possessions stuffed into two saddlebags.

He stopped at the A.Y. Ellis & Company store near the town square to inquire about the cost of a single bed, mattress, sheets, and pillow. Joshua F. Speed, one of the proprietors, figured it up: The total would be $17. Lincoln replied that the price seemed fair enough, but he just did not have the money. He had come to town to try "an experiment as a lawyer," he explained mournfully. Could credit be extended until Christmas? "If I fail in this," he confessed, "I do not know that I can ever pay you."

Speed had listened to one of Lincoln's political speeches and had been impressed, and he knew something of Lincoln's reputation. Perhaps to his own surprise, he said, "I have a large room with a double bed upstairs which you are very welcome to share with me." Lincoln asked, "Where is your room?" then carried his saddlebags up the stairs to the second floor. A few minutes later a happy Lincoln came down the stairs, without the saddlebags: "Well, Speed, I am moved!" It was the beginning of a lifelong friendship between the two young men. Joshua Speed became Abraham Lincoln's best friend. Born into a well-to-do Louisville family in 1814, Speed had been educated at a private school and at St. Joseph's Academy in Bardstown. In 1835 Speed moved to Springfield, where he worked in the Ellis store and helped edit a newspaper. He typified the considerable number of well-to-do Kentuckians who left the state in search of greater opportunities. Many of them, often attracted by the land survey system in the Old Northwest, crossed the Ohio River. Others moved westward to Missouri, which also had a strong Kentucky heritage. Joshua Speed was unusual in that after spending several years in Illinois he returned to Kentucky and became successful at home. He and his brother James were among Lincoln's most trusted advisers and supporters during the Civil War. Lincoln's first extended trip to Kentucky after leaving it as a boy was in 1841, when he visited Joshua and the Speed family at Farmington, their home outside Louisville.[5]

Lincoln won reelection to the state legislature in 1838 and 1840. During his eight years in the House he became adept at legislative procedures and politics. He was an effective debater and party leader, but even most of his political opponents liked him. Lincoln saw the need for an effective party organization in the state, and he worked diligently to perfect one. An active politician, he became well known in political circles across the state. His reputation for honesty sometimes surprised even his associates. His first presidential vote was cast in 1832 for Henry Clay, and he remained loyal to "Harry of the West" and his political principles when success seemed possible. During these legislative years he had become well acquainted with another rising young lawyer, Stephen A. Douglas, a Democratic partisan, whose defense of President Andrew Jackson's attack on the Second National Bank and his own stature earned him the name of "The Little Giant." As early as 1839 Lincoln and Douglas had begun public debates, which culminated in their famous exchanges in the senatorial race of 1858.[6]

During the 1840 presidential campaign Lincoln made the only political speech of his career in his native state. His efforts on behalf of "Tippecanoe and Tyler too" brought him to Shawneetown near the Ohio River. George W. Riddell and other Whig adherents in Morganfield, Kentucky, persuaded him to speak at a rally they had planned. The Shawneetown Whigs cooperated and prepared a float drawn by two white horses that featured lovely girls who represented the states of the Union. They also sent along a huge cannon that exploded when it was fired. No record was kept of Lincoln's remarks, but one must assume that it was typical of the others he delivered in the stirring campaign that elected Harrison as the first Whig president.[7] He was disappointed when John Tyler, who succeeded William Henry Harrison after the latter's death, proved to be more of an anti-Jackson Democrat than a Whig. Lincoln had supported Harrison in the 1840 campaign rather than Clay because the general stood a better chance of being elected.

Although politics was his great love, law was the profession in which he earned a living, and Lincoln's reputation also grew in that field. His close connections with Kentucky continued in that area of his life; all three of his law partners had a Kentucky background. Stuart's partner was moving out of the community, and in April 1837 Stuart invited Lincoln to join him in a partnership. Stuart had a flourishing practice, and Lincoln was exposed to a wide variety of cases. Most of them were routine, but for others, which were more complex, Lincoln had to master intricacies of the law that had eluded his study. The two lawyers occupied one room with a minimum of furniture and a tiny law library. Once Lincoln got over his initial awe of legal documents, his declarations became simple and clear. He enjoyed the work, including riding circuit as the circuit court moved from county to county, spending a week or two in each one, depending upon the length of the docket. Fees may have averaged about $5, and sometimes they were paid in commodities instead of cash. As the junior partner, Lincoln was responsible for keeping the record of the cases they handled and the fees charged. Neither partner was systematic in handling papers, and frantic searches often had to be made to locate important documents. After Stuart was elected to Congress, Lincoln assumed more of the office burdens and handled more of the cases that came to the firm. In May 1841 they dissolved the partnership by mutual consent and parted on good terms.[8]

Lincoln then became the partner of Stephen T. Logan, another Whig, who had practiced law in Kentucky for ten years, including a stint as commonwealth attorney, before moving to Springfield in 1833. Elected a circuit judge, he had resigned because of the inadequate pay. Logan had an exceptional knowledge of the law, but his bizarre appearance and a poor voice were handicaps in presenting jury cases. He taught Lincoln much about the importance of careful preparation of a case and the drafting of a comprehensive brief before representing a client in court. Logan was in great demand by persons who had cases coming before the Illinois Supreme Court, and Lincoln was gratified to find that such fees averaged $20. Logan later commented on Lincoln's standing as an attorney: "I don't think that he studied very much. . . . He would work hard and learn all there was in a case he had in hand. He got to be a pretty good lawyer, though his general knowledge of law was not very formidable. But he would study out his case and make about as much out of it as anybody."

Stuart and Lincoln had divided their income evenly, but Logan appears to have pocketed a two-thirds share. As Logan had hoped, Lincoln became adept in handling cases that went before a jury. He established good rapport with jurors, and he used his limitless supply of stories and anecdotes to make his points and to deflect those of his opponent. Lincoln placed much emphasis upon using short, clear, carefully prepared closing statements. As he told a young man who was studying law with the partners: "Billy, don't shoot too high—aim lower and the common people will understand you. They are the ones you want to reach."

Logan and Lincoln did not have much of a library, but after the state Supreme Court moved into the statehouse in 1841, they had access to the court's good library. Though Lincoln never became a legal scholar, he spent many hours in the library searching for precedents that would help his cause. He enjoyed appearing before the Supreme Court. The acquisition of a wife and family made the larger fees more welcome, and he had time for careful preparation of the briefs, on which the court depended more than it did on oral arguments. Lincoln's skill in preparing such briefs made him a formidable adversary, and his reputation grew across the state.

Logan and Lincoln dissolved their relationship in the fall of 1844. Logan wanted to go into partnership with his son, Lincoln probably felt that he was entitled to more than one-third of the income, and both men were anxious to go to Congress—which meant competing for the same seat. They parted gradually and amicably, and they occasionally worked together as long as Lincoln practiced law.[9]

One morning in the fall of 1844, Lincoln hurried into the firm's office and made a startling proposal to William H. Herndon, an apprentice studying law with the partners: "Billy, do you want to enter into a partnership with me in the law business?" Herndon recovered sufficiently to stammer his acceptance of the unexpected offer. Herndon was born in Green County, Kentucky, on December 18, 1818, but his family moved to Illinois two years later. His father, Archer Herndon, opened the Indian Queen Hotel about 1826 and had served in the legislature with Lincoln. William clerked for a time for Joshua Speed, enrolled in Illinois College for a year, then returned to the store, where he became acquainted with Lincoln. He left the store in 1842 and began studying law with Logan and Lincoln. Many members of the legal fraternity were surprised by the choice. Mrs. Lincoln developed a dislike for Herndon that evolved into hatred—a sentiment that he reciprocated in full. Lincoln's election as president suspended the partnership, but Lincoln indicated to Herndon that he wanted to resume their relationship when his term expired. After the assassination Herndon devoted most of the rest of his life to collecting information about Lincoln and writing and speaking about the man whose memory he revered. Unfortunately, since Herndon did not go to Kentucky to collect information himself, he had to depend on other sources, and his information for Lincoln's early years is inferior to what he found for the Indiana and Illinois experiences.

About five feet nine, a well-dressed dandy, a nonstop talker, an extensive reader on many subjects, Herndon was a decided contrast to his mentor. He was also a heavy drinker who later became an alcoholic; he was a strong abolitionist, and he didn't really like the law. Lincoln selected him in part because he wanted to be the head of his own firm; he sought an assistant, not an equal, and he was confident that with experience, Herndon would develop as a lawyer. Herndon also had connections with the nonaristocratic local element of the Whig party, whose support Lincoln needed if he expected to win his way to Congress. And, what was perhaps most important, he liked the young man and knew that he could depend upon his absolute loyalty. They were an odd couple in many respects. Lincoln was subject to bouts of melancholy, whereas Herndon was always optimistic. Herndon lacked a sense of humor whereas for Lincoln that trait probably permitted him to keep his sanity.

Their final office was a single room on the second floor of a brick building near the town square. The sparse furniture included an old sofa where Lincoln liked to stretch while thinking out his briefs, a couple of tables for desks, several cane-bottomed chairs, and a bookcase filled largely with Herndon's books. Dirt accumulated undisturbed, so that a law student later asserted that some fruit seeds that fell to the floor sprouted there. Neither man was orderly, and their papers were usually in absolute disarray. Lincoln often stored important documents in his stovepipe hat. Upon one occasion he apologized to a client for having misplaced his papers; he had bought a new hat and had forgotten to transfer the contents of the old hat to the new one. Papers were lost so often in the office that Lincoln kept a bundle tied with a string on his desk. It carried the notation: "When you can't find *it* anywhere else, look into this."

Herndon had other problems with Lincoln's family besides his mutual hatred with Mrs. Lincoln. He was beset by invasions of the office, often when they were working on Sunday, by Lincoln's undisciplined sons. Lincoln would work on, unaware of the havoc the boys were creating as they pulled books from the shelves and turned over chairs in addition to creating noise that upset Herndon until he "wanted to wring their little necks." But in deference to his partner, Herndon said nothing about the brats. During their long association, the partners always addressed each other as "Billy" and "Mr. Lincoln."[10]

In view of his later role in bringing slavery to an end in the United States, it is interesting to see that Lincoln represented both sides in fugitive slave cases. In the 1841 *Bailey v. Cromwell* case before the state Supreme Court, Lincoln secured freedom for an indentured Negro girl who had been sold in Illinois by one white man to another. Lincoln's argument was that the Northwest Ordinance of 1787 and the state constitution prohibited slavery in the state. Therefore, all persons, regardless of color, were free. And it was obviously illegal to attempt to sell a free person.

Six years later in the Robert Matson slave case, Lincoln defended a Kentucky slave owner who had brought several slaves across the Ohio River to work his Illinois land. Taking advantage of their presence on free soil, the slaves refused to return to Kentucky. Lincoln's opponent used the arguments that

Lincoln had employed in the *Bailey v. Cromwell* case, without, however, citing it. Lincoln argued that since the slaves had been brought into the state on a temporary basis and would have soon been returned to Kentucky, the Illinois law did not apply to them. He lost the case, but by 1847 he was sufficiently antislavery that he may not have been too disappointed by the result.[11]

His election to the state legislature had not satisfied Lincoln's political ambitions. In the short run, he aspired to the new Seventh Congressional District seat in the national House of Representatives. It would come vacant when John T. Stuart decided to return to his law practice at the end of his term. British-born Edward D. Baker was a possible candidate to succeed him. A flamboyant orator who liked to appear on a platform with an eagle that appeared abashed when Baker assailed the Democrats but spread its wings and screamed when he praised the Whigs, Baker was a popular figure. So was John J. Hardin, a former Kentuckian who had been educated at Transylvania University before moving to Illinois. Faced with such formidable opposition, Lincoln worked assiduously in 1843 to line up support. He asked a friend to deny any claims that Lincoln really did not want the post: "The truth is, I would like to go very much."[12] The Sangamon County Whig convention endorsed Baker, but the Pekin district party convention selected Hardin. Lincoln got the convention to go on record as endorsing Baker in 1844, thus establishing a principle of rotation in office after one term. This would mean that Lincoln would get his chance in 1846. He also secured the consent of the convention to continue using the convention as the way of making nominations. Its use, he insisted, would strengthen the party by creating a stronger organization.

Baker was nominated in 1844, and Lincoln campaigned vigorously on his behalf, as he also did for another of Henry Clay's futile efforts to capture the presidency. Baker was elected, and Lincoln started lining up votes for his own 1846 campaign. He had a scare when Hardin, who had enjoyed his term in the

House, gave signs of running again. Lincoln's most effective tactic was to emphasize that "turn about is fair play," and he rejected Hardin's efforts to return to the old system of independent candidates instead of using the convention to make nominations. Lincoln's many contacts in the district paid dividends, and Hardin, seeing inevitable defeat, withdrew from the race and volunteered for military service during the Mexican War.

Peter Cartwright, the noted Methodist circuit rider, was Lincoln's Democratic opponent. Active in the Great Revival in Kentucky and Tennessee, the "Kentucky Boy" had himself transferred to Illinois in 1824 because of his antislavery sentiments. He had defeated Lincoln in his try for the state House in 1832. Cartwright was not a good campaigner, but well into the race he asserted that Lincoln was an infidel. Lincoln issued a handbill in which he admitted that early in life he had argued for the "Doctrine of Necessity," the belief "that the human mind is impelled to action, or held in rest by some power, over which the mind itself has no control." He had abandoned that view some five years earlier, although he understood that some Christian denominations held that opinion. Though he was not a member of any Christian church, he stated, "I have never denied the truth of the scriptures; and I have never spoken with intentional disrespect of religion in general, or of any denomination of Christians in particular." He did not believe that he could support a man for office who was an open enemy of religion. Lincoln won the election easily, getting eight of eleven counties and nearly 57 percent of the vote.[13]

The Thirtieth Congress did not meet until December 1847, so Lincoln had to wait a year before taking his seat. Because his family was to accompany him to Washington, he rented their house for a year for $90. Herndon was to keep the firm going while Lincoln was gone. On October 25, 1847, Lincoln, Mary, and their sons Robert (4) and Eddie (1½) began a stagecoach-steamboat-railroad trip to Lexington. Mary had not returned there since her move to Springfield in 1839. Her father had visited his considerable family in Illinois, but the other Todds had not met Lincoln and the boys. The three leisurely weeks spent in Lexington constituted one of the few vacations Lincoln ever had. He was introduced to many Todd family friends, including Henry Clay. The Todds had a large private library, and Lincoln spent hours reading there, including a book of poetry of which he was especially fond. But he also visited with some of the city's noted lawyers, and he saw the darker side of slavery in the slave pens and the public auctions. On Thanksgiving Day the Lincolns resumed their tiring trip to Washington by taking the stage to Maysville, where they caught a steamboat. They found lodging in one large room in Mrs. Ann G. Sprigg's boardinghouse, just east of the Capitol; eight other Whig Congressmen also boarded there. Lincoln was a popular figure almost immediately, but Mary became bored with the cramped quarters and the complaints of other boarders about the noisy Lincoln sons. In the spring of 1848 she took the boys to her father's home in Lexington, Kentucky.

One of Lincoln's new friends was Alexander H. Stephens of Georgia, another Whig who hoped to revitalize the party. Lincoln had said little about the Mexican War, which had started in 1846; he believed that once it was under way a good citizen should support the war effort. Now, however, the war was almost won, and he saw an opportunity to attack the Democrats over the way in which it had started. In his December 1847 message to Congress, President James K. Polk repeated the assertion he had made in his war message of May 11, 1846, that the war had started when Mexico invaded the state of Texas, "shedding the blood of our citizens on our own soil."[14] On December 22 Lincoln introduced a series of resolutions that became known as "the Spot Resolution." He challenged the president to specify the spot of undisputed American soil on which the blood had been shed. He continued the attack in January in a lengthy speech in which he blamed the president and the Democratic party for starting the war.

Much to Lincoln's disappointment, his challenge was

largely ignored in Washington. He received considerable criticism in Illinois, where even some Whigs believed that he was undercutting the American armies in the field. Lincoln hastened to reassure Herndon, who relayed some of the complaints, that the intent was to hurt the Democrats in the 1848 presidential election. One way to dispel the disloyalty charge was to nominate Gen. Zachary Taylor for president. Practical politics led Lincoln to abandon Henry Clay, his political idol, whom he had supported faithfully for many years. "Our only chance is with Taylor," he wrote Jesse Lynch on April 10, 1848. "I go for him, not because I think he would make a better president than Clay, but because I think he would make a better one than Polk, or Cass, or Buchanan, or any such creatures, one of whom is sure to be elected if he is not."[15] A Kentuckian who deserted Clay explained his reason for doing so in somewhat more elevated terms. "I have voted for Mr. Clay all the time, have *bet* on him, and lost, until I am *tired,* and have finally concluded that Mr. Clay is *too pure a patriot* to win in these demagogueing times."[16]

Zachary Taylor's family had moved to Jefferson County, Kentucky, when he was less than a year old. He had grown up there, and Kentucky was his legal residence for much of his adult life. Later, he sold his Bluegrass farm and purchased extensive acres in Louisiana and Mississippi. Lincoln urged the party's nominee to stand above and apart from regional and local issues and to pledge himself as president to leave "the legislation of the country to rest with Congress, uninfluenced in its origin or progress, and undisturbed by the veto unless in very special and clear cases." That stance should apply, Lincoln argued, even to the subject of slavery, which was attracting more controversy. If the Wilmot Proviso (which would prohibit slavery in any of the territory acquired from Mexico) should pass Congress, Lincoln said, Taylor, although a large slaveholder, should not veto it. But, as he pointed out later, Lincoln had often voted for the Wilmot Proviso during his tenure in the House.[17]

Mary and the boys came back from Kentucky to accompany him on a speaking tour through several New England towns in the fall of 1848. Lincoln made a good impression with Whig audiences and party newspapers. It was important exposure for a man who was hoping and working to revitalize the Whig party—and for a man who was an ambitious politician.[18]

When Lincoln returned to Washington for the December 1848 opening of Congress, Mary and the boys remained in Springfield. He found that slavery, and especially the question of its expansion, had become the major issue in Congress. Though he was opposed to slavery, he was not an abolitionist. Lincoln did not believe that Congress had the constitutional right to interfere with slavery in the states that had it. He thought that if slavery was not allowed to expand, it would ultimately die. But he did believe that Congress had the power to abolish slavery in the District of Columbia if the people in the District requested it. On January 10, 1849, after careful discussions with a number of people, Lincoln introduced a resolution in which he proposed holding a referendum in which all free white male citizens of the District could vote. If a majority approved, slavery would be ended in the District except for the personal servants of federal officials. Slaves in the District would remain slaves, but the federal government would pay full value to owners who agreed to free them. Children born to slave mothers in the District after 1850 would be free. In a concession to proslavery advocates, Lincoln proposed that effective steps be taken to return to their owners fugitive slaves who had fled into the District.

The support that Lincoln thought he had obtained for his proposal disappeared when the idea came under public scrutiny. Attacked for doing too little or attempting too much, he did not bother to introduce a bill that was doomed to defeat.[19] He was especially discouraged by the failure of his efforts to unite the Whig party. In part he blamed President Taylor for not using his patronage to strengthen the party. Lincoln contended that preference should be given to Whig over Democratic candidates for offices, and he favored replacing strongly partisan Democrats who held office, even if they were performing their duties well. As a lame duck congressman with little influence, because of the rotation agreement, Lincoln was not very successful in placing persons whom he recommended for positions. In an effort to secure a cabinet post or a foreign mission for Edward D. Baker, Lincoln had Joshua Speed plead Baker's case with John J. Crittenden, then governor of Kentucky. Crittenden did not think highly of Baker, but he said, "There is Lincoln, whom I regard as a rising man—if he were an applicant I would go for him." Lincoln dismissed the flattery when he responded to Speed: "There is nothing about me that would authorize me to think of a first class office, and a second class one would not compensate me for being snarled at by others who want it for themselves."[20] But Governor Crittenden's flattering remarks recognized Lincoln's growing influence in the Whig party.

As patronage positions were filled, only the office of the commissioner of the General Land Office seemed within the reach of an Illinois Whig. It paid a good $3,000 per year, it had considerable power, especially in the West, and it included a number of patronage positions. Friends such as the massive Judge David Davis advised Lincoln to take the job; it would probably pay more than he could earn as a lawyer. Lincoln was not willing to abandon the law, and he had promised to support Cyrus Edwards for commissioner. A deadlock developed when Baker pushed the claims of James L.D. Morrison, and Lincoln was urged to take the post himself. He was dismayed when Whigs in the northern part of the state backed Justin Butterfield, a Chicago lawyer who had supported Henry Clay in 1848 rather than Taylor. Lincoln entered the contest to block Butterfield, and each man hurried to Washington to plead his case. Secretary of the Interior Thomas Ewing favored Butterfield, and the president resolved his problem by letting the secretary decide.

Secretary of State John M. Clayton then surprised Lincoln

by offering him the position of secretary to the governor of the Oregon Territory. Lincoln declined it. Then Secretary Ewing, perhaps realizing that he had snubbed an important Illinois Whig, asked Lincoln to become governor of the Oregon Territory. The offer was tempting, but Oregon was strongly Democratic, and when it became a state a Whig would have little chance to become state governor or to be elected to the U.S. Senate. When he declined the offer, Lincoln stated that his wife was strongly opposed to making a move to the Pacific Northwest.[21] His political career apparently at an end, Lincoln returned to Springfield and devoted himself to his law practice. Within the next few years he became one of the outstanding lawyers in the state.

During his formative years in Illinois, Lincoln was closely associated with a number of former Kentuckians who had also moved north of the Ohio River. His law partners, especially the first two, who did much to train him in the practice of law, had a great deal of influence in determining his development in law and politics. The three former Kentucky women with whom Lincoln had romantic attachments contributed much to his personal growth, especially Mary Todd, whom he married. Numerous other individuals with whom he had contact in Illinois also contributed to his personal growth. In Illinois, more than in Indiana, he was influenced by members of a social and economic class superior to his family background. He became associated with a number of former Kentuckians who were representative of the Kentuckians with whom he had to deal during the war years.

5

Lincoln
and Romance

When Abraham Lincoln moved to New Salem in the summer of 1831, he was twenty-two years old and an eligible bachelor despite his lack of a steady income. He became popular almost immediately with the males in the community, but he was shy and awkward with the females, especially those of marriageable age, and efforts to match him with various young women failed. Nevertheless, it was at New Salem that Lincoln had the first of the three more or less serious romantic attachments of his life. All three of the women had been born in Kentucky. They also increased his connections with Kentucky and thereby enhanced his understanding of the state and its people.

James Rutledge was a South Carolinian who moved to Kentucky. A daughter named Ann May Rutledge was born there on January 7, 1813. The family later moved to Illinois, where James was one of the founders of New Salem. He started the debating society that Lincoln joined, and Lincoln must have borrowed books from Rutledge's library of two or three dozen volumes. Later, Lincoln boarded at the Rutledge tavern, where he became better acquainted with Ann. She was described by those who knew her as being pretty, with fair skin, blue eyes, and hair that was either auburn or red. She was about five feet two inches tall and weighed between 120 and 130 pounds. In time, she and Lincoln were attracted to each other.

But there was a complication. She had become engaged to

John McNeil, a New Yorker who boarded at the Rutledge tavern. McNeil had prospered as a farmer and storekeeper, and they were to be married. Then he confessed to her that his name was really John McNamar. He had come west to recover the family fortune, and he had changed his name to avoid interference by family members. Now, he told Ann, he was able to go back to New York and bring his family west to live. Then he and Ann would get married. After he departed, McNamar's letters came frequently at first, then finally ceased. When Ann fell in love with Lincoln, she decided that she should break the engagement with McNamar before marrying Lincoln. By the time they married, he should have become a lawyer and would be in a better position to support a wife. Then in the summer of 1835 Ann became ill, probably with typhoid fever; she died on August 25. According to some versions of their romance, she called for Lincoln, who came to her deathbed for a final tearful parting. Lincoln then fell into one of his melancholy depressions, so severe that friends feared for his sanity and even his life. He was persuaded to spend some time on the farm of his friend Bowling Green, and there he recovered enough to resume his studies.[1]

Billy Herndon was responsible for making the Ann Rutledge story known after Lincoln's death. As soon as his partner was assassinated, Herndon began collecting information about Lincoln's life and career. Much of his information came from interviews, and a number of people from New Salem days mentioned the Ann Rutledge relationship. On November 16, 1866, when Herndon gave a lecture on Lincoln and the Ann Rutledge love affair in the Springfield courthouse, he presented Ann as the only true love in Lincoln's life. It was a devastating blow to Mary Todd Lincoln, and she and her supporters denounced the story as a fabrication. Herndon may have been influenced by his intense dislike of Mrs. Lincoln, but it is possible that he decided on the basis of his knowledge of Lincoln and the information acquired in his interview that Ann was truly Lincoln's great and only love. The Rutledge story appealed to many persons, and it became part of the Lincoln legend in numerous books, poems, and plays. Carl Sandburg was one of the best-known authors who accepted the tragic story and made it an important event in the development of Lincoln's life.[2]

In time many historians decided that the romantic tale was simply a myth, and a number of historical works either ignored the story or dismissed it as fiction. One damning indictment was that Lincoln never mentioned Ann in any of his writings. In recent years more research has restored credibility to the story. Herndon secured recollections from a number of persons from the New Salem days. William G. Green recalled that after Ann's death Lincoln had said, "I can never be reconciled to have the snow, rain and storms to beat on her grave," and Elizabeth Abell, also a New Salem friend, remembered Lincoln's saying on a stormy day "that he could not bear the idea of it raining on her grave." Isaac Cogdal said that he asked the president-elect if it was true that he had loved and courted Ann Rutledge. According to Cogdal, Lincoln replied, "It is true—true, indeed I did. I have loved the name of Rutledge to this day." Was it true that he had "run a little wild" over her death? "I did really. I ran off the tracks; it was my first. I loved the woman dearly and sacredly. She was a handsome girl, would have made a good loving wife, was natural and quite intellectual, though not highly educated. I did honestly and truly love the girl and think often, often of her now."[3] Some recent studies have accepted the validity of this relationship.[4]

If Lincoln's first romantic attachment contained the elements of tragedy, the second one bore traces of comedy or even farce. Mary Owens was born in Green County, Kentucky, on September 29, 1808, into a well-to-do family. In 1833 she visited her sister, Mrs. Bennett Abell, in New Salem for a month. Mary was described as a handsome woman with black hair, a fair skin, and very white teeth who stood five feet five inches tall and weighed some 150 pounds. She was well read, was a good conversationalist, and had a cheerful, lively disposition that won many New Salem friends. The normally shy Lincoln was much impressed by Mary, and after she returned to Kentucky he supposedly told Mrs. Abell, "If ever that girl comes back to New Salem I am going to marry her." When Mrs. Abell prepared to visit in Kentucky in late 1835 or early 1836, she asked Lincoln whether he would marry Mary if she returned to Illinois with her. Lincoln may have supposed that Mrs. Abell was jesting, but he was alleged to say that if they did not get married it would not be his fault.[5]

Mary Owens returned to New Salem in 1836, and Lincoln began to court her. She seemed to return his interest, and members of the little community who had been trying to find a mate for their tall friend must have been pleased with the prospect of success. When Lincoln wrote her from Vandalia on December 13, 1836, when he was in a legislative session, he dwelt on political affairs but then begged her to write "as soon as you get this, and if possible say something that will please me, for really I have not been pleased since I left you." His next extant letter to Mary was from Springfield on May 7, 1837. Addressed to "Friend Mary," he confessed being lonely. "I have been spoken to by but one woman since I've been here, and should not by her, if she could have avoided it." He had been thinking about what they had said about her coming to live in Springfield.

> I am afraid you would not be satisfied. . . . You would have to be poor without the means of hiding your poverty. Do you believe that you could bear that patiently? Whatever woman may cast her lot with mine, should any ever do so, it is my intention to do all in my power to make her happy and contented; and there is nothing I can imagine, that would make me more unhappy than to fail in the effort. I know I should be much happier with you than the way I am, provided I saw no signs of discontent in you. What you have said to me may have been in jest, or I may have misunderstood

it. If so, then let it be forgotten; if otherwise, I much
wish you would think seriously before you decide. For
my part, I have already decided. What I have said I will
most positively abide by, provided you wish it. My
opinion is that you had better not do it. You have not
been accustomed to hardship, and it may be more severe than you now immagine [*sic*]. I know you are capable of thinking correctly on any subject; and if you
deliberate naturally upon this, before you decide, then
I am willing to obey your decision.

This less than passionate declaration of true love indicates
that Lincoln had proposed marriage and then had become fearful that she might accept. He seemed anxious to break off the
engagement, if indeed there was one. As Mary became acquainted with Abraham, she became aware of some unpleas-
ant traits. On an outing with some other young couples, he had
not helped her across a stream as the other gentlemen had done
with their companions. She must have heard about his bouts
with melancholy and his depressed moods. His poverty, as he
admitted, was self-evident. Later, Mary commented, "Mr. Lincoln was deficient in those little links which make up the path
of a woman's happiness—at least it was true in my case."

Lincoln wrote Mary again on August 16, 1837, from
Springfield. If anything, his proposal of marriage was even less
certain than it had been in his last letter. "I want in all cases to
do right, and most particularly so, in all cases with women."
More than anything, he wanted to do right with her, if only
he knew what it was. To clarify the issue he continued:

I now say, that you can now drop the subject, dismiss
your thoughts (if you ever had any) from me forever,
and leave this letter unanswered, without calling forth
one accusing murmur from me. . . . if it will add anything to your comfort, or peace of mind, to do so, it is
my sincere wish that you should. . . . What I wish is,

that our further acquaintance shall depend upon your-self. . . . If you feel yourself in any degree bound to me, I am now willing to release you, provided you wish it; while, on the other hand, I am willing, and even anx-ious to bound you faster, if I can be convinced that it will, in any considerable degree, add to your happiness.

Then he added, "If it suits you best not to answer this—fare-well—a long life and a merry one attend you."[6] No answer to this passionate declaration is known to exist.

This romantic episode reveals a callow young man, unac-customed to dealing with women, who found himself almost committed to a marriage for which he was not yet ready to assume responsibilities. He longed to get rid of the commit-ment that he seemed to have made, but his sense of honor and fairness dictated that he could not abruptly terminate the un-derstanding—if there was one. On April 1, 1838, he sent an account of the affair to Mrs. Orville H. Browning, one of his most trusted female friends, who was safely married. Almost cruelly, he depicted Mary Owens as being so fat that she did not have the wrinkles that otherwise would have revealed her age, was missing teeth, and had an elderly, weathered face. "I was not all pleased with her," he wrote, but he felt bound to carry out his commitment to marry her. After delaying as long as he could, he proposed directly. To his surprise and relief, she firmly rejected his offer. "I verry [*sic*] unexpectedly found my-self mortified almost beyond endurance." He began to think for the first time "that I was really a little in love with her." Lincoln realized, he confessed, that he had made a fool of him-self. "I have now come to the conclusion never again to think of marrying; and for this reason; I can never be satisfied with any one who would be block-head enough to have me."[7]

She seems to have returned to Kentucky during the spring of 1838, and she married Jesse Vineyard in March 1841. Be-fore her death in 1877, she referred to Lincoln as "a man with a heart full of human kindness and a head full of common sense."[8] Their semicomic involvement showed Lincoln as a young man who did not know enough about women to avoid getting into an awkward situation from which he did not know how to extract himself gracefully. Both Mary Owens and Lincoln were probably pleased to reach the end of an embarrassing episode. Abraham Lincoln's third romantic attachment was with Mary Todd of Lexington, Kentucky. It ended in a sometimes stormy marriage that lasted until his untimely death.

The Todd brothers, John, Robert, and Levi, came to Kentucky during the frontier era. They acquired large acreages of land, they helped found Lexington, and they were active in the economic and political development of Kentucky as it became a state in 1792. A son of Levi Todd, Robert S. Todd, married Eliza Parker on November 26, 1812. Eliza's father, Robert Parker, had come to Lexington in 1790. Although not as successful as the Todds, he had also prospered as a merchant and landowner; he died in 1800. Widow Elizabeth Parker then built a house in Lexington. Robert Todd had graduated from Transylvania, then had become a lawyer who never practiced that profession. Instead, he concentrated on his business and land interests. He also became clerk of the lower house of the General Assembly, a position that paid poorly but provided many useful contacts. Eliza and Robert Todd had six living children when she died in childbirth on July 6, 1825. Mary Ann was born on December 13, 1818. Her two older sisters were Elizabeth and Frances; Ann was the youngest sister, and Mary had two younger brothers, Levi and George Rogers. Robert Todd's unmarried sister, Ann Maria, came to live with the thirty-four-year-old widower and his six children. Household slaves also helped care for them, but Robert Todd felt the need for a wife and a mother for them. By Christmas 1825 he was courting Elizabeth Humphreys, usually called Becky. She was connected with the Brown family that had also been prominent in the early history of Kentucky. They were engaged by October 1826, and Robert pressed for an early wedding. They were married in Frankfort on November 1, 1826, with John J. Crittenden as the groom's best man.

The widow Parker had opposed the remarriage of her son-in-law, and the family situation was not helped by the two homes' being separated by only some fifty yards. The dislike of the six children for their stepmother was intensified by the birth of her own children. Mary and her siblings were convinced that their stepmother was partial to her own offspring. Mary, nearly eight years old, was a complex child who could be loving and generous at times but was also headstrong and high strung. She clashed frequently with her stepmother over such issues as the clothing that was proper for a young girl to wear. When Mary lost that battle, she was said to have put salt in Mrs. Todd's coffee. Mary was also intellectually precocious, and a partial solution for the family strife was to give her an education that was rare for a girl of that era. Mary entered the academy of Dr. John Ward when she was about eight. Rector of Christ Church Episcopal, he was a New Englander who had come to Kentucky by way of North Carolina. His school was coeducational with some 120 pupils from many of the best families of the Bluegrass. Dr. Ward believed in discipline, and during the summer some classes started as early as five o'clock. Cousin and classmate Elizabeth Humphreys recalled that Mary was an excellent student, well in advance of others of her age. She had a retentive memory and a mind that quickly grasped the meaning of materials presented to her.[9]

After six years at Dr. Ward's academy, Mary enrolled in the boarding school of Mme. Victorie Charlotte LeClere Mentelle on the Richmond Pike, opposite Ashland, the estate of Henry Clay. The Mentelles had fled from the French Revolution in 1792 and by 1798 were living in Lexington. Well educated, they taught French and dancing before opening the boarding school. The Todd coach carried Mary to the school each Monday morning and picked her up each Friday afternoon to spend the weekend at home. Starting in 1832, home was a house that Robert Todd purchased on Main Street, about two blocks from the family's previous house, which was on Short Street. Considerably larger than the old home and located on lovely grounds with the Town Fork of Elkhorn Creek running along its lower edge, it had another advantage; it was more removed from his mother-in-law, who could not accept his remarriage.

Mme. Mentelle's purpose was to provide "a truly useful & 'Solid' English Education in all its branches." In addition to academic subjects, the pupils learned social skills, including a number of dances. Mary was an apt student of French, which she used for the rest of her life. She enjoyed her years at the boarding school, and few girls in the region were as well educated as she was when she left at the end of four years. At eighteen, she was short and somewhat plump but graceful, with lovely blue eyes, a broad, expansive mouth, and a face that dimpled when she smiled. Called brilliant, vivacious, charming, and impulsive, she also had a caustic wit that she sometimes unleashed without warning or thought of consequences. The daughter of a wealthy and popular citizen, after a reasonable amount of flirtation Mary might be expected to make a good marriage with a promising son of a similar family.

Mary's home life was not as ideal as it appeared to be, for friction continued between Robert Todd's children from his first marriage and their stepmother and his second family, which was increasing at regular intervals. Mary's oldest sister, Elizabeth, married Ninian W. Edwards, son of a former governor of Illinois, on February 29, 1832. The groom was a junior at Transylvania, and when he graduated they moved to Springfield, Illinois. In 1836 Frances Todd went to Springfield to live with them. Mary was the eldest daughter left at home, and in her efforts to achieve independence, she clashed with her stepmother. Later, after she married Lincoln and was staying in Lexington while her husband was in Congress, Mary wrote Lincoln about her stepmother: "She is very obliging and accommodating, but if she thought any of us were on her hands again, I believe she would be worse than ever."

In the summer of 1837, Mary went to Springfield to visit

sisters Elizabeth and Frances. Other relatives lived there in a sizable ex-Kentucky community: Uncle Dr. John Todd and three cousins, John T. Stuart, John J. Hardin, and Stephen T. Logan, who were lawyers. Mary was the belle of that social circle that summer, and although she apparently did not meet Abraham Lincoln, she heard a great deal about him before she returned to Lexington in the fall.[10] Two years later Mary decided to make an extended visit to her sisters in Springfield. This time she met Lincoln in the lively youthful society that centered around Elizabeth and Ninian Edwards at their mansion. Mary Todd was dangerously close to being called an old maid, and in an era in which a woman had few economic opportunities outside of marriage, she must have considered the young bachelors whom she met as possible husbands.

William Herndon described Mary when she came to Springfield:

> She was a young woman of strong, passionate nature and quick temper. . . . of the average height, weighing when I first saw her about a hundred and thirty pounds. She was rather compactly built, had a well rounded face, rich dark-brown hair, and blueish-gray eyes. In her bearing she was proud, but handsome and vivacious. . . . a good conversationist. . . . she wrote with wit and ability. She not only had a quick intellect but an intuitive judgment of men and their motives. Ordinarily she was affable and even charming in her manners; but when offended or antagonized, her agreeable qualities instantly disappeared beneath a wave of stinging satire or sarcastic bitterness, and her entire better nature was submerged. In her figure and physical proportions, in education, bearing, temperment, history—in everything she was the exact reverse of Lincoln.

He added that "she soon became the belle of the town, leading the young men of the town a merry dance." One of her admirers was Stephen A. Douglas, a leading Democrat in the state; the "Little Giant" did not tower over her. According to one story of their meeting, Lincoln said to Mary that he wanted to dance with her in the worst way. A friend who overheard asked her later if he had danced with her in the worst way, "Yes," Mary replied, "the very worst." Mary so fascinated Lincoln with her wit, charm, and general culture that he overcame much of his shyness when he was with her. They both loved poetry and politics, and he discovered that she was also a strong Whig and that his admired Henry Clay was a family friend. He had never known a woman of her intellect and manners, and he attended her whenever possible—dances, horseback rides, picnics, just so he could be with her. Mary found Lincoln interesting and perhaps something of a challenge; she was impressed by his ambition and his aspirations to move on to higher positions and offices. Friendship ripened into an engagement near Christmas of 1840. The Edwardses, who had at first disliked his prospects, had come to see him as a desirable match; they also recognized some unique qualities in their friend Abraham. Mary displayed some jealousy when she thought that Lincoln was paying too much attention to the lovely young Matilda Edwards.[11]

Having made a commitment, Lincoln began to have the same second thoughts that he had had during his Mary Owens entanglement. Could he give Mary Todd the type of life to which she was accustomed? Had he been maneuvered into proposing? Was he ready to make such a drastic change in his life? Biographer David Donald suggests that both Lincoln and Joshua Speed were "probably sexually inexperienced," and they were probably "anxious about their own, as yet untested sexual adequacy; in addition, they must have worried about how to go about transforming the adored object of chaste passion into a bed partner."[12] Lincoln's anxiety was made more acute because Speed had decided to sell his share of the store and return to Kentucky. Lincoln had to leave the room he had shared with Speed and find other lodging.

The accumulation of problems was just too much for him;

Lincoln decided that he must break the engagement. His first thought was to write Mary and tell her that he did not love her, but Speed had the wisdom to dissuade him from that course. Words spoken may be forgiven, he asserted; words put into writing can not be erased. Lincoln went to the Edwards home and told Mary that he did not love her. She burst into tears, and Lincoln kissed her and departed. Mary, who thought he might be in love with Matilda Edwards, released him from the engagement but indicated that she had not changed her mind.

As Lincoln pondered over his action and wondered if he had forever forfeited any chance of happiness, he fell into a deep depression. For a week he stayed in bed, unable to attend the legislative sessions, seeing only Joshua Speed and Dr. Anson G. Henry, who diagnosed hypochondria brought on by anxiety, overwork, and exhaustion. Speed was so fearful of suicide that he took away Lincoln's razor and knife. Some friends who had witnessed earlier bouts of melancholy were not as concerned, but when Lincoln was able to resume some semblance of a normal life they were shocked by the change in his appearance and manner. Ninian Edwards said Lincoln was "as crazy as a loon," but Elizabeth Edwards gave a better explanation of his plight. Lincoln, she observed, "went crazy because he wanted to marry and doubted his ability and capacity to please and support a wife." A friend who had left town was concerned when he wrote another friend: "We have been very much distressed on Mr. Lincoln's account; hearing that he had two Cat fits and a Duck fit since we left."[13]

When Lincoln wrote partner John T. Stuart in Washington on January 23, 1841, he was unable to give a complete account of political developments, for "I am now the most miserable man living. If what I feel were equally distributed to the whole human family, there would not be one cheerful face in the world. Whether I shall ever be better I can not tell; I awfully forbode I shall not. To remain as I am is impossible; I must die or be better, it appears to me." He was able to return to the legislature before the end of January, and from then until adjournment in March he participated actively in the work of the House. In May 1841 he and Stuart dissolved their law firm, and he formed another partnership with Stephen T. Logan. Speed had sold out and returned to Kentucky, and when Lincoln wrote him on June 19 to describe a spectacular murder case, he added, "I stick to my promise to come to Louisville."[14]

In August Lincoln visited Farmington, the Speed estate outside Louisville, for a few weeks. It was his first experience with luxurious living made possible by slavery. A household slave was assigned to make him comfortable, and he relaxed in that environment. He and Mary, Joshua's half sister, became friends, and he had long talks with Mrs. Speed, who gave him a Bible, which he promised to read regularly when he returned home. Lincoln enjoyed walking into town and visiting James, Joshua's brother, in his law office and borrowing some of his books. He and Joshua took long walks and had lengthy talks. They could unburden their hearts to each other as to no one else. Lincoln's spirits lifted when he discovered that his romantic problems were not unique. Joshua was courting Fanny Henning, and Lincoln found her to be "one of the sweetest girls in the world" with "heavenly *black* eyes." The only flaw he discovered was "a tendency toward melancholly," but "This, let it be observed, is a misfortune not a fault."

Years later when he was visiting a Union army camp, seeing an officer's sword reminded Lincoln of a scary experience he had while visiting at Farmington:

> That is a formidable weapon, but it don't look half as dangerous to me as once did a Kentucky bowie-knife. One night I passed through the outskirts of Louisville when suddenly a man sprang from a dark alley and drew out a bowie-knife. It looked three times as long as that sword, though I don't suppose it really was. He flourished it in front of me. It glistened in the moonlight, and for several seconds he seemed to try to see

how near he could come to cutting off my nose without doing it. Finally he said, "Can you lend me five dollars on that?" I never reached in my pockets for money so quick in the whole course of my life. Handing him a bill, I said: "There's ten dollars, neighbor. Now put away your scythe."

Speed was having the same second thoughts as the ones that had plagued Lincoln. In Kentucky, and from Springfield upon his return, Lincoln sought to reassure his anxious friend. As the date of the wedding approached, he wrote Speed, "In two or three months, to say the most, you will be the happiest of men." After the marriage, Lincoln was delighted to receive Speed's assurance that he was happier than he had ever expected to be; that news made Lincoln happier "than the total sum of all I have enjoyed since that fatal first of Jany. '41." Seeking absolute proof of Speed's happiness, Lincoln inquired later if he was still as happy as he had been soon after the event. "From any body but me, this would be an impertinent question not to be tolerated; but I know you will pardon it in me."[15]

In trying to help Speed, Lincoln provided therapy for himself, and he began to resolve some of his doubts. But this time he was determined to be cautious. When he wrote Speed on July 4, 1842, he declared that "before I resolve to do the one thing or the other, I must regain my confidence in my own ability to keep my resolves when they are made."[16] He had once prided himself upon his ability to do that, but it had been lost and he had not regained it.

Friends of both Mary and Abraham had regretted the breakup of their engagement, and in the summer of 1842 some of them decided to bring them back together. The traditional story is that Eliza Francis, wife of the editor of the *Sangamo Journal*, invited them separately to her home and told them to be friends. They began meeting secretly at her home with only Dr. Henry and Julia Jayne, Mary's closest friend, aware of their reconciliation.[17] A recent study of the relationship suggests that

John J. Hardin, one of Mary's cousins, and his wife, Sarah, were the friends who were most responsible for bringing the estranged couple back together.

A political incident may have helped heal the breach. Democratic state auditor James Shields properly ordered nonacceptance of the notes of the State Bank of Illinois when it failed in 1842. Posing as "Rebecca," an uneducated but shrewd countrywoman, Lincoln wrote a letter to the newspaper in which he made fun of Shields and the policies of his party. Shields lacked a sense of humor, and Mary and Julia added some touches to Lincoln's letter. It was so well received that the two ladies rashly wrote another letter of their own. Outraged, Shields demanded that the editor reveal the name of the author. To protect the ladies, Lincoln authorized Francis to tell Shields that Lincoln was the sole author. On September 17, 1842, Shields sent Lincoln a letter demanding full retraction. Its implication was clear: retract or face a duel. Although Lincoln was opposed to dueling, he was egged on by a bellicose Dr. Elias H. Merryman until he found himself challenged. Once again, as he had in the affair with Mary Owens, Lincoln found himself in a serious situation without understanding quite how he got there and not knowing quite how to extricate himself from it. Because of the Illinois law against dueling, the encounter was scheduled for a spot in Missouri across the river from Alton. As the challenged party, Lincoln had the choice of weapons, and he selected the broadsword, a weapon with which his height and strength would work to his advantage. When the parties arrived at the dueling ground, friends intervened to halt the proceedings. Shields withdrew his insulting note and Lincoln declared that the letters were written for political purposes without any intention of reflecting on Shields's personal character. The principals shook hands and returned to Illinois. This aborted duel was one of the most embarrassing moments in Lincoln's life, and he and Mary agreed never to discuss it. But she must have been impressed by his willingness to risk injury and even death in her defense.[18]

Assured by Joshua Speed that he was supremely happy after several months of matrimony, Lincoln renewed his proposal of marriage and was again accepted. They kept their intent to marry a secret until almost the last moment. Ninian and Elizabeth were not informed until the morning of November 4. Appalled by the short notice but resigned to the event, Elizabeth did what she could to stage a wedding suitable for a Todd. Late in the afternoon Lincoln asked James H. Mathery, a friend in the circuit clerk's office, to be his best man. When Lincoln was blacking his boots and getting dressed, the son of his landlord asked where he was going. "To hell. I reckon," the apprehensive groom replied. Despite the late notice (the wedding cake was said to be still warm from the oven), two dozen or so friends were present at the Edwards's home to witness the ceremony, performed by Episcopal minister Charles Dresser. Lincoln placed on Mary's finger a ring that he had had inscribed "Love Is Eternal."[19]

Lincoln's marriage to the daughter of a Kentucky aristocrat gave him connections with the state's leaders that he would have had difficulty achieving on his own. The Todds, one of the state's first families, had many connections by marriage and friendship with other families in the state. Much of Lincoln's knowledge and understanding of the upper-class Kentuckians with whom he had to deal during the secession crisis and the war years came from his marriage to Mary Todd.

Mr. and Mrs. Abraham Lincoln started married life in a small room at the Globe Tavern on Adams Street in Springfield. It rented for $4 per week, and they ate in the common dining room with other boarders and transient guests. For Mary, it was a sharp contrast to the comforts to which she was accustomed; for Lincoln, it may have been the most comfortable lodgings he had ever had except for his stay at Farmington. Lincoln was gone most of the days, and it was Mary who had to cope with the noisy, crowded environment, away from her sisters and friends. Any sexual anxieties proved groundless, and on August 1, 1843, a son was born and named Robert Todd after Mary's father. Lincoln then dropped other names for his wife and called her "Mother." She adhered to the formal style of the period and called him "Mr. Lincoln."

The room was too crowded with the baby, and in the fall of 1843 Lincoln rented a small three-room house on South Fourth Street. When the proud grandfather came to see his namesake and the other members of his family who lived in Springfield, he handed Mary a gold coin and promised her $120 a year for as long as he lived. He also gave each daughter a deed to eighty acres of Illinois land. Robert Todd liked his new son-in-law and employed him to handle some Illinois land cases.

By dint of long hours and hard work, Lincoln raised his earnings to about $1,500 a year in the mid-1840s, a good income for that area at that time. In January 1844 he purchased a story-and-a-half frame house and lot on Eighth and Jackson Streets for $1,200 and a town lot valued at $300. The house, within easy walking distance of his office, had a parlor, a sitting room, and a kitchen downstairs and two small bedrooms upstairs, where the ceilings were so low that there was only one small area where Lincoln could stand erect. A privy and a stable were in the back yard. A cistern and a well provided water; heating was done by fireplaces and wood-burning stoves. Lincoln was also able to chip away at his "National Debt," which had plagued him for over a decade. A second son, born in the new home on March 10, 1846, was named Edward Baker for Lincoln's British-born friend.

The Lincolns were indulgent parents, seldom disciplining their sons. Mary became hysterical if a boy wandered out of her sight or had a minor accident. Lincoln enjoyed getting down on the floor and playing with his sons. Their love for their children was one of the enduring bonds between Mary and Abraham. It was strengthened by the birth of William Walker on December 21, 1850, and Thomas (Tad) on April 4, 1853. The parents were brought even closer together by their grief when Eddie died in 1850 at age four and Willie died in the White House on February 20, 1862, when he was eleven.

Mary's insecurities included a fear of poverty. She sometimes fought it by indulging in extravagant shopping sprees—which made her even more fearful that they might end up in poverty. She was also terrified by thunderstorms, which brought on headaches that sometimes sent her to bed for days. Mary had an intense need for affection and constant assurances that she was loved, and Lincoln was not by nature a very demonstrative person. Mary was extremely jealous, and she sometimes went into uncontrollable tantrums when she thought her husband was paying too much attention to other women.[20] Her frequent illnesses may have been caused in part by her attempts to hold Mr. Lincoln's attention. Lincoln's circuit-riding appearances, on which much of his income depended, kept him away from home for nearly half the year, and even sitting in their parlor he often became so lost in thought that he was unaware of her presence. Mary had a quick and sometimes violent temper; she needed a good argument occasionally to get it out of her system. Lincoln would frequently refuse to argue and would seek refuge by going to his office. She was annoyed by some of his habits: opening the door himself instead of letting the maid do so; meeting guests in his sock feet; his careless dress; his failure to use his butter knife; his uncouth pronunciation of some words; his use of country terms. In time she was able to smooth over some of his rough edges, but she never achieved complete reform. With all his faults, Mary loved him dearly, and she shared with him an intense interest in politics. She was as ambitious for him as he was for himself. Once when someone compared him with Stephen A. Douglas, Mary snapped: "Mr. Douglas is a very little, little giant by the side of my tall Kentuckian, and intellectually my husband towers above Douglas just as he does physically."

As exasperated as Lincoln must have been at times with his wife, he admired her education, her culture, and the social skills that made her a gracious hostess. She was the mother of his sons, and she lavished care and concern upon them. He could and did talk serious politics with her. They had some serious quarrels, but they always made up. Both Mary and Abraham would have been difficult persons for anyone to live with; psychiatrists and psychohistorians are still trying to understand that odd couple. Perhaps the key to comprehending their sometimes troubled relationship may be found on Mary's wedding band: love is eternal.

Between 1831 and 1842 Abraham Lincoln underwent what Douglas L. Wilson calls "years of a remarkable transformation" as he moved successfully from one world to another. A callow, awkward youth in 1831 who was uncertain of his future and apprehensive of unmarried females had become a quite different person in a much different world by the end of 1842. By then he was well established in a profession, he had become a successful politician, and he was married to a woman of a higher social status who contributed much to his adjustment to his different world. The more mature Lincoln had a much better understanding of himself, and he had tighter control over his emotions and actions. He had regained faith in his ability to hold fast to the resolutions that he reached. He had distanced himself from much of the world in which he had lived prior to 1831.[21] The years 1831 to 1842 were truly Abraham Lincoln's formative years.

6

Lincoln and Slavery
to 1854

After Lincoln completed his term in Congress, he concentrated for several years on building up his law practice. He and Herndon worked well together, with Billy doing much of the general research required to prepare a case and calling Lincoln's attention to significant information. Lincoln was adept at drafting clear and logical briefs, and he was much better than Herndon in presenting cases before a jury. Herndon often remained in Springfield when Lincoln rode the circuit twice a year. They did considerable business in the federal courts in the state, Lincoln becoming noted for his presentations before the Supreme Court of Illinois. Without any inherited wealth, Lincoln's income consisted almost entirely of the proceeds from his legal practice, and he was not able to start building an estate until the 1850s. The census of 1860 recorded real estate worth $5,000 and a personal estate of $12,000.[1] From the mid-1850s Lincoln's services were used more and more by the rapidly growing railroads; the Illinois Central Railroad became one of his most profitable clients.

Although Lincoln refused to run again for a House seat in 1850, he remained active in the Whig party in the state. Some of his speeches in the midcentury were attacks on the Democratic party and its policies. His association with the Todd family gave him contacts with the Whig leaders in Kentucky, and through his Kentucky friends and his newspaper-reading, he remained aware of political happenings in the state of his birth.

As a senior member of the Whig party in Illinois, Lincoln was called upon to deliver eulogies for President Zachary Taylor when he died in 1850 and for Henry Clay after his death in 1852.

His Taylor eulogy was perfunctory and consisted largely of a brief sketch of Taylor's career. On July 22 Lincoln received the request that he deliver it, and he did so in Chicago on July 25. He probably accepted in order to keep his name before the party members in the northern part of the state. Lincoln credited Taylor's youthful years in Kentucky, "where his taste for military life, probably inherited, was greatly stimulated," for much of his later success. Occasionally he resorted to oratorical flights not typical of Lincoln's best addresses. "Anon the anxious brethren meet; and while hand strikes hand, the heavens are rent with a loud, long, glorious, gushing cry of victory! victory! victory!" just is not vintage Lincoln.[2]

He did better by Clay. Lincoln had more time in which to prepare, and Clay was more his hero than Taylor was. Clay died in Washington on June 29, 1952, too ill to make a final journey to Ashland. On July 6 in Springfield the Reverend Charles Dresser conducted a memorial service in the Episcopal church; then Lincoln delivered his eulogy in the hall of the House of Representatives.[3] When Lincoln said in his debate with Stephen A. Douglas on August 21, 1858, that Henry Clay was "my beau ideal of a statesman, the man for whom I fought all my humble life," he did not exaggerate his devotion to Clay and his ideas. Lincoln had fought hard to get Clay nominated for the presidency and to get him elected to that position. He had tried but failed to get Clay to visit Illinois in 1848, and he had gone to Lexington that year to hear Clay speak. One of Lincoln's greatest political disappointments came in 1848 when he found it necessary to support Taylor instead of Clay for the Whig nomination for president. His political sense told him that Taylor could be elected, whereas Clay could not. In October 1861, when President Lincoln was given Thomas H. Clay's nominations of two men for postmaster positions, his endorsement was

"For the sake of Kentucky and the memory of Henry Clay, I would like these appointments to be made as soon as possible."[4] Thomas Hart Clay was a son of Henry Clay.

In his eulogy Lincoln paid tribute to Clay's eloquence, which on at least three occasions had quelled serious crises. He "exorcized the demon which possessed the body politic, and gave peace to a distracted land." Clay's achievement, despite the lack of an early education, "teaches that in this country, one can scarcely be so poor, but that, if he *will*, he *can* acquire sufficient education to get through the world respectably." Clay's great eloquence was not based upon elegant techniques, "but rather of that deeply earnest and impassioned tone, and manner, which can proceed only from great sincerity and a thorough conviction, in the speaker of the justice and importance of his cause." What Clay did was for the whole country, for he believed "that the world's best hope depended on the continued Union of these States, he was ever jealous of, and watchful for, whatever might have the slightest tendency to separate them."[5] In thus extolling the virtues of Henry Clay, Lincoln might have been describing himself.

After discussing some of Clay's compromise efforts, Lincoln turned to Clay's views on slavery. Throughout Clay's career he was "on principle and in feeling, opposed to slavery," and for half a century he had tried to get Kentucky to adopt gradual emancipation. Although an owner of slaves, Clay could not see "how it could be at *once* eradicated, without producing a greater evil, even to the cause of human liberty itself. His feeling and his judgment, therefore, ever led him to oppose both extremes of opinion on the subject." Clay was an early member of the American Colonization Society, and he served as its president. Its success was one of his most cherished dreams. Twenty-five years earlier Clay had suggested that colonization of Africans in Africa would be "the possible ultimate redemption of the African race and African continent." That hope remains, Lincoln said, a hopeful solution for the slavery question today.[6]

Here again, Clay might have been voicing Lincoln's own thoughts. Lincoln had gradually become more interested in the slavery issue and its ultimate solution as slavery and its expansion had come to be a major concern of the nation. The nation had faced one of its greatest crises at midcentury when the future of slavery in the territories acquired from Mexico threatened the country with sectional conflict. The Compromise of 1850, as inadequate as it was, had appeared to satisfy a majority of the citizens, but the slavery issue lurked in the background as a threat to the Union that both Clay and Lincoln loved. Somewhat against his will, Abraham Lincoln was being forced to pay more attention to slavery.

As a boy Lincoln must have seen some slaves in Kentucky, for Hardin County reported 940 slaves in the census of 1810 in a total population of 7,531. But his family did not dwell among slaveholders, and Lincoln did not see large numbers of blacks until he made his first flatboat trip to New Orleans in 1828. During his second trip to New Orleans in 1831, Lincoln was supposed to have vowed, after seeing a comely mulatto girl rudely treated in a slave market, "If I ever get a chance to hit that thing, I'll hit it hard." That statement in all probability was added to the Lincoln legend at a later date.

When Lincoln wrote to Mary Speed, Joshua's sister, in September 1841 after his visit to Farmington, he described in some detail seeing a group of Kentucky slaves who were being sold South.

A gentleman had purchased twelve Negroes in different parts of Kentucky and was taking them to a farm in the South. They were chained six and six together. A small iron clevis was around the left wrist of each, and this fastened to the main chain by a shorter one at a convenient distance from, the others; so that the Negroes were strung together precisely like so many fish on a trot-line. In this condition they were being separated forever from the scenes of their childhood, their friends, their fathers and mothers, and brothers and sisters, and many of them, from their wives and children, and going into perpetual slavery where the lash of the master is proverbially more ruthless and unrelenting than any other where; and yet amid all those distressing circumstances, as we would think them, they were the most cheerful and apparently happy creatures on board. One, whose offence for which he had been sold was an over-fondness for his wife, played the fiddle almost continually; and the others danced, sung, cracked jokes, and played various games with cards from day to day. How true it is that "God tempers the wind to the shorn lamb," or in other words, that He renders the worst of human conditions tolerable, while He permits the best, to be nothing better than tolerable.[7]

Although Lincoln recognized the distress that such separation might be expected to cause, his description did not contain the outraged protests that would have come from a William Lloyd Garrison.

After his marriage to Mary Todd, Lincoln also saw a benign form of slavery when he visited the Lexington home of his in-laws. Chaney was the treasured cook, Mammy Sally had charge of the nursery, Nelson supervised the stables except when he was called upon to concoct mint juleps for special guests.[8] But Lexington also had slave markets, and there Lincoln witnessed a quite different aspect of the peculiar institution from the one he saw in the Todd home. Through his Kentucky connections Lincoln also became familiar with Cassius Marcellus Clay, a member of a wealthy slaveholding family who became antislavery. Clay's violent physical encounters obscured the mildness of his views, for he was an emancipationist who favored colonization. In 1845 when he started publishing the *Lexington True American,* a Committee of Sixty seized his press while he was ill and shipped it to Cincinnati. With characteristic modesty, Clay later claimed that he had been a major factor in developing Lincoln's antislavery views.[9] As an avid newspaper reader, Lincoln was aware of the failure of antislavery forces in Kentucky to include some provision for emancipation in the new constitution that was adopted in 1850. Not a single antislavery candidate was elected to the 1849 convention, and the slavery article in the old constitution was repeated in the new one. In a speech at Bloomington, Illinois, on May 29, 1856, Lincoln was alleged to have been critical of Kentucky's failure to provide for some means of emancipation in the constitutional convention of 1849. "In Kentucky—my state—in 1849, on a test vote, the mighty influence of Henry Clay and many other good men could not get a symptom of expression in favor of gradual emancipation on a plain issue of marching toward the light of civilization with Ohio and Illinois; but the state of Boone and Hardin and Clay, with a nigger under each arm, took the black trail toward the deadly swamp of barbarism."

In 1851 Cassius M. Clay ran for governor on an Emancipation Party ticket. Calling for gradual emancipation, he argued that the free men of Kentucky were being hurt by the presence of slave labor. He received just over 3 percent of the votes cast, but most of them came from former Whigs, and Clay was convinced that he had contributed to the downfall of the Whig party in the state. The Democrats elected Lazarus W. Powell, the first Democratic governor in Kentucky since 1834. The failure to secure even mild change made it clear that the large majority of Kentucky voters who did not own slaves supported the institution of slavery.

In a speech made at Springfield on July 17, 1858, Lincoln summarized his views on slavery prior to the Kansas-Nebraska Act of 1854. "Although I have ever been opposed to slavery, so far I rested in the hope and belief that it was in course of ultimate extinction. For that reason, it had been a minor question with me. I might have been mistaken; but I had believed, and now believe, that the whole public mind, that is the mind of the great majority, had rested in that belief up to the repeal of the Missouri Compromise."[10] Though he deplored the existence of slavery, Lincoln accepted its inclusion in the Constitution, and he recognized that it was an integral part of the fabric of Southern social and economic life. Confident in his belief that slavery would some day cease to exist, Lincoln remained somewhat aloof from the developing antislavery sentiment in the North. He disliked extremists, whether they were pro- or antislavery.

The acquisition of the Mexican Cession and the argument over the future of slavery there revealed that the fire of sectional controversy that had been smothered by the Missouri Compromise had not been extinguished. On January 29, 1850, Henry Clay, once again in the Senate in Washington, introduced a series of resolutions designed to compromise the differences between the North and the South over the slavery issues. The elderly statesman proposed to bundle most of his proposals in an "Omnibus Bill" that he hoped would be passed as a unit. When it became obvious that the combined opposition to sections of the bill would be enough to kill it, Illinois senator Stephen A. Douglas assumed the major role in breaking the bill into its parts and steering them to passage. Five bills were passed, all of them by different counts: (1) California was admitted as a free state. Never again would there be as many slave as free states. (2) New Mexico was organized as a territory without any restriction on slavery. When it became a state, the status of slavery there would be determined by what provision was in the state constitution. Texas gave up its claims to a large part of New Mexico in return for a payment of $10 million made by the United States. (3) Utah was created as a territory on the same terms as New Mexico received. (4) A harsh Fugitive Slave Act modified the relatively mild act of 1793. It became much easier to seize a person accused of being a fugitive slave. (5) The slave trade, but not slavery, was ended in the District of Columbia.

Lincoln was not pleased by portions of the compromise, especially the possibility that slavery might expand into New

Mexico and Utah and the Fugitive Slave Act, which was so loaded against a person accused of being a fugitive. But the admission of California as a free state and the end of the slave trade in the District of Columbia were clear gains for the antislavery forces. What was more important, the compromise was endorsed by both major parties; it apparently ended another sectional crisis that had threatened national unity. If it was not the final solution to the slavery, it might at least last for another generation. Lincoln continued to expand his increasingly lucrative legal practice and to remain active in state politics.

At midcentury Lincoln's views on slavery were much like those of Henry Clay. Although he opposed slavery on principle, he accepted it for the present because he was sure that at some future date it would be ended in the United States. He did not believe that blacks and whites should have perfect social and political equality; their physical differences would prevent their living together on equal terms. But he believed strongly that blacks were entitled to the rights described in the Declaration of Independence—life, liberty, and the pursuit of happiness, which meant the right to earn a decent living.

The ideal solution to the racial problem, Lincoln believed, was colonization of the blacks once they had been freed. The program of the American Colonization Society suggested a way that might be done. Sending free blacks to Africa, Lincoln thought, would appeal to both the North and the South, and it would allow the blacks to improve their status by showing that they could make a success of a self-governing community. In fact, colonization never had a chance of success, but Lincoln continued to cling to the idea until well after the Civil War started. The vast majority of blacks had no desire to go to Africa; few slaveholders were willing to free their bondspersons; and the costs of an effective program were prohibitive. Since Lincoln could not see how slavery could be abolished—except that he believed it would be in time if not allowed to spread— he paid little attention to the question immediately after the Compromise of 1850 was put in place.

Four years later the fires of the slavery controversy flared up again, and this time they were not extinguished until the Civil War brought an end to the infamous institution. In 1854 Douglas undid the compromise that he had done so much to pass. On January 4, 1854, as chairman of the Senate committee on territories, Douglas introduced a bill to create a huge Nebraska Territory in the northern part of the Louisiana Purchase, where slavery had been prohibited by the Missouri Compromise. The area's swelling population justified the formation of a territorial government, and its creation would probably enhance the prospects of building a Northern transcontinental railroad—an outcome greatly desired by Douglas. Previous efforts to organize such a territory had been blocked by Southerners who feared it would lead to the admission of one or more free states. They wanted the transcontinental railroad to run through the South. To appease Southerners, Douglas proposed that when a state or states from that territory entered the Union, it could have or not have slavery as its constitution provided. Thus the issue of slavery there would be based on the "popular sovereignty" concept that had been applied to New Mexico and Utah in the Compromise of 1850. The bill implied that the prohibition on slavery in that area had been superseded, but the Southerners wanted it made explicit. Douglas agreed to outright repeal and the creation of two territories, Kansas and Nebraska. After several months of bitter debate, the bill passed.

Lincoln did not respond publicly to the bill until late summer. He was deeply involved in an important case before the Illinois Supreme Court, and he was wary of the sudden strength of the Native American or Know Nothing Party. Lincoln was a crafty, experienced politician, and he had learned to be silent when there was nothing to be gained by a gratuitous expression of opinion. In July Cassius M. Clay went to Springfield to denounce the Kansas-Nebraska Bill and to urge the creation of a party that would unite to repeal it. In his self-serving autobiography, Clay told of Lincoln's lying on the grass under a tree while Clay spoke. "I shall never forget his long, ungainly form, and his ever sad and homely face. *He*, too, was a native Kentuckian; and could bear witness, in his own person, to the depressing influence of slavery upon all the races. . . . So I flattered myself, when Lincoln listened to my animated appeals for universal liberty for more than two hours, that I sowed there also seed which in due time bore fruit."[11]

Clay's claim was exaggerated, for the bill had dismayed Lincoln. Any possible expansion of slavery into previously forbidden territory made less certain his hope and expectation of its ultimate extinction. Lincoln took a public stand on August 26, 1854, when he addressed the Whig convention in Scott County and denounced "the great wrong and injustice of the repeal of the Missouri Compromise and the extension of slavery into free territory." His main purpose then was to secure the reelection of Congressman Richard Yates, and Lincoln spoke there and elsewhere as a state leader of the Whig party. Later, in Springfield, Lincoln would claim that the passage of the Kansas-Nebraska Act had convinced him that "the institution was being placed on a new basis—a basis for making it perpetual, national and universal. Subsequent events have greatly confirmed me in that belief. I believe that bill to be the beginning of a conspiracy for that purpose. So believing, I have since then considered that question a paramount one."[12]

Nonetheless, he recognized the complexity of the problem and the difficulties involved in finding a solution. Lincoln made a point of disclaiming prejudice toward Southerners. "They are just what we would be in their situation. If slavery did not now exist amongst them, they would not introduce it. If it did now exist amongst us, we should not instantly give it up. . . . When southern people tell us they are no more responsible for the origin of slavery, than we; I acknowledge the fact. When it is said that the institution exists; and that it is very difficult to get rid of it, in any satisfactory way, I can understand and appreciate the saying. I surely will not blame them for not doing what I should not know to do myself. If all earthly power were given me, I would not know what to do, as to the existing institution. My first impulse would be to free all the slaves, and send them to Liberia,—to their own native land." He hoped for this solution in the long run, but its sudden execution was impossible: they would perish within ten days. Free them but keep them as underlings? Would that improve their condition? he asked. "Free them, and make them politically and socially, our equals? My own feelings will not admit of this," and neither would the feelings of the great mass of white people. "We can not, then, make them equals. It does seem to me that systems of gradual emancipation might be adopted; but for their [Southerners'] tardiness in this, I will not undertake to judge our brethren of the South."[13] During this campaign Lincoln clarified and solidified his antislavery views. He became even more convinced that the long-range solution was to prevent any further expansion of slavery.

Once he decided to enter the fight over the Kansas-Nebraska Act, Lincoln became an active participant. He spoke at a number of Whig meetings, and he studied carefully the history of slavery in the territories to find weaknesses in Douglas's defense of the measure. Douglas defended his action and the principle of popular sovereignty as giving the people of a territory the democratic right to decide for themselves the future of slavery in their state. Douglas tried to avoid appearing on a platform with Lincoln, but when he completed a speech at Springfield on October 3, 1854, Lincoln shouted from the stairway that he or Lyman Trumbull would reply the next day in the Hall of Representatives. He invited Douglas to attend and promised him an opportunity to reply.

The next afternoon, collarless and tieless, Lincoln spoke for nearly three hours before a large crowd. After asserting that the constitutional protection of slavery applied to the states that had it, not to the expansion of slavery beyond the limits of the states, Lincoln admitted that the North was as responsible as the South for the origins of slavery and that he did not believe it possible to free the slaves and make them the social and political equals of whites. Then he carefully traced the history of the expansion of slavery. The right of Congress to exclude slavery in the territories had been accepted until Douglas had reversed his previous position. Inhabitants of a territory had the right to make their own laws, Lincoln admitted, but the issue of slavery had to be decided on whether the Negro was a man. Because the Negro was a man, there could be no moral right to the institution of slavery. "No man is good enough to govern another man, *without that other's consent.*" Since, Lincoln asserted, Douglas simply did not see the Negro as a human, he thereafter denied any question of morality.[14]

This sense of moral outrage was Lincoln's major contribution to the argument. The Declaration of Independence had recognized the equality of all men, and the founders of the Constitution had tried to limit slavery as much as they could under the conditions that existed then. The American struggle over slavery, Lincoln maintained, must be viewed as part of the world's struggle for freedom. The United States was the world's best hope for expanding freedom, and the nation must not forfeit its world leadership by allowing slavery to expand into new territories.

Douglas then defended his position in a two-hour speech. Public reaction to the debate depended largely upon political affiliation, but Lincoln's speech had considerable impact. A small meeting that evening was followed by a larger one the next day, at which Ichabod Codding and Owen Lovejoy moved to form a Republican party in the state to halt the expansion of slavery. Lincoln was still not prepared to join such a movement, but his speech, repeated at several places, did much to rally support in opposition to the Kansas-Nebraska Act and its sponsors. Lincoln gained increased recognition across the state as a powerful speaker who was firmly opposed to any expansion of slavery. When the radical antislavery men organized the beginnings of the Republican party, Lincoln was made a member of the Illinois central committee. He neither accepted nor denied membership. He could not yet be associated with the nascent party, but he needed the group's support for his intended race for the U.S. Senate. Lincoln was still a Whig, not a Republican, and he was antislavery but not an abolitionist.[15] Some strong antislavery men were suspicious of Lincoln because of his Kentucky background. Charles H. Ray of the *Chicago Tribune* voiced his distrust to an associate: "He is southern by birth, southern in his associations and southern, if I mistake not, in his sympathies. . . . His wife, you know, is a Todd, of a pro-slavery family, and so are all his kin."[16]

Lincoln refused election to the state House of Representatives in order to be eligible for election as one of Illinois's U.S. senators. When the legislature started voting on the candidates on February 8, 1855, he had forty-five votes, more than anyone else but short of the number required for election. Lincoln's vote dwindled, and he had only fifteen left when Democratic governor Joel A. Matteson reached forty-seven, only three votes from election. To prevent that result, Lincoln released his loyal supporters to vote for Lyman Trumbull, an anti-Nebraska Democrat, who was elected on the tenth ballot. Although disappointed by his failure, Lincoln found solace in the fact that he had not been defeated by a popular vote. And he would be free to oppose Douglas in 1858 when the "Little Giant" came up for reelection.[17]

In the summer of 1855 Judge George Robertson of Lexington visited Springfield. He missed seeing Lincoln, who was riding circuit, but the judge left Lincoln a copy of his *Scrap Book on Law and Politics, Men and Times*. Long active in Kentucky politics, he had been in the Old Court Party, which had succeeded in abolishing the New Court in Kentucky in the 1820s. Robertson had served on the Court of Appeals from 1828 to 1843, much of the time as chief justice. Returning to the practice of law, he had been the local counsel for the heirs of Robert S. Todd in a suit he had filed against Robert Wickliffe before his death in 1849. Robertson had been in the U.S. House of Representatives from 1817 until 1821 and had been involved in the passage of the Missouri Compromise. As Lincoln read Robertson's book, he was surprised to learn that Congress had acted upon the question of slavery in a territory in 1819 before the Missouri Compromise was passed. Robertson had moved for the organization of the Arkansas Territory on December 16, 1818. On February 18, 1819, Representative Taylor of New York had proposed an amendment to prohibit slavery and involuntary servitude in the territory. Taylor's amendment had failed by just two votes. In fighting it, Robertson had admitted that Congress could prohibit slavery in a territory, but he argued that such a decision should be left to the people who lived there. Against their will, Congress should neither force slavery upon them or prohibit them from having it. If Congress did insist upon legislating upon slavery in the territories, Robertson suggested that a line be drawn, perhaps at the 37th parallel, which would allow slavery below that line and prohibit slavery north of it. With accurate prescience, Robertson warned that if the majority of Congress should impose the Taylor amendment, "that majority will heedlessly sow wind, and may, in time to come woefully reap the whirlwind. They may, and I fear will, recklessly raise a storm that will scatter the seeds of discord over this favored land. . . . that may destroy its heart forever."

In his 1854 Peoria speech, Lincoln claimed that Congress in adopting the Northwest Ordinance of 1787 had established a policy of prohibiting slavery in a new territory, a policy from which it had not deviated except by compromise until the passage of the Kansas-Nebraska Bill. Lincoln was surprised to learn of the earlier incident from Robertson's book; but when he wrote Robertson, he argued that the situation in 1855 was far different from that in 1819. In 1819 Robertson had spoken of "the peaceful extinction of slavery" and had indicated his belief that it would come to an end. Since then, Lincoln argued, "we have had thirty six years of experience; and this experience has demonstrated, I think, that there is no peaceful extinction of slavery in prospect for us." The failure of Henry Clay and others to effect any move toward gradual emancipation in Kentucky in 1849 was proof of that. During the Revolution we had proclaimed as a self-evident truth that all men were created equal; nearly half the states had then adopted schemes of eman-cipation. Now, we reject that great principle, and not a single state has adopted emancipation since then. "The Autocrat of all the Russias will resign his crown, and proclaim his subjects free republicans sooner than will our American masters volun-tarily give up their slaves. Our political problem now is 'Can we, as a nation, continue together *permanently—forever*—half slave, and half free?' The problem is too mighty for me. May God, in his mercy, superintend the solution."[18] As the contro-versy unleashed by the Kansas-Nebraska Act continued dur-ing the rest of the decade in different forms, Abraham Lincoln had an increasingly important role in its development.

7

The Gathering Storm

One of the many portents of change for Lincoln in the 1850s was his reluctant decision to become a Republican. Whigism was in his political bones, but that party was crumbling fast, and with its disappearance went one of the bonds of national union. In sharp contrast, the Republican party would be a sectional party without a Southern branch to encourage compromise. Lincoln expressed his dilemma in a long letter to Joshua Speed on August 24, 1855.

Speed had suggested in a May letter to Lincoln that they probably differed now on political matters. We are not that different in regard to slavery, Lincoln replied; I detest it, and you admit that in the abstract it is wrong. "But you say that sooner than yield your legal right to the slave—especially at the bidding of those who are not themselves interested, you would see the Union dissolved." He was not asking Speed to yield that right; that matter was left up to him. But he said, "I do oppose the extension of slavery. . . . If for this you and I must differ, differ we must." What if Kansas is admitted as a slave state by unfair means? Lincoln asked. He had looked upon the Nebraska Bill as violence from the beginning; he assumed that Kansas would form a slave constitution and be admitted under it, but "by every principle of law, ever held by any court, North or South, every Negro taken to Kansas is free." He would oppose the admission of Kansas as a slave state, Lincoln warned, but he and others who felt that way might well be defeated. "If we are, I shall not, on that account, attempt to dissolve the Union." You say that as a Christian you would rejoice if Kansas fairly votes itself free. "All decent slave-holders *talk* that way, . . . But they never *vote* that way. . . . you would vote for no man for Congress who would say the same thing publicly. . . . The slave breeders and slave-traders, are a small, odious and detested class among you; and yet in politics, they dictate the course of all of you and are as completely your masters, as you are masters of your own negroes."

"You inquire where I now stand. That is a disputed point. I think I am a whig; but others say there are no whigs and I am an abolitionist." He had voted forty times for the Wilmot Proviso in Congress, and no one tried to unwhig him for that. "I now do no more than to oppose the *extension* of slavery." Certainly he was not a Know-Nothing. "How can any one who abhors the oppression of negroes, be in favor of degrading classes of white people? Our progress in degeneracy appears to me to be pretty rapid. As a nation, we began by declaring that '*all men are created equal.*' We now practically read it, 'all men are created equal, *except negroes.*' When the Know-Nothings get control, it will read 'all men are created equal, except negroes, *and foreigners, and catholics.*' When it comes to this, I should prefer emigrating to some country where they make no pretense of loving liberty—to Russia, for instance, where despotism can be taken pure, and without the base alloy of hypocracy [*sic*]." Lincoln concluded this lengthy statement of his views "Your friend forever."[1]

By 1856 Lincoln had reluctantly concluded that the only practical course was to form a new political party in Illinois made up of all opponents to the expansion of slavery. He was the only nonjournalist at a Decatur meeting of antislavery editors on February 22, and he guided the group in the formulation of a series of conservative declarations against the expansion of slavery. A state convention was called for at Bloomington on May 29, but Lincoln rejected suggestions that he should be the gubernatorial candidate. An anti-Nebraska Democrat would be a better choice. But he indicated that he would welcome the opportunity to run for the U.S. Senate in 1858. His 1855 defeat still rankled, and he longed for a chance to unseat Douglas, whom he blamed for much of the current slavery controversy.

Lincoln was apprehensive over the support that would be indicated at the Bloomington convention, but he was reassured by the presence of some 270 delegates who came to organize the Illinois Republican party. Rejecting extremist demands, the convention adopted a moderate platform. On the slavery issue it merely asserted that Congress had the power to exclude slavery from the territories and should do so. Called upon to deliver the last major speech at the convention, Lincoln made what may have been the best speech of his career up to that point. It became known as his "Lost Speech," because it was said that reporters were so fascinated by his remarks that they neglected to take notes. He charged slavery with being the cause of the nation's problems, and he accused the Democrats of beginning to accept the South's demand that slavery be extended to white laborers. He was ready, Lincoln asserted, "to fuse with anyone who would unite with him to oppose the slave power."[2]

Similar movements were occurring in other free states, but little time remained for the formation of a national party that could run a candidate for president in the fall election, 1856. The Democrats had nominated "doughface" James Buchanan of Pennsylvania, who had avoided most of the Kansas-Nebraska controversy by being out of the country. As a further sop to the South, his running mate was the youthful John Cabell Breckinridge of Kentucky. The American Party, as the Know-Nothings preferred to be called, had nominated ex-President Millard Fillmore. Because so many members of the new Republican party were former Whigs, Lincoln urged the nomination of John McLean of Ohio, one of two justices on the Supreme Court who would oppose the Dred Scott decision. The national convention bypassed its most prominent figures and nominated John C. Fremont, whose exploits in exploring the West had made him well known. The Illinois delegates supported Lin-

coln for vice president, and the 110 votes he received testified
to his growing reputation outside the state. He was pleased with
that support, but he modestly suggested that the votes must
have been intended for a famous Lincoln (Governor Levi Lincoln) from Massachusetts. William L. Dayton of New Jersey
was the nominee for vice president.

Lincoln delivered some fifty speeches on behalf of the
ticket, most of them in the southern and central parts of the
state. Because of the number of former Kentuckians who lived
in those areas, Republican editors stressed Lincoln's Kentucky
birth and associations. He tried to convince American Party
voters that they should not waste a vote on Fillmore, who had
no chance of being elected. Lincoln avoided sensational topics
such as the continuing struggle in Kansas. Instead, he talked
calmly of the necessity to halt the expansion of slavery. Lincoln encountered some opposition within his household. Mary
was much interested in politics, and she wrote her sister Emilie,
"My weak woman's heart was too Southern in feeling to sympathize with any but Fillmore," who had been a good president, was a just man, and would keep foreigners "within
bounds." If Mrs. Lincoln had been able to vote, she would have
canceled her husband's ballot.[3]

Buchanan won the election, but the new Republican party
made an amazing showing for its first presidential effort. The
popular totals were Buchanan, 1,838,169; Fremont, 1,335,264;
Fillmore, 874,534. The electoral vote was Buchanan 174, Fremont 114, Fillmore 8. The Republicans had carried eleven free
states, whereas the Democrats had won five free and fourteen
slave states. Fillmore's only victory was in Maryland. In Illinois the Republicans won four of nine congressional seats and
elected all the state slate, including the governor. Despite the
presence of the popular John C. Breckinridge on the ticket, the
Democrats got 69,509 votes in Kentucky to 63,391 for the
American Party. Only 314 independently minded Kentuckians
voted Republican.

As Lincoln saw it, the Republicans could win in 1860 if

they could capture most of the Fillmore voters. They had little or no chance to carry a Southern or even a border state, but by winning the support of other antislavery groups, Republicans were almost sure of victory in 1860. And, more to the point, Lincoln should be able to defeat Douglas and remove him from the Senate. That Senate seat was Lincoln's political goal.

Lincoln had neglected much of his legal work in 1856; in 1857 he concentrated on earning money. Part of it went to remodeling and enlarging their simple cottage into a two-story house, which Mary furnished in an expensive style that reflected the status they had attained. She knew the value of political entertaining, and in the enlarged house she could do much more. Dinners were usually for six or eight guests, but in February she invited five hundred guests—and regretted that a rain storm held attendance to only three hundred. This was the sort of entertaining suitable for a Todd.[4]

The Kansas situation had settled into an uneasy truce, but on March 6, 1857, the Supreme Court opened another explosive phase of the slavery controversy. Two days earlier, Buchanan had announced that the Supreme Court was about to decide the slavery issue, once and for all. The Dred Scott 7–2 decision was read by Chief Justice Roger B. Taney, but every member of the court wrote an opinion. Taney ruled that Dred Scott could not sue for freedom on the grounds that he had been in a free state and a free territory because as a Negro he was not a citizen of the United States. Blacks had been considered so inferior that they had not been granted citizenship by the Constitution. Furthermore, restrictions, including the Missouri Compromise, that prohibited slavery in national territories were not valid because they restricted property rights guaranteed under the Fifth Amendment. Proslavery advocates could not have asked for more than what they received in this decision. They became even less likely to compromise; why should they do so when the Supreme Court had ruled that they were right?[5]

Despite his reverence for the law and the judicial system, Lincoln decided that the Supreme Court had erred. He believed that the Declaration of Independence had included blacks as well as whites. When Douglas defended the decision at Springfield in June, Lincoln responded with the Republican answer on June 26.[6] The decision was erroneous, he declared. The Court that made it had often overruled its own opinions, and "we shall do what we can to have it to over-rule this. We offer no *resistance* to it" (401). Lincoln accused Douglas of trying to depict his antislavery foes as favoring "an indiscriminate amalgamation of the white and black races" (405). Lincoln protested "against that counterfeit logic which concludes that, because I do not want a black woman for a *slave,* I must necessarily want her for a *wife.* I need not have her for either, I can just leave her alone. In some respects she certainly is not my equal; but in her natural right to eat the bread she earns with her own hands without asking leave of anyone else, she is my equal, and the equal of all others" (405). The Declaration of Independence did not intend "to declare all men equal *in all respects*" (405); but they were declared equal "in certain unalienable rights, among which are life, liberty, and the pursuit of happiness" (406). Are you, he asked Democrats as well as others, willing to let the Declaration "be thus frittered away?" (407). Slavery itself was the greatest source of amalgamation, and the only way to prevent it was to separate the races—which meant that colonization should be used for the blacks.[6]

Most Kentuckians, including even a majority of nonslaveholders, welcomed the Dred Scott decision as the final solution to the slavery question, but there were some dissenters. William Shreve Bailey, a mechanic who became an editor, started the antislavery *Newport News,* sometimes called *The South,* in 1850. Despite physical and legal harassment, he denounced both the Dred Scott Decision and the Kansas-Nebraska Bill in his paper. Cassius M. Clay let the *True American* die, but he remained active in politics, and in April 1856 he was one of the few Madison County Republicans who held a convention to select delegates to the national convention. He spoke widely in free states during the presidential campaign, and he provided some assistance to John G. Fee in establishing an antislavery church and school at Berea in the foothills of the mountains. He was ably assisted by others, such as John A.R. Rogers. Although a nonviolence pacifist, Fee held radical antislavery views; he and Clay were the odd couple of the antislavery movement in Kentucky during their period of cooperation. After Clay withdrew his support, a Committee of Sixty ordered the Bereans to leave the community. Appeals to the proslavery governor, Beriah Magoffin, produced no help. A public meeting in Mason County on January 21, 1860, resolved that "no Abolitionist has a right to establish himself in the slaveholding community and disseminate opinions and principles destructive of its tranquillity and safety." Kentuckians had not interfered with Northern rights, and "we desire and demand to be '*let alone*'" by "our officious and philanthropic friends at the North." Most Kentuckians would have echoed those sentiments.[7]

When President Buchanan accepted the proslavery Lecompton Constitution for Kansas after its adoption in a rigged election that most antislavery men boycotted, Senator Douglas broke with the president of his own party. What happened in Congress, Douglas stormed, was a flagrant violation of his cherished principle of popular sovereignty. "I care not whether slavery is voted down or voted up," he insisted. His objection was to the method by which the vote was obtained. Lincoln wanted the Republicans to stand aside and let the Democrats tear their party to pieces, but he began to fear that the Republicans were falling into a trap by supporting Douglas in his anti-administration stand. Herndon and other Illinois Republicans rejected suggestions from eastern members of the party that they support Douglas for reelection in 1858. Lincoln's supporters arranged for him to be unanimously nominated at the party's state convention on June 16.

Confident of his nomination, Lincoln had carefully prepared his acceptance speech. On the evening of June 16 he gave the "house divided" speech, the one for which he was best known prior to 1861. More than four years ago, he said, the nation started a policy that was designed to put an end to the slavery question. Instead, agitation had increased.

> In my opinion, it *will* not cease, until a *crisis* shall have been reached and passed.
> "A house divided against itself cannot stand."
> I believe this government cannot endure, permanently, half *slave* and half *free*.
> I do not expect the Union to be *dissolved*—I do not expect the house to fall—but I *do* expect it will cease to be divided.
> It will become *all* one thing, or *all* the other.
> Either the *opponents* of slavery, will arrest the further spread of it, and place it where the public mind shall rest in the belief that it is in the course of ultimate extinction; or its *advocates* will push it forward, till it shall become alike lawful in *all* the states, *old* as well as *new*—*North* as well as South.

As he continued this speech, Lincoln charged that Douglas was part of a plot designed to nationalize slavery. His Kansas-Nebraska Act had opened national territory to slavery, thus changing a national consensus of many years. Lincoln saw the Democratic presidents and Chief Justice Taney working in tandem to make the change. Admitting that there was no absolute proof of the conspiracy, he blamed the Northern Democrats for the attack. Unless the power of the Democratic party was broken, he could foresee a future Supreme Court decision that would rule that a state could not exclude slavery. Since he had no trust in Douglas, Lincoln probably believed sincerely in his conspiracy theory. He refrained from blaming "the slave power," although the Southern Democratic votes were vital to the success of the party. Only the Republicans, Lincoln asserted, could be trusted to halt the movement to nationalize slavery; Douglas must be defeated.

The house divided statement had appeared in three books of the Bible, and Lincoln had used it as early as 1843 and several times since. Other speakers, North and South, had used it during the slavery controversy, but Lincoln's use of it caught the nation's attention. It was one of the most radical Republican speeches of the year. Although he denied that he had pledged the Republican party to wage war against slavery in the states that had it, many who read Lincoln's speech assumed that he meant for such warfare to be waged. Abraham Lincoln was seen by many antislavery people as the crusader who could lead them to victory over the infamous institution; he was seen by many proslavery people as a dangerous radical who would destroy slavery if given an opportunity to do so.[8]

Douglas knew that Lincoln would be a formidable foe. "I shall have my hands full," he was reported to have said. "He is the strong man of his party—full of wit, facts, dates—and the best stump speaker, with his droll ways and dry jokes, in the West. He is as honest as he is shrewd, and if I best him my victory will be hardly won."[9] Douglas had broken with the Buchanan administration when it had made a mockery of popular sovereignty in Kansas, and for a time some people hoped—or feared—that he might even become a Republican. Instead, "the Little Giant" girded himself for what became the nation's most noted senatorial election of that era.

Douglas began his campaign with a speech from the balcony of the Tremont House in Chicago on July 9, 1858. He claimed credit for defeating the proslavery Lecompton Constitution in Kansas. Popular sovereignty, he maintained, meant that Congress had no right to force a slave status upon an unwilling people; and it meant that Congress had no right to force free status upon unwilling people. "It is no answer," he declared, "to say that slavery is an evil and hence should not be tolerated." The people who are concerned must decide on the issue. Lincoln was seated on the balcony behind him, and Douglas acknowledged him as "a kind, amiable, and intelligent gentleman, a good citizen and an honorable opponent" who did not understand "the great principles upon which our government rests" and who advocated a sectional war between the North and the South. Our government, Douglas maintained, was founded on a white-only basis in which blacks had no part.[10]

Lincoln responded to Douglas the next evening from the same balcony, and for the next few weeks he continued to follow Douglas around the state. When Douglas finished a speech, Lincoln would rise and announce to the audience that he would reply either that evening or the next day. His advisors told Lincoln that that approach was a poor tactic. It appeared undignified to trail his opponent, and the format allowed Douglas to keep him on the defensive. This pattern changed when Lincoln challenged Douglas to a series of face-to-face debates. Douglas accepted reluctantly, for he did not like to attract publicity to his less-well-known rival, and he was already committed to an exhausting schedule of speeches. But he could not afford to appear to be afraid of Lincoln, and they agreed upon a series of seven debates, beginning on August 21 and ending October 13. One would be held in each Illinois congressional district except for two in which they had already spoken. They would alternate the openings and closings. One would speak an hour, the other would have an hour and a half, and the initial speaker would have half an hour in which to respond.[11]

Both men had a number of other speaking engagements, but the seven debates attracted the most attention, not only in Illinois but across the nation as they were widely reported. Large crowds attended the debates, with special trains often bringing citizens from other parts of the state. Douglas was the more skillful debater; Lincoln was at his best when he had time for careful preparation. They swapped charges and countercharges on a number of issues. Lincoln posed four questions for Douglas at Freeport on August 27. One of them asked, "Can the people of a United States Territory, in any lawful way, against the will of any citizen of the United States, exclude slavery from its limits prior to the formation of a State Constitution?" Lincoln assumed, rightly, that Douglas would stand by his doctrine of popular sovereignty. Douglas responded that the people could exclude slavery by failing to pass laws to protect it: "Slavery cannot exist a day or an hour anywhere, unless it is supported by local police regulations." With this declaration Douglas widened his split with the Buchanan administration, which held that the Dred Scott decision had answered the question in the negative. After his answer, Douglas would be supported by few proslavery Democrats. They would not accept a candidate who did not accept the Dred Scott decision.[12]

At Quincy on October 13, Lincoln restated what he called the fundamental issue of the campaign: the difference in the way slavery was viewed.[13] Republicans "think it is a moral, a social and a political wrong" (254), whereas the Democrats did not see it as a wrong. Douglas suggested that Lincoln's plan to prevent the spread of slavery was genocidal, for his call for "ultimate extinction" (265) really meant the extermination of the Negro race. If the voters would return to the principle of self-government that had been recognized from the start of the nation, "this republic can exist forever divided into free and slave States" (274). Douglas also charged Lincoln with varying his principles, depending on whether he was or was not in an abolition county.

In his presentation on October 15 in Alton, the most pro-Southern of the seven debate sites, where many of those who attended were from Kentucky or had close ties to it, Lincoln quoted extensively from Henry Clay to substantiate his views on slavery.[14] Lincoln emphasized that he had "never sought to apply these principles to the old States for the purpose of abolishing slavery in those States" (305). He had never proposed that Missouri or any other slave state should emancipate her slaves. As to Judge Douglas's repeated references to Lincoln's "house divided" speech, Mr. Crittenden had said that when the Nebraska Bill was introduced "*there was no slavery agitation at that time to allay*" (305). Douglas was the one who had stirred up the issue again, and since then the people in Kansas had not had the advantages of self-government. Lincoln repeated his belief that slavery must be placed in a position where the public would believe that it was in the course of ultimate extinction, or that it would become lawful in all the states. He believed that the founding fathers had wanted to place slavery in a position leading to its ultimate extinction. Why else had they provided that the African slave trade should be cut off after twenty years? Why did they provide that slavery would be forever prohibited in the new territory that we owned then? Why did they not use the terms "slavery" or "the Negro race" in the Constitution? The reason was that they wanted no mention of slavery in that document after slavery had ended. "And when I say that I desire to see the further spread of it arrested, I only say I desire to see that done which the fathers have first done" (308). They found the institution among us, and they found it impossible to remove it at that time.

Then Lincoln turned to Douglas: "*I turn upon him and ask him why he could not let it alone?* . . . I have proposed nothing more than a return to the policy of the fathers" (308). We have had peace in the Union when the institution of slavery remained quiet where it was. Except for the nullification controversy, the nation's major problems have resulted from efforts to spread slavery. This issue divides the people more than any other.

"I agree with him very readily that the different States have the right . . . to decide the whole thing for themselves" (311). Our concern, Lincoln reiterated, is for the territories. "We agree that when the States come in as States they have the right and the power to do as they please" (311). What we insist on is "that the new Territories shall be kept free from it while in the Territorial condition" (311). Judge Douglas charges that we want to introduce perfect social and political equality between the white and black races. It is a false issue.[11] The real issue in this controversy ". . . is the sentiment on the part of one class that looks upon the institution of slavery *as a wrong*, and of another class that *does not* look upon it as a wrong" (312). A way to treat a wrong is to make sure that it does not grow larger. "Has anything ever threatened the existence of this Union save and except this very institution of slavery?" (313). The Democrats, Lincoln charged, never treat slavery as being a wrong. Judge Douglas looks to no end to slavery; he has been the most prominent instrument in changing the position of slavery which the fathers of this government had expected to be ended before now.

Lincoln was totally opposed to the Dred Scott decision, and he wanted to do whatever was possible to see that it was reversed. Though he disliked the Fugitive Slave Act, he would accept it because it implemented a constitutional right. Douglas, Lincoln asserted, argued that unfriendly legislation could deprive a slaveholder of his right to hold a slave in a territory; that same approach could be used to nullify the Fugitive Slave Act.

Douglas challenged most of Lincoln's assertions. Lincoln and his party could win only with the aid of the federal administration. He accused Lincoln of opposing the Mexican War after it had been declared and the army was fighting. As to Lincoln being a Henry Clay Whig, Douglas claimed that Lincoln had turned against Clay in 1847 and 1848. He had helped stir up the strife that Douglas had helped Clay put down. Slavery was only one subject that had disturbed the peace of the country. Despite what Mr. Lincoln claimed, the country was founded with each state free to have or to reject slavery. "I look forward to a time when each State shall be allowed to do as it pleases. . . . I would not blot out the great inalienable rights of the white men for all the negroes that ever existed" (322). Our fathers did not foresee many things, Douglas exclaimed, such as the telegraph and the railroad, but that does not change the principles of government such as self-government. How does Mr. Lincoln put slavery in the course of ultimate extinction if he does not intend to interfere with it in the states where it now exists? His idea is to prohibit slavery in the territories, thus making them come into the Union as free states. He would cordon off slave states and let the slaves multiply until they die of starvation. And he would do this in the name of humanity and Christianity. Lincoln, he charged, would govern a territory without a representative, much as George III had done before the American Revolution. The people in Kansas could decide what they wanted to do in regard to slavery, for "the absence of local legislation protecting slavery excludes it as completely as a positive prohibition" (324). There would be peace between the North and the South if we would only live up to the great principles of self-government. We must stand by the Constitution as our fathers made it, obey the laws as they are passed, and sustain the proper decisions of the Supreme Court.

The speeches were high political drama, although they contained much repetitive material. In their concentration on slavery, the antagonists largely ignored other important topics. They agreed upon a number of points, such as wanting Kansas to enter the Union as a free state; they emphasized their differences. Douglas believed that the fundamental difference was on the principle of self-determination, the power of the people in a state or territory to determine their own government and their own social institutions. Lincoln contended that the moral issue of slavery was most important, and he stressed it throughout the debates. No majority, he maintained, had the right to deny a minority its rights to life, liberty, and the pursuit of happiness.

Election day was November 2. Since the state legislature elected senators, the names of Lincoln and Douglas did not appear on the ballot. The Democrats carried most of the counties in the southern part of the state and along the Illinois River. The Republicans won most of the northern counties. The central counties, where most of the debates had taken place, were evenly divided. If Douglas had not broken with the national administration, the Democrats would have had a clear majority. As it was, the Republicans won about 50 percent of the vote and got about 47 percent of the seats in the House; with some 47 percent of the popular votes, the Democrats captured 53 percent of the House seats. When the legislators voted on January 5, 1859, Douglas was reelected 54 to 46.[15]

Sorely disappointed by the result, Lincoln was sure that his officeholding days were over, but he remained active in the party. He wrote Dr. Anson G. Henry on November 19, 1858, when he was sure of what the vote would be, "I am glad I made the late race. It gave me a hearing on the great and durable question of the ages, which I could not have had in no other way; and though I now sink out of view, and shall be forgotten, I believe that I have made some marks which will tell for the cause of civil liberty long after I am gone."[16]

One of the things that had bothered Lincoln during the campaign was the report that John J. Crittenden of Kentucky, a politician whom Lincoln respected and admired as a Whig successor to Henry Clay, was so anxious to see Douglas win that he had pledged to write Illinois friends to that effect. "It is not in character with you as I have always estimated you," Lincoln wrote in an effort to secure a denial of the rumor. He believed that nearly all of Crittenden's friends in Illinois would be "mortified exceedingly by anything of that sort from you." Crittenden replied on July 29 that he had "openly ardently and frequently expounded" in committee his belief that Douglas's reelection was a necessity. He had written no letters to persons in Illinois, Crittenden said, and only a few replies to letters from elsewhere. Later, Crittenden did respond to some inquiries from Illinois, but at his request they were not published. But when a Republican newspaper reported that Crittenden had written a gentleman in Springfield that he "wanted Douglas crushed," the Democrats published Crittenden's endorsement of Douglas and a statement that he had not written any statement critical of Douglas. Lincoln believed that he had been hurt by Crittenden's action, but he did not blame him for malicious intent. Mary Lincoln must have been bitterly disappointed. Crittenden had been one of her father's closest friends and had been his groomsman at his second wedding.[17]

After his defeat Lincoln spent more time with his legal practice, but he also worked diligently to keep the Republican party intact and to prepare it for the 1860 election. It was in debt and it had been rent with internal disputes. Lincoln suspected Douglas, whose party had removed him from his chairmanship of the Senate Committee on Territories, of trying to attract Republicans to a new central party that Douglas would head. In several speeches, Lincoln in effect continued to debate Douglas in an effort to forestall such a move. More than he had in the Lincoln-Douglas debates, Lincoln stressed the adverse effect that slave labor had upon the labor of white men. The territories must be kept free, he argued, so that settlers there would not be in competition with unpaid slave labor.

Even before the end of 1858, some newspapers in Illinois and elsewhere began to mention Lincoln as a possible candidate for president or vice president. During the 1858 campaign he told journalist Henry Villard that he doubted his ability to be an effective senator, but Mary Lincoln was confident that one day he would be president. Lincoln laughed at the idea: "Just think, of such a sucker as me as President." As suggestions that he run came to his attention in 1859 his stock answer was "I must, in candor, say I do not think myself fit for the Presidency." Indeed, he appeared superficially to be much less well qualified than anyone who had ever held the office. He had little formal education, he had no administrative experience, he had served only one term in the House of Representatives, he had lost both of his attempts to become a U.S. senator.

But he had become a successful lawyer, he had considerable experience in the state legislature, and he was well known in the Republican party. Lincoln realized that none of the front runners for the nomination was sure of securing the nomination; each of them had strong handicaps. Ambition had always been a strong trait of Lincoln, and he began quiet moves to strengthen himself for a possible candidacy without campaigning openly for the nomination. He collected the records of the Lincoln-Douglas debates and had them published as a book. At the request of Jesse W. Fell, a Bloomington politician, he supplied some biographical information for his first political biography. Then he accepted an invitation to speak at the

Brooklyn church of Henry Ward Beecher. By the time he arrived in New York, dressed in a new black suit that cost $100, the address was being sponsored by the Young Men's Central Republican Union and had been moved to the Cooper Union Hall in Manhattan.[18]

Lincoln's speech on February 27, 1860, was a success; it was a masterful introduction to eastern Republicans. His careful examination of the founding fathers showed that a majority of the signers of the Declaration of Independence had believed that the federal government could control slavery in the territories. He said Republicans were the true conservatives on the slavery issue; Southern fire-eaters were the radicals who sought to change a stable situation that had existed for years. He called upon Republicans to stand firm in refusing to let slavery expand into national territories. He did not mention his "house divided" concept, nor did he attack any of the party leaders who might be presidential candidates.[19]

One topic was new. John Brown's raid on Harper's Ferry had occurred on October 16–18, 1859. Brown had been tried in a Virginia court, had been found guilty of treason and of criminal conspiracy to incite a slave insurrection, and had been hanged on December 2. Outraged and alarmed Southerners had blamed the "Black Republicans" for being responsible for the raid. Lincoln praised Brown's courage and unselfishness and agreed with his hatred of slavery, but he concluded that Brown was insane. He had violated the laws in a futile attempt that could not bring about the eradication of a great evil. There had been no slave revolt, Lincoln emphasized; white men had tried to start one, but the slaves did not join it. A congressional investigation had failed to find any evidence of a Republican connection with the affair. Yet some Southern fire-eaters had declared that the 1860 election of a Republican president would result in the Union being dissolved. "That is cool," Lincoln exclaimed. "A highwayman holds a pistol to my ear, and mutters through his teeth, 'Stand and deliver, or I shall kill you, and then you will be a murderer!'"[20]

After his New York triumph, Lincoln went to New England to visit his son Robert, who was enrolled at Phillips Exeter Academy. He accepted as many speaking engagements as possible and continued to win praise. But the trip was tiring, and he wrote Mary from Exeter, "If I had foreseen it, I think I would not have come east at all."[21] Nevertheless, this eastern exposure was important for his political aspirations. He was still unwilling to become an open candidate, and he still had doubts that he could secure the nomination of the party if he sought it, but the political fires were beginning to burn within him. Lincoln began to think more of a possible presidential nomination in 1860 than a possible rematch with Douglas for the Senate in 1864.

Lincoln and Sen. Lyman Trumbull corresponded frequently on party affairs, and in April 1860 Trumbull asked Lincoln what his intentions were. Lincoln admitted on April 29, "The taste *is* in my mouth a little." Then he added, "Let no eye but your own see this."[22]

8

An Election, a War, and Kentucky's Neutrality

During most of the nineteenth century, presidential candidates did not campaign openly; the post was supposed to seek the man. Lincoln remained true to that tradition, but a number of managers pushed his campaign. Some dealt with particular constituencies; Gustave Koerner, for example, was Lincoln's main link with German Americans. Judge David Davis, who weighed some three hundred pounds and thus was allowed the luxury of sleeping alone while riding circuit, came closest to being the campaign manager. When Mark W. Delahay, who hoped to be elected senator from Kansas, asked for financial assistance, Lincoln replied, "I can not enter the ring on the money basis—first, because, in the main, it is wrong; and, secondly, I have not, and can not get, the money.... With me, as with yourself, this long struggle has been one of great pecuniary loss." But for some purposes in a political campaign, spending money is both right and necessary. If Delahay was a delegate to the Chicago convention, Lincoln would send him $100 for expenses. (Delahay went to Chicago but not as a delegate; Lincoln sent the money anyway.) When E. Stafford suggested that Lincoln raise a campaign chest of $10,000, the candidate replied, "I could not raise ten thousand dollars if it would save me from the fate of John Brown. Nor have my friends, so far as I know, yet reached the point of staking any money on my chances of success."[1]

Lincoln expected to have the support of the Illinois del-

111

egates at the national convention, plus some scattered votes from other states. He was the second choice of many other delegates, and if William H. Seward did not win on the first ballot, Lincoln hoped to gain on the second voting. The Republican choice would depend somewhat on the Democratic nominee. If it was Douglas, the Republicans would need a western candidate to counter the strength of the "Little Giant" in that region. Lincoln worked hard to be assured of the unanimous support of the state delegation. An invaluable campaign gimmick came his way at the state party convention in Decatur on May 9–10. Richard J. Oglesby, a young local politician, consulted with John Hanks, a first cousin of Lincoln's mother, and found a rail fence that Hanks and Lincoln had built in 1830. On the first day of the convention during a lull in the proceedings, Oglesby introduced Hanks, who, with an assistant, marched down the center aisle with a sign on two decorated rails they carried:

ABRAHAM LINCOLN
The Rail Candidate
FOR PRESIDENT IN 1860
Two rails from a lot of 3,000
made in 1830 by
Thos. Hanks and Abe Lincoln—
whose father was the first pioneer
of Macon County

Their approach caught the fancy of the crowd, despite some inaccuracies in the slogan. Called to the platform, Lincoln admitted that he had built a cabin and some fences near Decatur in 1830. Although he could not vouch for the two rails being displayed, he "had maulded many and many better ones since he had grown to manhood." He became "the Rail Splitter," or "Honest Abe, the Rail Splitter," and an election myth of incalculable worth was created; Lincoln rails were displayed widely during the campaign. The convention voted to instruct the state delegates to the national convention to vote as a unit for Lincoln.[2]

Lincoln was a serious candidate from the first day of the national convention as it met in the "Wigwam" in Chicago on May 16. Meeting in his state was a definite asset, and his managers were able to pack the seats for spectators with vocal Lincoln supporters. He was a moderate who had not made enemies of any of the other contenders. Judge Davis and his assistants worked the state delegations to get Lincoln at least one hundred votes on the first ballot and to keep Seward from winning on that vote. Stephen T. Logan, a former Kentuckian and once Lincoln's partner, was assigned to the Kentucky delegation. Some of Lincoln's adherents wanted to cut some deals to gain votes, but the alarmed candidate sent an urgent message to Davis: *"Make no contracts that will bind me."* That instruction was carried out with some exceptions, notably Pennsylvania, where Simon Cameron may have been promised a cabinet post if his state went for Lincoln after the first ballot.[3]

The Republican party in Kentucky played a minor role in the preconvention campaign. Cassius M. Clay ran for governor in 1851 on an Emancipation Party platform. Though he received only 3,621 votes, his participation helped defeat the Whigs and contributed to the downfall of that party in the state. Clay decided that the slavery question would have to be solved on a national basis, and he soon joined the Free Soil Party. It also proved to be unsuccessful; in the 1852 election it received only 256 votes in Kentucky. Next Clay turned to the new Republican party, which he hoped could be directed into an antislavery organization. At the February 1856 Pittsburgh convention at which the national party was organized, a letter from Clay helped bring about the adoption of an antislavery resolution. Clay corresponded with a number of leaders in the party, and in his mind he ranked among them. In the 1856 national convention he received a few complimentary votes for vice president. The small Kentucky Republican party made a gesture toward waging a campaign, but Cassius Clay spent most of his time campaigning for Fremont in the Northern states. At an outdoor speech in Springfield, he met Lincoln for the first time, although he had known Mary Todd Lincoln since childhood days. Afterward, Clay claimed credit for converting Lincoln to antislavery. Clay's speeches in the North attracted considerable attention to him, but the Republicans polled only three hundred votes in Kentucky in 1856.[4]

Clay wrote Seward in regard to the 1860 election, "We must have one candidate of the two, in this next canvass, *South* of the line." Obviously, he hoped to be that one, and by January 1860 he was actively seeking support. Clay was pleased by the warm reception he received when he spoke at Cooper Union in New York; the next speaker in the series of programs was to be Abraham Lincoln. When Clay appealed to Thurlow Weed of New York for his assistance, Clay mentioned several reasons why he should be the Republican candidate. One of them was "that I will form a Southern wing of the party which is necessary to a safe administration of the government, and thus put down all hope of *disunion*."[5]

During the preconvention months, Clay deluded himself into thinking that if one of the "old leaders" such as Chase or Seward was not nominated at once, the convention would turn to "a new man"—who would most likely be Cassius Marcellus Clay. His Kentucky location would eliminate the cry of sectionalism. Of course as he advanced his case, Clay was careful to deny that he sought such recognition. Clay addressed a Covington convention of Republicans before the Chicago convention met. He decided not to go to Chicago, but he convinced himself that he was at least the second choice of many of the state delegations. On the first ballot the twenty-three Kentucky delegates divided their votes among five candidates, one of whom was Cassius Clay. On the second vote Seward gained two Kentucky votes, and Clay picked up three. When Lincoln won a clear majority on the third ballot, the convention moved to make the decision unanimous.[6]

The nomination of Lincoln ended any hope that Clay had

to be nominated for the vice presidency. He and Lincoln were both from Kentucky, and both had been Whigs; the party needed a better-balanced ticket. Hannibal Hamlin of Maine received 194 votes on the first ballot; Clay with 101½ was his only serious challenger. When Hamlin won on the second ballot, George D. Blakely of the Kentucky delegation moved to make the vote unanimous, and Cassius Clay received three cheers from the grateful delegates.[7]

The presidential nomination at Chicago required 233 votes. On the first ballot, Seward, as expected, led with 173½. Lincoln had 102, Edward Bates 48, Cameron 50½, Salmon P. Chase 49. The rest of the ballots were widely scattered. When Pennsylvania switched to Lincoln on the second vote, his total rose to 181 while Seward's only increased to 184½. All the other candidates lost votes. Seward retained most of his votes on the third count, but Lincoln's total increased to 231½. An Ohio delegate got the floor and switched four votes to make "the Rail Splitter" the party's nominee. Other switches lifted his total to 364, and the Seward faction moved to make the vote unanimous. Lincoln received news of his victory at the Springfield telegraph office. He accepted congratulations from those who waited there with him, joked for a bit, then excused himself to go home: "Well Gentlemen there is a little short woman at our house who is probably more interested in this dispatch than I am."[8]

An official delegation came to Springfield on May 19 to notify him of his nomination (and was served only ice water). Four days later, after studying the platform, Lincoln formally accepted the nomination.[9] Pressure mounted on the candidate as letters and visitors inundated him. Governor John Wood graciously offered the use of his office, and Lincoln gratefully accepted. John G. Nicolay, a German American newspaperman, was paid $75 a month by some of Lincoln's friends to be the candidate's invaluable secretary and assistant. The flood of mail was so overwhelming that John Hay, a recent graduate of Brown University who was reading law, was soon added to the overworked staff. He and Nicolay served Lincoln faithfully until his death. Photographs were made, material was given out for campaign biographies, ruffled feathers of party notables were smoothed, job applications were deflected.[10] Forbidden by custom and the advice of his managers from campaigning, Lincoln stayed at home during the course of the campaign.

He did, of course, follow political developments with intense interest. The Democrats had met in Charleston, South Carolina, on April 23. Party rules required a two-thirds majority to make a nomination, and front runner Douglas was unable to attain it. After fifty-seven ballots, the convention adjourned; by then delegates from eight Southern states had withdrawn. The Kentucky delegates were committed to the candidacy of James Guthrie, who had been secretary of the treasury from 1853 to 1857 after an active political career in Kentucky. In 1860 he had become president of the Louisville and Nashville Railroad. Guthrie was sixty-eight years old, and a number of the delegates preferred John C. Breckinridge, then the youthful vice president of the United States. Breckinridge had considerable support in the North as well as the South, but he insisted that the state delegation give Guthrie solid support, and his name was not added to those nominated until the thirty-fifth ballot. Guthrie was then in second place, but Douglas had triple his total of votes.

When the adjourned Democratic convention met in Baltimore in June 18 with many Southerners absent, the Douglas men were in firm control. Some other delegates left the convention, and after considering the matter overnight, the Kentuckians also walked out. With more than a third of the original members missing, Douglas was nominated by what was largely a Northern Democratic convention. Alabama senator Benjamin Fitzpatrick was selected as his running mate to balance the ticket.[11]

Before the Southern Democrats held their convention, also in Baltimore, a group of Northern men consulted with Breckinridge about his views on the political situation. He assured them that his primary concern was to restore unity to the Democratic party. He was devoted to the Constitution and the Union, and he condemned the idea that the election of Lincoln would result in secession. After George Loring of Massachusetts visited Breckinridge, he insisted that a vote for Breckinridge would be a vote against secession. Breckinridge was nominated easily on the first ballot, and Joseph Lane of Oregon was picked as the vice-presidential candidate. The presidential nominee faced a dilemma. If he accepted the nomination, the Democrats were split and Lincoln's election was almost assured. Breckinridge's first thought was to decline the nomination.

Then Sen. Jefferson Davis invited him and a few other party leaders to dine with him. Davis suggested that Lincoln could be defeated if Breckinridge, Douglas, and John Bell, the candidate of the Constitutional Union party, all withdrew in favor of a mutually acceptable candidate. But Robert Toombs insisted that if Breckinridge accepted the nomination, he would be so sure to sweep the South that within forty days Douglas would have to withdraw. The Kentuckian decided to accept the nomination, but he promised Davis that he would withdraw if Douglas and Bell also did so. Bell agreed to the plan, and so did Benjamin Fitzpatrick, Douglas's running mate. Douglas refused. If he withdrew, he argued, most of his supporters would switch to Lincoln. He stayed in the race, now with Herschel V. Johnson of Georgia as his vice-presidential candidate. Douglas still believed that he could win; and if he lost, he was at least determined to control his party. He could not understand why Southerners were so opposed to him. Douglas did not see that his cherished doctrine of popular sovereignty did not give the South what the Dred Scott decision did.

Not only did Douglas remain in the race, he broke with political tradition and actively campaigned. Displaying considerable courage, he went into the South to plead his case. Asked if the Southern states would be justified in seceding if Lincoln was elected, Douglas was blunt: "To this I emphatically answer

NO." If a state tried to secede, it would be the president's duty to prevent it, as Andrew Jackson had done with nullification.[12]

John Bell of Tennessee was the fourth candidate. The Constitutional Union party had one plank: the preservation of the Union. Bell was nominated on May 10; Edward Everett of Massachusetts became the vice-presidential candidate. Most of this party's strength came from the old Whig and American parties, and most of its members were in the Upper South.

After the Democratic split, Lincoln was reasonably sure of being elected if the Republicans stayed together, so he labored to hold all factions within the party. The party's platform contained a number of economic promises that appealed to different groups. Since any important statement could be misinterpreted, Lincoln maintained a discreet silence.

Kentucky Democrats were dismayed by the split in their party, for it made almost certain a Bell victory in the state. Most state Democrats favored the popular Breckinridge, who in 1859 had already been elected to a Senate seat that he would assume after retiring as vice president. Douglas also had a party following, and at a Louisville convention in August his supporters denounced any proposal or policy that disturbed the harmony of the party or endangered the existence of the Union.[13] The Breckinridge Democrats had to defend themselves from the charge that they were the ones who most favored secession. Breckinridge told a Frankfort audience in July, "I am an American citizen, a Kentuckian, who never did an act or cherished a thought that was not full of devotion to the Constitution and the Union." Yet the support he received in the Lower South seemed to belie his protests. In a Lexington speech in September before a crowd estimated at fifteen thousand, he reaffirmed his devotion to the Union and his abhorrence of secession.

At the election in November, Breckinridge's personal popularity was not enough to win even a plurality of the Kentucky vote. Bell received 66,016 votes, Breckinridge 52,836, Douglas 25,644, and Lincoln 1,364. Fayette County gave Lincoln just five votes; only two of them came from Lexington, his wife's hometown.[14] Since Breckinridge had disavowed secession, a number of citizens who voted for him turned out to be Unionists.

Billy Herndon persuaded Lincoln to vote on November 6, but the Republican candidate cut off the part of the ballot that had the names of electors so that he would not be voting for himself. That evening he and friends went to the telegraph station to await the election returns. They came in slowly from the critical eastern states, and some Republican ladies served a late supper. Word arrived about two o'clock in the morning that he had carried New York and won the election. "I went home," Lincoln recalled later, "but not to get much sleep, for I then felt as I never had before, the responsibility that was upon me."[15]

When the national count was complete, the popular votes were: Lincoln, 1,866,452; Douglas, 1,376,957; Breckinridge, 849,781; Bell, 588,879. Lincoln had just under 40 percent of the popular vote. Lincoln received 180 electoral votes; Breckinridge 72; Bell 39; and Douglas 12. Lincoln did not receive a single vote in ten of the slave states; he won in all the free states except New Jersey, where he and Douglas split the electoral vote. Had Lincoln's three opponents been combined behind a single candidate, and had the votes remained as they were cast, Lincoln would still have won by a comfortable 169–134 margin.

The secession movement started quickly, although moderates pointed out that it would be March 1861 before Lincoln actually became president, that it would be another election and at least two years before the Republicans could control Congress, and that the Supreme Court that had rendered the Dred Scott decision was still intact. But many Southerners had convinced themselves that the election of a "Black Republican" would be the handwriting on the wall as far as slavery was concerned. Why wait until they were actually hurt when they could prevent it by leaving the Union and thus get rid of the increasing pressure against their peculiar institution? Secession was too important to leave to a state legislature whose members might have been elected sometime earlier when the question of secession was not before the voters. The legislature must call a special convention whose members would be elected on the specific issue of secession. The resulting action of the convention would then reflect the sovereign will of the people. Some cautious individuals and states even believed that a convention decision still had to be ratified by a direct popular vote.

A generation earlier South Carolina had taken the lead in the nullification controversy; it took the leadership again in 1860. A difference was that this time South Carolina did not stand alone as it had in 1832–1833. The state legislature called for a convention as soon as Lincoln's election was certain, and on December 20 by a unanimous vote it dissolved South Carolina's association with the United States of America. A Declaration of Immediate Causes issued on December 24 blamed the North's long-continued attack on slavery, the victory of a sectional party, and the election of a president who was hostile to slavery as the reasons for its action. During the next several weeks six other states followed South Carolina's example: Mississippi, Florida, Alabama, Georgia, Louisiana, and Texas. The four states of the Upper South (Virginia, North Carolina, Tennessee, and Arkansas) did not secede then, but they warned that they would oppose any effort by the federal government to coerce a state. Four border slave states also remained in the Union: Kentucky, Maryland, Missouri, and Delaware. Sizable Unionist minorities existed in several of the seceded states, and a few Southern leaders tried to halt the movement. Few secessionists wanted their states to remain independent, and at Montgomery, Alabama, convention delegates hurriedly formed a provisional government called the Confederate States of America. Jefferson Davis of Mississippi was elected president, with Alexander H. Stephens of Georgia as vice president. Work continued on establishing a permanent government.

As his vote indicated, Lincoln had little support in Kentucky. A young man in Lexington wrote a friend on November 26, 1860, "Old Abe Lincoln—is an infernal old Jackass. I would relish his groans and agonies if I could see him put to torture in hell or anywhere else. He has chosen to become the representative of the Republican Party and as such I would like to hang him. I am not for Disunion, but I am for resistance to the Republican Party as long as there is breath in it or any of its members; fight it to the last but preserve the Union." Some Kentuckians were more sanguine of what the Republican administration might do. A Lexington gentleman who had known Lincoln for some years noted that "Lincoln has grown great since we knew him. His speeches in reply to Douglas show him to be a man of sound mind and clear head. Those who know him best have entire confidence in his firmness. I hope and pray he may be found equal to the trying trust."[16]

Lincoln was especially pleased to receive a congratulatory letter from Joshua Speed written on November 14. Their differences on slavery had threatened their friendship, but now Speed offered, "If it would be agreeable to you I will come & see you—and I think I can impart to you some information as to men and public sentiment here which may be valuable." Lincoln hastened to reply. He would be in Chicago on November 22 and for a day or two thereafter. "Could you not meet me there?" Since Mary would be with him, perhaps Mrs. Speed could also come? He wanted to keep the meeting private, added the president-elect. This gesture must have cheered Lincoln, and it gave him a Kentucky ally in whom he had complete confidence. According to Speed's later recollection, Lincoln appeared to be leading up to an offer of a cabinet post, which Speed forestalled by saying that he did not want any kind of appointment. Lincoln then asked him to sound out James Guthrie of Louisville about the possibility of becoming secretary of war, but Guthrie declined because of advanced years and poor health.[17] Joshua and his brother James Speed would be two of Lincoln's staunchest supporters in Kentucky until his death.

As the postelection crisis developed with the secession of several states and the formation of the Confederacy, much of the nation waited anxiously to see what Lincoln's policies would be. Nothing could be expected from the lame duck Buchanan administration. Some critics said unkindly that the president prayed each night that nothing too bad would happen before the end of his term. Lincoln was inundated by a flood of mail, much of it requesting a job or other favor, and a constant stream of visitors. He started a beard after an eleven-year-old New York girl suggested that a beard would go well with his thin face—and promised to get her brothers to vote for him if he grew one. Some visitors, including ex-governor Charles S. Morehead of Kentucky, disliked Lincoln's endless jokes and anecdotes. Some he told because they amused him; some he told to deflect or avoid giving answers to questions or requests that he wished to sidestep.[18] What he did not do was deliver speeches or issue statements on such vital issues as secession and the future of slavery, although in private letters to individuals he trusted, he discussed such issues. When John A. Gilmer of North Carolina wrote on December 10, 1860, asking for responses on several specific points, Lincoln responded in a "Strictly confidential" letter. "May I be pardoned if I ask whether even you have ever attempted to procure the reading of the Republican platform, or my speeches, by the Southern people? If not, what reason have I to expect that any additional production of mine would meet a better fate? It would make me appear as if I repented for the crime of having been elected, and was anxious to apologize and beg forgiveness. To so represent me, would be the principal use made of any letter I might now thrust upon the public."[19]

During this period after the election before the electoral votes were officially counted on February 13, 1861, Lincoln underestimated the strength of the secession movement and overestimated Unionist strength in the South. Threats of disunion had been made on previous occasions, but compromises had always been worked out. Surely, Unionists in the South-

ern states would rally to block drastic action. Even the secession of South Carolina did not convince him that it would
succeed elsewhere. He was more concerned when six other
states followed its leadership, but he still hoped that the remaining eight slave states might be kept in the Union. He allowed
Senator Trumbull to say in a speech in Springfield on November 20 that the states would be as free to govern their own affairs in his administration as they had ever been. Assumed to
be an official statement from Lincoln, it was assailed in both
the North and South. Lincoln made one point to several individuals. If the federal forts in the South "shall be given up before the inauguration, then General Scott must retake them
afterwards." He asked Elihu B. Washburne to say to General
Scott confidentially, "I shall be obliged to him to be as well
prepared as he can to either *hold,* or *retake,* the forts, as the case
may require, at, and after the inauguration."[20] Seventy-five-year-
old Gen. Winfield Scott was the general-in-chief of the army.

Many Kentuckians became gravely concerned over the
political situation after Lincoln's election. The state had strong
ties with both the North and the South. One of the first statements of states' rights had come in the Kentucky Resolutions
of 1798 and the Kentucky Resolution of 1799, but Kentucky
also had a long tradition of supporting nationalism. For nearly
half a century the state had backed Henry Clay unionism, and
the block of native marble inserted in the Washington monument carried these words "Under the auspices of Heaven and
the precepts of Washington, Kentucky will be the last to give
up the Union."[21] Slavery was an obvious strong tie to the South,
but Kentucky had some antislavery sentiment even before statehood, and the large majority of Kentuckians were not
slaveholders. The state's rivers had created economic ties with
the South and through New Orleans to other parts of the nation and the world. But the advent of railroads had somewhat
changed that situation; Kentucky in 1860 was tied more closely
by rail to the North than to the South. If the nation divided,
Kentucky would be on the frontier regardless of which section

the state joined, and slavery in the commonwealth would be jeopardized. Joseph Holt, the recent secretary of war, wrote James Speed on May 31, 1861, that if Kentucky joined the Confederacy, slavery would perish "as a ball of snow would melt in a summer's sun."[22] Nearly a third of a million former Kentuckians lived in free states and in Missouri in 1860, far more than had gone to the Lower South. Furthermore, Kentucky had nearly sixty thousand foreigners in 1860, more than any slave state except for Missouri, and nearly twenty-five thousand Kentuckians had come from the free states north of the Ohio River.

The question of secession had come up during the presidential campaign, and a number of state political leaders had rejected the idea. Massive Humphrey Marshall, a John C. Breckinridge supporter, was asked about it at a Covington speech in August 1860. "We are asked if Lincoln succeeds do you propose disunion? I would answer emphatically no! It is a remedy for no evil under heaven. It would be political suicide, and Kentucky would be the very last state to give up the Union." The Democratic Party, he asserted, would fight for its rights, but it would do so within the Union.[23]

Gov. Beriah Magoffin was a key figure in determining Kentucky's path through the developing crisis. Active in the Democratic party, he had won the governorship in 1859. He accepted slavery without question, and he was convinced that Southern rights had been violated in regard to slavery in the territories and the return of fugitive slaves. Although he believed in the right of secession, he hoped that it could be avoided. On December 9, 1860, he wrote the governors of the slave states with a proposal for settling the controversy. His main point was the adoption of a constitutional amendment that would divide the territories into slave and free at the 37th parallel. A constitutional amendment should eliminate the "Personal Liberty Laws" that some Northern states used to restrict the return of fugitive slaves. And another amendment should give the South protection from laws dealing with slavery. Magoffin may have been thinking of something like requiring a two-thirds vote in the Senate to pass such legislation.[24]

Gov. Andrew B. Moore of Alabama sent Kentucky-born Stephen F. Hale to Kentucky to seek cooperation in the secession movement under way in Alabama. Hale arrived in Frankfort on December 26, 1860. The next day he addressed a lengthy letter to Magoffin in which he paid tribute to the Kentucky Resolutions in stating the compact theory of the nature of the Union.[25] The election of Lincoln, Hale wrote, was "the last and crowning act of insult and outrage upon the people of the South. . . . nothing less than an open declaration of war" (23,24). If the Republicans were allowed to carry out their program, Southerners would "be degraded to a position of equality with free negroes. . . . or else there will be a eternal war of races, desolating the land with blood and utterly wasting and destroying all the resources of the country" (25). When the two races were continually pressing together, "amalgamation or the extinction of the one or the other would be inevitable" (25). The South had to depend on its own efforts to provide protection; if it was successful, it had a bright and joyful future.

W.S. Featherson of Mississippi had been in Frankfort on December 19–21 on a similar mission to recruit Kentucky into the secession movement, but he had not elicited a public response from Governor Magoffin. On December 28 Magoffin answered the Alabama appeal.[26] Hale had not exaggerated the wrongs heaped upon the South. Because of her geographical position, Kentucky might be more fully aware of the problems than the states in the Lower South. "Our safety, our honor, and our self-preservation, alike demand that our interest be placed beyond the reach of further assault." Though Kentucky would make every effort to preserve the Union, "Kentucky will never submit to wrong and dishonor, let resistance cost what it may." The best approach to their problems, Magoffin suggested, "should be determined in a full and free conference of all the Southern States" (29). If such a conference presented a uniform demand for protection of their rights, "our just demands would be conceded, and the Union be perpetuated stronger than before" (30). If such an effort failed, the South would be more united than ever before. Such demands should be presented before the incoming administration began a policy of coercion. It would force Mr. Lincoln and his advisors to abandon any thought of "a force policy." His convention approach, Magoffin wrote, would be more effective than sending commissioners to different states. "You have no hope of redress in the Union. We yet look hopefully to assurances that a powerful reaction is going on at the North. . . . You would act separately; we unitedly" (31).

In a November 16, 1860, letter to the editor of the *Frankfort Tri-Weekly Yeoman*, Magoffin had insisted that Lincoln's election did not constitute grounds for secession; he and his party would not control Congress or the Supreme Court. Kentucky should wait "for an overt act, and then Kentucky can and will join her sister Southern States." The slave, the governor declared firmly, "is *morally, socially, and religiously a better and happier man than he could be under any other condition.*"

On December 27 Magoffin called a special session of the General Assembly to convene on January 17, 1861, to consider the state of the commonwealth. After recalling his futile efforts to hold a convention of all slaveholding states, Magoffin concluded, "It is now too late. The revolution has progressed beyond that point." The Republicans, "obstinate in spirit and sullen in temper," had blocked every effort to arrive at a reasonable compromise. He recommended that the legislature call a convention that would determine Kentucky's course of action. In the meantime, Kentucky should send delegates to a conference of border states to meet in Baltimore in early February. And action should be taken at once to provide adequate defense for the state.[27]

Kentucky's anxiety over the crisis was indicated by its willingness to participate in almost any effort that might find a compromise solution. On December 18, 1860, U.S. Senator Crittenden introduced his compromise proposals that would have divided the territories at 36°30' and by constitutional amendment provided for the protection of slavery in the states that had it. They were defeated for the usual reason: the Republicans would not accept the expansion of slavery into any territory. Some Kentuckians believed that the Crittenden proposals would have been accepted if they had been submitted to the people for a decision. On January 25 the General Assembly proposed that a national convention (last used in 1787) be called to draft amendments that would then go to the states for ratification without being referred to Congress. Such a convention required a call by Congress, and that was never done.[28] On January 26 the General Assembly appointed six commissioners to attend the Peace Conference in Washington that had been called by Virginia. In a burst of generosity, the legislature provided $500 to each commissioner for expenses. Although the Peace Conference remained in session until February 27, its proposed amendments, much like those of Crittenden, failed to get approval because of the expansion-of-slavery issue.

During the hectic weeks of the secession crisis, several influential Kentuckians tried to form and direct public opinion in the state. On January 4, 1861, Robert Jefferson Breckinridge, uncle of the vice president, delivered a lengthy address in Lexington. He urged a moderate course, and he warned the state against precipitate haste in leaving the Union for a place in the Southern Confederacy. Printed as a pamphlet, his remarks were distributed widely across the state. The Douglas and Bell leaders held separate meetings in Louisville on January 8. Archibald Dixon, Joshua F. Bell, and Garret Davis were leaders in moving to combine their strength and to agree upon a program for what amounted to a new party. They admitted that the South had endured many wrongs but advised against secession. Lincoln's election was not cause for separation; such drastic action should not come before overt hostile acts of the federal government. Instead, they sought the support of moderate men in the North to secure adoption of the Crittenden amendments. The states agreeing to adopt those amendments should form a confederation of their own. They warned that a Union "held together with a sword" was "not worth preserving." A Union State Central Committee included the influential editors George D. Prentice of the *Louisville Journal* and J.H. Harney of the *Louisville Democrat*.[29]

Governor Magoffin assumed leadership of the Breckinridge Democrats. He had supported the Crittenden compromise until it became obvious that it would not be accepted. In his call for a special session of the legislature, he asked for a convention that would determine "the future of Federal and interstate relations of Kentucky." He was critical of the hasty secession of the Southern states, but he rejected the use of force to coerce them. Political battle lines within the state were drawn over his proposed convention. Most Kentuckians agreed that only a convention could pass an ordinance of secession. Therefore, the first defense of the Unionists against secession was to prevent the calling of a convention. Those favoring secession hoped that if a convention were called, the Southern wave of secession would sweep Kentucky along into the Confederacy.

Robert Jefferson Breckinridge, a Presbyterian minister, was one of the most determined opponents of the calling of a convention. This irritable divine had proved on many theological and political issues how obstinate he could be. On the great issue confronting the state, he advised using all possible methods to delay or prevent the calling of a convention. If by some misfortune a convention was called and passed a secession ordinance, he would demand that it be submitted to a popular vote. His son Joseph declared that the Unionists in the Danville area were about ready to fight if that was necessary to prevent a convention from taking Kentucky out of the Union. Such drastic measures were unnecessary, for the Unionists in the General Assembly refused to permit a convention to be called.

The General Assembly made another attempt to reach a compromise by calling for a convention of the border states to meet in Frankfort on May 27. A special election was held to select twelve Kentucky delegates to it, but the Southern Rights

Party (also called the State Rights Party) withdrew its candidates before the election, so that only Unionists were elected. The 110,000 votes cast were equal to nearly two-thirds of Kentucky's votes in November 1860; they indicated clearly that a majority of Kentuckians were Unionists who were determined to remain in the Union.[30]

During the interlude between the election in November and the inauguration in March, Lincoln spent some time working on his address, which he hoped would calm the South, encourage Southern Unionists, and arrest the secession movement. Mary went on a shopping trip to New York for attire suitable for a first lady; she began to run up heavy debts and to accept favors from individuals who hoped to influence the president-elect. Near the end of January Lincoln made an emotional farewell visit to his beloved stepmother and for the first time visited his father's grave. He rented their Springfield house for $350 per year, insured it and the outbuildings for $3,000, and tied up the family trunks and shipped them to the White House.

On February 11, 1861, Lincoln left Springfield on a twelve-day circuitous route with frequent whistle-stop appearances and a few pauses for more important addresses. Allan Pinkerton, head of his National Detective Agency, warned of an assassination plot in Baltimore when the Lincoln party would have to transfer from one station to another. Lincoln, to his later regret, was persuaded to adopt a partial disguise and proceed by a special train to Washington ahead of the rest of his party. During the ten days before his inauguration, he worked on the composition of his cabinet, dealt with countless office seekers, and attended a number of receptions. Among the many persons who made courtesy calls were Vice President John C. Breckinridge and the other two defeated candidates in the recent presidential election.

On March 4, 1861, Gen. Winfield Scott took elaborate precautions to protect Lincoln from any attempt on his life. Lincoln was introduced by his Illinois friend, Edward D. Baker.

When he rose to deliver his address, he was uncertain what to do with his tall hat. Douglas took the hat and held it during the address. Then Chief Justice Roger B. Taney, nearly eighty-four years old, administered the oath of office.[31]

In his address Lincoln repeated his pledge not to interfere with slavery in the states that had it; expansion of slavery was the only real issue between the sections, he declared. The Union of States was perpetual, and it was considerably older than the Constitution itself. No state could leave the Union on its own motion. He promised to execute the laws of the nation faithfully in all of the states to the best of his ability. There would be no bloodshed or violence unless it was forced upon the national authority. No constitutional right had been denied to those who had decided to attempt to leave the Union. The principle of secession, Lincoln warned, would create a precedent that would wreck the government that the minority tried to form; "the central idea of secession, is the essence of anarchy." The true course for those who have been defeated was the next election. Lincoln called upon all who were dissatisfied to take time to think seriously upon the course they were considering. "In *your* hands, my dissatisfied fellow countrymen, and not in *mine,* is the momentous issue of civil war. The government will not assail *you.* You can have no conflict, without being yourselves the aggressor." At the suggestion of Secretary of State William H. Seward, Lincoln softened the conclusion he had originally planned. "I am loth to close," he said, and he expressed the hope that "the mystic chords of memory" would prevail when touched by "the better angels of our nature."[32]

By April the national situation had become more complex and more threatening. On April 12, 1861, after unsuccessful negotiations, Confederates opened fire on Fort Sumter in Charleston Harbor. By then it was one of only two Federal forts in the South still flying the Union flag. A relief expedition was on the way to resupply the garrison, and a controversy has raged from then to the present over whether or not President Lincoln provoked and tricked the Confederates into firing the first shot. Kentuckian Maj. Robert Anderson commanded the fort. After Lincoln was assured by those who knew Anderson that he was totally loyal to the Union, Lincoln placed full trust in him. If it became necessary, Anderson was authorized to surrender his small force.[33] After a heavy bombardment that killed no one, Anderson surrendered with honors of war on April 14. The Civil War had begun.

Since the entire army of the United States in 1860 was just over sixteen thousand men, most of whom were located on the frontier, more troops were urgently needed. On April 15 President Lincoln called for seventy-five thousand men to put down the rebellion. The rebels were ordered to return to a peaceful status within twenty days. To implement the request for troops, Secretary of War Simon Cameron sent telegrams to the governors. Magoffin was asked to supply four regiments of militia. The governor answered the same day. "Your despatch is received. In answer, I say, *emphatically*, Kentucky will furnish no troops for the wicked purpose of subduing her sister Southern States."[34] After the surrender of Fort Sumter, Virginia, North Carolina, Tennessee, and Arkansas joined the Confederacy. Four slave states remained in the Union; Delaware, Maryland, Missouri, and Kentucky.

After the fall of Fort Sumter and before Lincoln's call for troops could be met, Washington appeared to be defenseless. Rumors abounded that Confederate forces were poised to seize the nation's capital. Some semblance of order was created by senator-elect of Kansas James H. Lane, who organized the Frontier Guard, and Cassius M. Clay of Kentucky, who headed the Clay Battalion. Clay had campaigned actively for Lincoln in the North, and he believed that he was entitled to a senior cabinet position. But appointing Clay would have angered many Kentuckians, and Lincoln was determined to hold his birth state in the Union. Clay finally agreed to accept the post of minister to Spain, then switched to Russia when that position became available. He was in Washington to receive instructions when he hastily organized his small command. With three pistols strapped to his waist and carrying both a sword and his favorite knife, he was an inspiring sight at his headquarters in Willard's Hotel. With his usual modesty, Cassius Clay claimed that he enjoyed the full confidence of the president.[35]

Sentiment for a neutral stance in the war had been growing across the state. In a major address in Lexington on April 17, Crittenden declared that Kentucky had made every effort possible to avert the war; now the state must take no part in it except to act as a mediator. Two days later a mass meeting in Louisville, directed by Unionists Archibald Dixon and James Guthrie, led the audience into an open acceptance of neutrality. "Can he [Lincoln] make Kentucky help him kill?" asked Dixon. "No; they will never lend themselves to such a course. But Kentucky will stand firm with her sister border States in the center of the Republic, to calm the distracted sections. This is her true position, and in it she saves the Union and frowns on secession." The meeting adopted resolutions rejecting Lincoln's call for troops, opposing secession, and providing military force "if necessary, to make the declaration [neutrality] good with her strong right arm."[36] On April 20 in his *Louisville Journal,* Prentice trumpeted a call to his fellow citizens: "KENTUCKIANS! YOU CONSTITUTE TODAY THE FORLORN HOPE OF THE UNION." Would they accept that responsibility?

Other Kentuckians were still trying to find some way to take the state out of the Union. Blanton Duncan inquired as early as March 6 whether the Confederacy would accept a regiment of Kentucky troops. Secretary of War Leroy Pope Walker replied that it would depend on whether war came and on whether such troops could be received without damaging the friendly relations between Kentucky and the Confederate States of America. Magoffin apparently gave tacit permission for Confederate recruiters to operate within the state. After Fort Sumter, John Hunt Morgan sent a telegram to President Davis: "Twenty thousand men can be raised to defend Southern liberty against Northern conquest. Do you want them?" Duncan even arranged with the governor of Louisiana to enlist fifteen hundred Kentuckians as a part of that state's quota.[37] On April 22 the Confederate secretary of war called upon Magoffin for a regiment to be sent to Harper's Ferry. Magoffin refused the request, for it would have upset the movement toward neutrality that was well under way. Magoffin then withdrew the tacit understanding that allowed Confederate recruiting agents in Kentucky.[38]

Some Kentuckians feared an invasion from the states immediately north of the Ohio River. Gov. O.P. Morton of Indiana rebuffed Magoffin sharply when the Kentuckian tried to form a block of neutral states. No state, the Hoosier lectured, had a right to stand aside from the struggle and act as a mediator; Kentucky should take her place beside Indiana to help save the Union. Ohio's response to a neutral block was also negative; because of Lincoln, Illinois was assumed to be negative.

An effort was then made between leaders of the Union and Southern Rights parties to decide on a policy for Kentucky to follow. The Union Party selected Crittenden, Dixon, and Samuel S. Nicholas to confer with the Southern Rights representatives, Magoffin, John C. Breckinridge, and Richard Hawes. After the Unionists rejected the calling of a convention, the six men agreed upon a policy of neutrality and arming the state for self-defense. Magoffin was so distrusted by the Unionists that they insisted on placing the state's military force under the control of a five-man board instead of using the governor as the head of the military forces. This scheme collapsed when the Southern Righters made Magoffin one of its two members. The Unionists were so incensed by this attempt that they refused to participate in the plan even after Magoffin was removed.[39]

Garret Davis, a strong opponent of secession, met with President Lincoln about April 23 to discuss Kentucky's situation. The president still hoped that Kentucky would supply its four regiments, but he assured Davis that he did not intend to compel obedience. He did not intend to invade any state unless the state or its people made it necessary by resisting the laws of the United States. If Kentucky or its citizens seized the post at Newport, he might attempt to retake it, but he "contemplated no military operation that would make it necessary to move any troops over her territories, although he had the unquestioned right at all times to march the United States troops into and over any and every state." If Kentucky made no demonstration of force against the United States, he would not molest Kentucky. Shortly thereafter Lincoln repeated the assurance to Warner L. Underwood of Bowling Green, a Unionist slaveholder.[40]

Given this assurance, the Kentucky House of Representatives resolved on May 16: "That this State and the citizens thereof should take no part in the civil war now being waged, except as mediator and friends to the belligerent parties; and that Kentucky should, during the contest, occupy the position of strict neutrality." It was adopted 69–26. Then the House voted 89–4 to approve a resolution supporting Magoffin's refusal to supply troops to the federal government. On May 20 Magoffin issued a proclamation of neutrality without waiting for the Senate to act. He warned all states against invading Kentucky's neutrality, and he warned Kentuckians to avoid "any warlike or hostile demonstrations" and to stay quietly at home. On May 24, as it prepared to adjourn, the Senate by a vote of 13–9 also adopted resolutions agreeing to neutrality. Its first resolution stated firmly "that Kentucky will not sever her connection with the national government" nor side with either belligerent, but that she would arm herself to pursue "tranquility and peace within her own borders."[41]

Neutrality was no more constitutional than secession, but it was much less of a threat to the Union. Lincoln saw how important Kentucky was in the struggle, and he determined to hold his birth state in the Union even if he had to accept this irregular measure to do so. In an oft-quoted letter to Orville H. Browning, he explained why he considered Kentucky so important. "I think to lose Kentucky is nearly the same as to lose the whole game. Kentucky gone, we can not hold Missouri, nor, as I think, Maryland. These all against us, and the job on our hands is too large for us. We would as well consent to separation at once, including the surrender of the capital."[42] Lincoln was also reputed to have said that he hoped to have God on his side, but he had to have Kentucky.[43] He was in the position of a fisherman who hooks a large fish on a slender line. Play the fish carelessly and it is lost. Lincoln played Kentucky's neutrality skillfully and cautiously; he did nothing that would drive the state into the Confederacy. The period of neutrality allowed the Unionists in the state to consolidate their position until they had a clear majority in the General Assembly and any chance of secession was gone.

Kentucky was relatively a much larger and more important state in 1861 than it has been in the twentieth century. Although before 1860 its population was growing slower than that of the nation as a whole, Kentucky still ranked ninth among the states in population. Kentucky was seventh in the value of farms, fifth in the value of livestock. In an era when armies still depended heavily upon animals for mobility and cavalry was still an important arm of the service, her horses and mules were of untold value. The state's diversified agriculture produced large quantities of corn, wheat, fruit, tobacco, hay, hemp, and flax. An unconfirmed theory holds that the fate of the Confederacy was decided when the usual supply of Kentucky bourbon was denied the South. Agriculture was much more important than industry in 1860, but Kentucky did rank thirteenth in the cost of raw materials used and fifteenth in both the amount of capital invested in manufacturing and in the annual value of manufactured goods.[44] Kentucky would have ranked high in industry among the Confederate states, and her accession to the Confederacy would have strengthened the economy of the nascent nation. Having Kentucky would have given the Confederacy a defense line along the Ohio River, and an army located there would have posed a threat to split the Union by driving to the Great Lakes.

Kentucky derived considerable economic advantage from her neutrality.[45] By allowing free trade on the Mississippi River, the Confederacy hoped to pull Kentucky and other states along that stream and its many tributaries into the Confederate States of America. The Louisville and Nashville Railroad had been completed in 1859, and by rail, river, and road vast quantities of goods flowed into Kentucky for transshipment to the South. The traffic was largely one way. Of every one hundred rail cars loaded at Louisville for Nashville, ninety-five returned empty. Once the war started, Unionists complained strongly about this trade with the Confederacy. Cincinnati, a bitter trade rival of Louisville, was especially incensed, and the Queen City attempted to interdict the objectionable trade. A river war seemed so probable that Governor Dennison of Ohio sent a personal envoy to Governor Magoffin in an effort to defuse the situation. Cincinnati vigilante groups continued to interfere with such commerce, and pressure soon forced Dennison to accept laws passed by the legislature to end the trade of goods destined for the Confederacy. Indiana faced similar problems. Illinois posed particular problems for Kentucky after the war started, for Governor Yates imposed what amounted to a blockade. On May 2 General Scott and the War Department ordered the blockade relaxed because of the adverse affect it might have on Kentucky and other states that depended heavily on river traffic. But that modification was rescinded six days later, and the blockade was renewed. The federal government soon took it over from the state. Lincoln moved slowly and cautiously in dealing with the trade problem; he feared that a too drastic policy might tilt Kentucky toward the South, and it might also influence the delicate situation in Missouri. Though restrictions were gradually imposed, he did not order commerce with the Confederacy closed until August 16. By then Unionists were firmly in control in Kentucky.

Louisville was the collecting point for most of the goods that were to be sent South, and Lincoln came under heavy pressure to do something there to halt the traffic. When he was slow to act, Governors Dennison, Yates, and Morton met on May 24 to see what they could do. Dennison wanted to seize the main river ports in Kentucky and thus strangle the trade. Ex-governor of Kentucky Charles S. Morehead (1855–1859) charged that Lincoln was "daily preventing supplies of food to the helpless women and children and slaves of the South, in order that under the desperation of starvation the slaves may be excited to servile insurrection." Lincoln gradually ordered enforcement of existing rules, and extralegal inspection of goods bound for Kentucky was made. Items suspected of being sent on to the South were often confiscated, but a great deal of deceptive shipping and outright smuggling occurred.

On June 21, 1861, the surveyor of customs at Louisville announced that after June 24 no goods could be shipped over the L&N without a permit from his office. Kentuckians, especially those trading with the Confederacy, howled in protest. Goods were often hauled in wagons to a shipping point south of Louisville and loaded aboard railcars there. Towns such as Franklin that were close to the Tennessee border experienced a boom in imports, which were then carried across the state line. Goods were also carried to Smithland and Paducah at the mouths of the Cumberland and Tennessee Rivers, respectively, and sent on South by steamboat. Some trade also went through Columbus for Memphis, but shippers had more trouble getting goods to Columbus on the Mississippi River.

The Confederacy also affected the trade that was flowing through Kentucky. On May 21 the Confederate Congress ordered a halt to the exportation of cotton. Some Confederates believed that the sooner a cotton shortage developed in Europe, the sooner the Confederate States of America would receive aid from England and France. Half a dozen staple crops were added to the prohibited list on August 2. The Confederacy cut off most of its products from going to the United States, but that policy probably helped keep Kentucky in the Union. Lincoln's cautious trade policy was in keeping with his thoughts on Kentucky's neutrality.

The situation in Kentucky in 1861 reflected the national crisis. The nation was dividing into North and South after failing to reconcile the principles on which it had been founded with the institution of slavery, which challenged those principles. The political machinery had failed to resolve problems created by clashes between the will of the nation and the rights of individual states. After the election of Lincoln in 1860, a majority of the slave states decided to secede. Kentuckians were also divided over these great questions. Kentucky's decision was uncertain but vital to the outcome of the national struggle.

Abraham Lincoln perhaps saw the problems more clearly than any other public figure. He realized that unless the Union was preserved, slavery would continue indefinitely in the South. Given time, he hoped that the spirit of unionism would prevail, but time expired nationally in April 1861 and the Civil War began. Kentucky's adoption of neutrality gave him more time in the state of his birth. Lincoln understood Kentucky and Kentuckians, and he worked skillfully and successfully with state Unionists to ensure that Kentucky remained loyal, although a Provisional Confederate Government was created. Some loyal Kentuckians disagreed strongly with such Lincoln policies as those dealing with slavery and the use of black troops, but by April 1865 the war was drawing to a close, and slavery was on its way to extinction by constitutional amendment.

9

The War Enters Kentucky

The Border State Convention that Kentucky had called met in Frankfort on May 27, 1861. Only Kentucky and Missouri were represented, plus one person from Tennessee, who was not officially admitted. The convention called for constitutional amendments to protect states' rights, continued Kentucky neutrality, and a national convention to find a way to end the war and reunify the nation.[1] This effort failed, as had so many others in recent months; matters had gone too far to be solved by any method short of war.

The governor, the General Assembly, and numerous private citizens had coupled neutrality with a state military force strong enough to command respect and to defend the state if that should become necessary. The traditional state militia was obviously inadequate for that task. It had languished after the War of 1812, with volunteers doing the state's fighting in the Mexican War. The new constitution of 1850 did not even provide for a militia. A legislative act revived it in 1851, but three years later the General Assembly decreed that starting in 1859 a regimental muster would be held only once in six years. Gov. Charles S. Morehead was correct when he stated in 1856, "There is in fact, no organized militia in the State," although some volunteer military units did exist. The "gathering storm" prompted Governor Magoffin to propose a new militia act in 1860, which was passed. Members were divided into three categories, volunteer, enrolled, and reserve, but the volunteers constituted the only effective force. Called the Kentucky State Guard, it was headed by an inspector general.[2]

Simon Bolivar Buckner was appointed to that position. A West Point graduate in 1844, he had resigned from the army in 1855 because of slow promotion. He had practiced law in Chicago and Louisville, and in the latter he had organized a volunteer company called the Citizens Guard. As inspector general, he built the State Guard into a body of more than four thousand men when the state declared neutrality. Most of the men had had some training, but many did not have adequate weapons. Almost from its inception, the State Guard was seen as being pro-Southern. When Magoffin sought bank loans to purchase weapons, only a few banks responded to his request. Early efforts to strip the governor of his control of the military forces failed, but an agreement was reached in the May 1861 special session of the legislature. Magoffin, Samuel Gill, George T. Wood, Gen. Peter Dudley, and Dr. John B. Peyton constituted a Military Board on which the governor had only one vote of five. Buckner was not a member of the board, which could issue orders to him. The board could borrow money to provide arms and to build powder mills. Home Guards were added to the existing State Guards; the two organizations were to share equally in the available funds. Since the Home Guard was not militia, it could not be called out of its county. From the start, the Home Guard was seen as being pro-Union.

Buckner worked closely with Magoffin to preserve Kentucky's neutrality. On June 8, 1861, he met in Cincinnati with Gen. George B. McClellan, who commanded federal troops north of the Ohio River. McClellan promised to respect Kentucky's neutrality; Buckner promised that the state would enforce that policy and the laws of the United States. If Confederates invaded the state and Buckner could not expel them, federal troops would do so and then withdraw from Kentucky. Buckner then went to Tennessee and secured a promise from Gov. Isham Harris that his state would also respect Kentucky's neutrality. In July Buckner traveled to Washington and in company with John J. Crittenden conferred with President Lincoln to make sure that the president's position toward Kentucky had not changed. After their talks, Lincoln wrote out a statement that he refused to sign but handed to Crittenden to attest to its authenticity as he saw fit. The senator initialed the paper, which read: "So far I have not sent an armed force into Kentucky, nor have I any present purpose to do so. I solemnly desire that no necessity for it may be presented; but I mean to say nothing which shall hereafter embarrass me in the performance of what may seem to be my duty." This masterful noncommitment may have lulled some Kentuckians into thinking that neutrality would last longer than it did.[3]

Buckner apparently impressed Lincoln when they conferred, for on August 17, 1861, the president sent a note to the secretary of war: "Unless there be reason to the contrary, not known to me, make out a commission to Simon Buckner, of Kentucky, as a brigadier general of volunteers. It is to be put in the hands of General Anderson, and delivered to General Buckner or not, at the discretion of General Anderson. Of course it is to remain a secret unless and until the commission is delivered." Anderson, the hero of Fort Sumter in the North, had been promoted to brigadier general and placed in command of the Military Department of Kentucky, which included all areas of the state within one hundred miles of the Ohio River. When Buckner accepted a commission as brigadier general on September 14, 1861, it was in the army of the Confederate States of America.

In respect of Kentucky's neutrality, Anderson maintained his headquarters in Cincinnati, but federal recruiting in the state was intensified. Recruits were directed to centers north of the Ohio River, such as Camp Joseph Holt across from Louisville and Camp Henry Clay opposite Newport. On May 7, 1861, Lincoln empowered Anderson, who was promoted to brigadier general on June 17, to recruit into federal service as many volunteer regiments from Kentucky and the western part of Virginia as would enlist for three years. For the moment, this recruiting was done among Kentuckians who crossed to the north side of the Ohio River. Later, Lincoln believed that some more direct participation by Kentucky troops would be helpful in dispelling the idea that the war was entirely sectional, and on July 29, 1861, he addressed a note to the "Gentlemen of the Kentucky Delegation who are for the Union" with this appeal: "I somewhat want to authorize my friend, Jesse Boyles, to raise a Kentucky regiment, but I do not wish to do it without your consent. If you consent, please write so at the bottom." Although nine of the ten congressmen from Kentucky were Unionists, only five of them signed the request: Robert Malory, Henry Grider, George W. Dunlap, James S. Jackson, and Charles A. Wickliffe. Nothing was done then, but on August 5 President Lincoln repeated his request for "Col. Boyle to raise a Regiment of cavalry, whenever the Union men of Kentucky desire, or consent to it." This attempt was contingent upon the approval of General Anderson, which then was not forthcoming. Boyle enrolled the men of the Fourth Cavalry Regiment, USA, in Louisville on December 13, 1861, and they were mustered in on December 24, 1861.[4]

Both the Home and the State Guards needed weapons, but so did the United States and the Confederate States of America. The result was a mad scramble for weapons, and prices soared. When weapons could not be bought, they were sometimes taken by stealth or force. Six cannon and nine hundred muskets disappeared in Paducah, then mysteriously surfaced in Tennessee. William Nelson, a native of Maysville and a naval lieutenant, was much concerned over the arms shortage for Kentucky Unionists, and he convinced Lincoln that weapons should be supplied at once to loyal Kentuckians. The president sent Nelson into the state to distribute five thousand "Lincoln guns." Anderson was told of Nelson's involvement and informed that he could call upon John J. Crittenden, James Guthrie, and Joshua Speed for assistance. Lincoln especially recommended Speed: "I have the utmost confidence in his loyalty and integrity, and also in his judgment on any subject which he professes to understand."[5]

"Bull" Nelson, standing some five inches over six feet and weighing an estimated three hundred pounds, was one of the most unusual undercover agents of the Civil War. He hastened to Frankfort, where at an all-night Unionist session plans were made for agents to distribute the guns. Allocations were made to various points around the state, and a reliable Unionist was appointed at each place to distribute the muskets at a nominal price of $1 each. The men agreed upon that night were James Harlan, Frankfort; James Speed, Louisville; Garret Davis, Paris; Samuel Lusk, Lancaster; John H. Ward, Bowling Green; Thornton F. Marshall, Augusta; John H. Lord [?], Frankfort; Charles H. Wickliffe, Bowling Green. Others were probably added later, and distribution spread out from the original points. Anderson carefully stayed clear of the operation so that he could not be accused of violating Kentucky's neutrality. James Speed was sent to Indianapolis to obtain ammunition for the weapons. Most of the guns were sent to Louisville for distribution, but those intended for central Kentucky were shipped from Cincinnati to Lexington over the Kentucky Central Railroad. Maysville was the port at which shipments for eastern Kentucky were received.

Knowledge of this operation could not be kept secret, and Confederate sympathizers attempted to intercept and seize the guns for their own use. One shipment left Cincinnati for Lexington on the Kentucky Central Railroad but was turned back when it was learned that it was to be seized in Cynthiana. Instead, the guns went to Louisville by boat, then were sent to Lexington by rail. Pro-Southerners in Lexington were determined to take the guns, and an open battle was barely avoided by the intercession of John C. Breckinridge and M.C. Johnson. The pro-Confederates were less successful in arming their partisans. The State Guard demanded an equal share of the state money available for armaments, but the Military Board gave the available funds to the Home Guard until it should be as well armed as its rival. As sentiment in Kentucky tilted toward the Union, protests were voiced that "Our State has supported a camp of instruction for the Southern Confederacy quite long enough." Before the end of the summer the Military Board voted "that no more money will be appropriated at present for the purpose of training men who may at any moment abandon the service of the State to join others in hostility to the State of Kentucky and the Government of the United States." The board even tried to recall arms from the State Guard units but with little success. In September, when Kentucky's neutrality ended, the legislature abolished the State Guard. By then many of its members were serving in the Confederate army.[6]

Two elections held during the summer of 1861 revealed that the state's neutrality was tinged with Unionism. Lincoln's call for a special session of Congress resulted in an election on June 20 for the ten members of the House of Representatives. All ten seats were contested, but Henry C. Burnett, who won the seat in the First District in the Jackson Purchase, was the only successful pro-Confederate candidate, and his Unionist opponent won 41 percent of the vote. The presence of slavery appeared to have little influence upon the results; some of the counties with the highest percentage of slaves were strongly pro-Union.[7] John J. Crittenden, Kentucky's Nestor, was the best-known member of the state's delegation. The total votes were less than half the number cast in 1860 in the presidential election; many Southern Rights adherents, recognizing their inevitable defeat, had boycotted the election. Since this was the first important election after the adoption of neutrality, the results were considered to be an endorsement of that unique policy.

On July 22 Representative Crittenden introduced a resolution that the House accepted in two parts by votes of 121–2 and 117–2. The nays were cast by Henry C. Burnett of Kentucky and John W. Reid of Missouri. It read:

> Resolved, That the present deplorable civil war has been forced upon the country by the disunionists of the Southern States, now in arms against the constitutional government, and in arms around the capital; that in this

national emergency, Congress—banishing all feeling of mere passion or resentment—will recollect only its duty to the whole country; that this war is not waged on their part in any spirit of oppression, or for any purpose of conquest or subjugation, or purpose of overthrowing or interfering with the rights or established institutions of those states, but to defend and maintain the *supremacy* of the constitution, and to preserve the Union with all the dignity, equality and rights of the several states unimpaired; and that as soon as these objects are accomplished the war ought to cease.

A few days later Sen. Andrew Johnson of Tennessee introduced an almost identical resolution that passed the Senate 30–5. There the dissenters were John C. Breckinridge and Lazarus W. Powell of Kentucky, Truston Polk and W.P. Johnson of Missouri, and Lyman Trumbull of Illinois.[8]

Kentuckians voted for members of the General Assembly on August 5, 1861. All members of the House were elected and half of the senators. Earlier in the year some Southern Righters seemed confident that they would capture control of the General Assembly, which would then call a convention that would take Kentucky out of the Union and into the Confederacy. Blanton Duncan had written the Confederate secretary of war, Leroy Pope Walker, on March 29 that he had "a strong confidence in our ability to carry it in August. If we do, we shall join you about the 1st of January." That expectation had faded well before August. Some determined Unionists worked hard and successfully to make sure that when neutrality ended, Kentucky would be in the Union. On the day that the state Senate voted for neutrality, Joshua Speed wrote Joseph Holt, who had been secretary of war in 1860–1861, for help in guiding Kentucky in the right direction. "Kentucky is nervous and excited, & the people struggling between loyalty to the Government and deep seated distrust of the policy of the administration in regard to war. . . . For Heaven sakes aid us if you can."[9]

Holt responded on May 31, 1861, in a letter designed to be published. Printed in pamphlet form, more than thirty thousand copies were distributed across the state. Holt denounced neutrality as being no more constitutional than secession, although its result was better. The South, he charged, had plotted for years to destroy the Union by refusing to compromise; the South would either rule or destroy the Union. In one of his more damaging statements, Holt asserted that the South wanted Kentucky to secede so that the Southern people would be sheltered behind her; Kentucky would be sacrificed to protect the South. If Kentucky joined the Confederacy, she would be taxed to death, and with the inevitable collapse of the Confederacy, Kentucky would find that she had sacrificed everything and gained nothing in return. Holt returned to Kentucky and waged an active campaign to elect Unionists to the legislature. A popular and effective speaker, he lambasted the Confederacy in speeches across the state and denounced neutrality as being unworthy of Kentuckians. Why would they even consider standing aside and watching the best government in the world destroyed? In anticipation of an election victory, he predicted that "not many weeks can elapse before this powerful commonwealth will make an exultant avowal of her loyalty, and will stand erect before the country, stainless and true as the truest of her sisters in the Union."[10] Holt did not work alone, but he may have been the most effective campaigner for the Union during the summer of 1861. The editor of the *Frankfort Tri-Weekly Commonwealth* may have helped sway borderline Unionists by reminding them in the issue of July 10 that one could be "for the Constitution and the Union, and not for Mr. Lincoln" or his misguided policies.

Many pro-Confederates stayed away from the polls on August 5, and the new legislature had a Unionist majority of 76–24 in the House and 27–11 in the Senate, although only half of the Senate seats were up for election. Thereafter, Governor Magoffin's vetoes became only a temporary obstacle until they were overridden by large majorities. Peace Democrats would complain throughout the war that the United States had held Kentucky in the Union by force, but a careful study of the 1861 elections denies that charge: the army played no part in the elections won by Unionists in 1861.

Kentuckian E.F. Drake warned Secretary of the Treasury Salmon P. Chase against relying too much upon the apparent Unionism in Kentucky as indicated by the results of the election for members of the General Assembly. The truth was, Drake warned, that "nearly all the old men are Unionists at heart and in action while their sons, living in their fathers' houses, are heading rebellion. There is another large class, who sympathize with the rebels, yet from policy vote and talk Union, and almost *every* Union man considers the South aggrieved, and expects an end of war only by agreeing to any demand by way of guarantee which the south may demand. . . . I am sure that Kentucky is only a Union state for fear of the consequences of being the seat of war as a border Confederate State." Samuel McDowell Starling, a slaveholding Unionist, had written a daughter in early May, "I wish the South would get a good whipping, perhaps then she will come to her senses & behave herself. She only wants Kentucky to stand between her & danger, to be her battle ground."[11] Such suspicions of Confederate motives in seeking Kentucky's support must have had some effect upon the formation of public opinion during the months of Kentucky's neutrality.

A step toward breaking the neutrality came on July 1, 1861, when William Nelson was authorized to start raising five regiments of Tennessee troops and three regiments of Kentucky troops from within the state. On loan to the army, Nelson was provided with ten thousand arms, six cannon, and an ample supply of ammunition. He set up a base at Crab Orchard and began recruiting. Frank L. Wolford and Thomas E. Bramlette were among the early volunteers who were commissioned and told to raise regiments. These moves could not have been taken without the president's consent, although he was careful not to attach his name to direct orders. After the August election,

Nelson opened Camp Dick Robinson in Garrard County and increased his recruiting efforts, much to the dismay of some conservative Union men who cherished their neutrality. George D. Prentice and Paul R. Shipman complained to John J. Crittenden on August 11 that sending weapons to Camp Dick Robinson was "as fearfully equipped for mischief as if it had been contrived by the Secessionists themselves or by the Devil himself. It is reckless in the last degree. It is insane." When Crittenden arrived home in the late summer, he feared that Nelson's activities might provoke an armed clash that would endanger or even end Kentucky's neutral status. He assured Lincoln that the newly elected legislature would soon take a Unionist stance, and he requested that nothing be done to endanger the situation until that was achieved. Governor Magoffin protested Nelson's activities to President Lincoln in a letter dated August 19, and he sent William A. Dudley and Frank K. Hunt to Washington to urge the removal of Nelson and his growing force from Kentucky. No danger existed in the state, Magoffin argued, that justified this violation of Kentucky's neutrality.[12]

When he responded on August 24, Lincoln was reasonably sure that there was no longer any danger that Kentucky might secede and join the Confederacy. Though he disclaimed "full and precise knowledge upon the subject," he believed that it was true that a small military force, acting upon U.S. authority, was within Kentucky and that some arms had been furnished by the United States. This force consisted of local Kentuckians who did not in any way threaten that part of the state. He had "acted upon the earnest solicitations of many Kentuckians, and in accordance with what I believed, and still believe, to be the wish of a majority of all the Union-loving people of Kentucky." Only the governor and the men who carried his letter had urged him to remove the military from the state. "Taking all the means within my reach to form a judgment, I do not believe it is the popular wish of Kentucky that this force shall be removed beyond her limits; and, with this impression, I most respectfully decline to so remove it." He also hoped to preserve "the peace of my own native State, Kentucky; but it is with regret I search, and can not find, in your not very short letter, any declaration, or intimation, that you entertain any desire for the preservation of the Federal Union."[13] Lincoln's careful policy to hold Kentucky in the Union had succeeded. The only questions remaining as the summer of 1861 neared its end were when and how the state's neutrality would cease.

In a letter dated August 24, 1861, Governor Magoffin asked Jefferson Davis to explain the attitude of the Confederate government toward Kentucky's neutrality. George W. Johnson of Scott County was the state commissioner sent to Richmond to receive the answer. Davis assured Magoffin that Confederate troops were stationed near Kentucky's southern boundary only to guard against a possible Union invasion; he did not intend to interfere with Kentucky's neutrality. But if that policy was to be respected, it "must be strictly maintained between both parties." Confederate recruiters had been withdrawn from Kentucky after the announcement of neutrality, but a growing number of Kentuckians had gone south to enlist in the Confederate army, particularly at Camp Boone in Montgomery County, Tennessee. On August 8, 1861, the Confederacy had begun accepting Kentucky troops, and on August 30 the Confederate Congress passed a law authorizing recruiting stations inside Kentucky. On the same day the Confederate Congress passed a secret appropriation of $1 million to be spent at the discretion of the president "to aid the people of Kentucky in repelling any invasion or occupation of their soil by the armed forces of the United States."[14]

Kentucky's precarious neutrality ended because of an impetuous Confederate general. Gideon Pillow, who commanded Confederate troops in western Tennessee, was obsessed with the strategic importance of Columbus on the Mississippi River in Hickman County, Kentucky. He believed that it was essential to controlling the vital river traffic on the Mississippi. Refused permission by Magoffin to occupy the town in May 1861, Pillow was restrained by Buckner from seizing it on his own initiative during the summer. But Pillow became convinced that a federal occupation of the area was imminent. His superior commander, Gen. Leonidas Polk, asked Magoffin on September 1 about the condition of the Southern party in Kentucky: "I think it is of the greatest consequence to the Southern cause in Kentucky or elsewhere that I should be ahead of the enemy in occupying Columbus and Paducah." When Ulysses S. Grant's federal troops occupied Belmont, Missouri, across the river from Columbus, on September 2, it was seen by Polk and Pillow as a preparatory move to seizing Columbus. Polk authorized the eager Pillow to occupy Columbus, which he did on September 3, 1861. U.S. Grant then occupied Paducah with Union troops.[15]

Confederate secretary of war Walker told Polk to order Pillow to withdraw from Columbus and to explain why it had been occupied at all. Tennessee governor Isham Harris also objected to the occupation; he had pledged to respect Kentucky's neutrality. However, President Davis concluded that military necessity had justified the move, and the Confederate troops were not ordered to withdraw. It had been an act "of self-defense on the part of the Confederate States, but also by a desire to aid the people of Kentucky," Davis explained. Polk defended the movement in a letter of September 8 to Governor Magoffin, but he promised to withdraw from the state if the federal troops would also do so and would promise not to occupy any part of Kentucky in the future. Buckner was convinced that the occupation was a great political blunder; if the Confederates withdrew, he could raise thousands of troops to expel the Union forces.[16] But all efforts to restore neutrality failed. It had been at best a temporary expedient; sooner or later Kentucky would have to become involved in the conflict. It had allowed time for Lincoln to make sure that the Unionists were in solid control of affairs in the state. Kentucky remained in the Union.

Magoffin wanted to demand that both sides withdraw from

A contemporary drawing of Lincoln's assassination.
Courtesy of the Audio-Visual Archives, Special
Collections and Archives, University of Kentucky
Libraries.

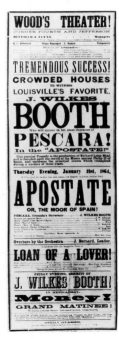

"Louisville's Favorite,"
J. Wilkes Booth
appeared there in
Apostate on January
21, 1864. Courtesy of
the Audio-Visual
Archives, Special
collections and
Archives, University
of Kentucky Libraries.

Above, The Lincoln Memorial near Hodgenville was dedicated by President William Howard Taft in November 1911. Courtesy of the Kentucky Department of Travel. *Below*, Some logs in the "birth cabin" in the Lincoln Memorial may have been in the original structure. Courtesy of the Kentucky Department of Travel.

Above, Henry Clay was Lincoln's "beau ideal of a statesman." This daguerreotype of Henry and Lucretia Clay was probably taken at their fiftieth wedding anniversary on April 11, 1849. Courtesy of The Filson Club Historical Society, Louisville. *Below*, Joshua Speed, Lincoln's best friend, married Fanny Henning before Lincoln married Mary Todd. Courtesy of The Filson Club Historical Society, Louisville.

These daguerreotypes of Abraham Lincoln (*opposite*) and Mary Todd Lincoln (*above*) probably were made in 1847. Courtesy of the Audio-Visual Archives, Special Collections and Archives, University of Kentucky Libraries.

Above left, Farmington, near Louisville, where Lincoln visited the Speeds in 1841. Courtesy of the Kentucky Department of Travel. *Above right*, The Todd House in Lexington at which the Lincolns stayed when they visited the family. Courtesy of the Kentucky Department of Travel. *Right*, John J. Crittenden failed to find a compromise to the sectional controversy. His sons split between the North and the South. Courtesy of the Library of the Kentucky Historical Society, Frankfort.

Lincoln offered a Union commission to brother-in-law Benjamin Hardin Helm, who refused it. Confederate Brigadier General Helm was killed at Chickamauga on September 20, 1863. Courtesy of the Audio-Visual Archives, Special Collections and Archives, University of Kentucky Libraries.

Above, The hastily raised Cassius M. Clay Battalion helped protect Washington in the spring of 1861 before regular troops arrived. President Lincoln and his cabinet are in the center; Mrs. Lincoln is in the third second story window from the left. J.T. Dorris, *Old Cave Springs* (1936), courtesy of Eastern Kentucky University Libraries, Special Collections and Archives Section. *Below*, Kentucky's unique neutrality as depicted in *Harper's Weekly*, June 29, 1861. Courtesy of the Kentucky Library, Western Kentucky University.

The Union opened Camp Dick Robinson, Garrard County, for volunteers in August 1861 despite the protests of Governor Magoffin. *Harper's Weekly*, November 1, 1862, courtesy of The Filson Club Historical Society, Louisville.

STOP THIEF!

The *Honorable* and *Neutral* Position occupied by the Hon. JOHN C. BRECKINRIDGE, of Kentucky. *(Drawing his Salary as U. S. Senator and furnishing Valuable Information to JEFF DAVIS at the same time.)*

Sen. John C. Breckinridge's awkward position in 1861 as seen by *Harper's Weekly*, October 12, 1861. Courtesy of the Kentucky Library, Western Kentucky University.

Above left, Gov. Beriah Magoffin (1859–1862) resigned on August 18, 1862, when confronted by large Unionist majorities in the General Assembly. Courtesy of the Library of the Kentucky Historical Society, Frankfort. *Above right*, Gov. James F. Robinson (1862–1863) completed Magoffin's term. Courtesy of the Library of the Kentucky Historical Society, Frankfort. *Left*, Gov. Thomas Elliott Bramlette (1863–1867) supported the Union war effort but disagreed with many of President Lincoln's policies. Courtesy of the Library of the Kentucky Historical Society, Frankfort.

Above left, Gen. Jeremiah T. Boyle, as military commander in Kentucky, antagonized many citizens with his zeal for the Union cause. John Hunt Morgan enjoyed taunting Jerry. Courtesy of The Filson Club Historical Society, Louisville. *Above right*, Gen. Stephen Gano Burbridge, military commander of Kentucky after Boyle, angered many Unionists, including Governor Bramlette. Courtesy of Prints and Photographs Division, Library of Congress.

MARTIAL LAW PROCLAIMED!

This town is declared under **Martial Law.** All citizens and soldiers except the guard, will retire to their quarters at 8 o'clock, P. M. A strong force will be stationed in the town. All persons found in the streets will be arrested.— Any one attempting to fire any building will be shot without trial. **W. J. HARDEE,**
Bowling-Green, Feb. 13th, 1862.   Maj. Gen.

Martial law was proclaimed by both sides in Kentucky during the Civil War. Confederate general W.J. Hardee issued this one as the Confederates were withdrawing from Bowling Green and Southern Kentucky. Courtesy of the Kentucky Library, Western Kentucky University.

Part of Bowling Green's town square was burned in mid-February 1862 as the Confederates withdrew from the state. This is the only known representation of the courthouse with its cupola. Courtesy of the Kentucky Library, Western Kentucky University.

Left, Gen. Don Carlos Buell lost Lincoln's confidence and his command after he allowed the Confederates to leave the state without a decisive battle following the Battle of Perryville on October 8, 1862. Courtesy of The Filson Club Historical Society, Louisville.

Above, A wartime photograph of President Lincoln. Courtesy of The Filson Club Historical Society, Louisville.

Above left, George D. Prentice of the *Louisville Journal* was one of Lincoln's favorite editors and one of his trusted advisors during the Civil War. Courtesy of The Filson Club Historical Society, Louisville. *Above right,* Robert Jefferson Breckinridge, Presbyterian minister, an effective state superintendent of education (1847–1853), and a frequent controversial-ist on many issues, was a staunch Unionist despite splits in his family. Courtesy of the Library of the Kentucky Historical Society, Frankfort. *Bottom right,* John Hunt Morgan became famous for his raids into Kentucky. He became less effective after his marriage to Martha Ready of Murfreesboro on December 12, 1862. Courtesy of the Audio-Visual Archives, Special Collections and Archives, University of Kentucky Libraries.

Washington, D.C. Nov. 14, 1861

Mrs Margaret Kellogg.

    Dear Madam

        Yours of the 10th is received — I comply with your request so far as I consistently can — I can not safely authorize any one to pass our lines without the approbation of the Military Commander in the vicinity, and some representative men of the citizens. With this explanation, the card I inclose will be intelligible —

        Yours truly

        A. Lincoln

This may pass Mrs Todd, and Mr Kellogg through our Military lines, if approved, and endorsed by Gen. Buell, and Hon. James Guthrie, at Louisville, Ky

    A. Lincoln.

Nov. 14. 1861.

President and Mrs. Lincoln were often criticized during the war because several members of her family were Confederates. Lincoln tried to oblige them with travel passes whenever possible. Mrs. Margaret Kellogg was a half sister of Mrs. Lincoln; Mrs. Todd was Mrs. Lincoln's stepmother. Courtesy of Eastern Kentucky University Libraries, Special Collections and Archives Section.

Left, Sue Mundy (Marcellus Jerome Clarke) was one of Kentucky's most notorious guerillas before he was captured and hanged in Louisville in March 1865. Courtesy of The Filson Club Historical Society, Louisville.

Below, Lincoln may have seen slave auctions such as this one on Cheapside in Lexington during his visit there. This photograph was probably taken in the 1850s. Courtesy of the J. Winston Coleman Photograph Collection, Transylvania University Library.

President Lincoln reads the Emancipation Proclamation to his cabinet on July 22, 1862. From left to right: Secretary of War Edwin M. Stanton, Secretary of the Treasury Salmon P. Chase, Lincoln, Secretary of the Navy Gideon Welles, Secretary of State William H. Seward, Secretary of the Interior Caleb B. Smith, Postmaster General Montgomery Blair, and Attorney General Edward Bates. Based on the painting by Francis B. Carpenter, courtesy of Prints and Photographs Division, Library of Congress.

the state, but the General Assembly required only the Confederates to do so.[17] More troops poured into the state, with the Union forces occupying the northern part of the state and the Confederates moving into the southern portions. The Green River region became a sort of no man's land in which numerous small clashes occurred as inexperienced soldiers began to learn something about fighting a war.

Kentucky's decision to remain in the Union was an embarrassment to the ardent pro-Confederate Kentuckians who had gone south before September or who fled to avoid arrest after the war came to their state. John C. Breckinridge, a member of the U.S. Senate, was one of the most prominent Kentuckians who fled to avoid arrest; former governor Charles S. Morehead was one of the most prominent citizens who did not flee and was arrested in Kentucky. Despite the results of the summer elections in the state, some exiled Kentuckians deluded themselves into believing that the majority in the state were really pro-Southern but were held in thrall by the Frankfort government, backed by the army of the United States. Representatives from thirty-two counties, often self-appointed, met in Russellville on October 29–30, 1861, to discuss what they could do to remedy their plight. Their leaders included John C. Breckinridge and George W. Johnson of Scott County. After condemning the Frankfort government as being unrepresentative of the people, the convention members decided to appeal to the inalienable right of a people "to alter, reform, or abolish their government in such manner as they think proper." They called for a sovereignty convention to meet in Russellville on November 18, and they appointed a planning committee to make arrangements.

Henry C. Burnett of Trigg County, the only pro-Confederate elected to the national House of Representatives in the summer election, presided over the November convention, which had some 115 delegates from some 68 counties. George W. Johnson, the key member of the planning committee, took the lead in directing the work of the convention. Appealing to

151

"the ultimate right of revolution possessed by all mankind against perfidious and despotic government," the delegates voted to "forever sever our connection with the Government of the United States, and in the name of the people, we do hereby declare Kentucky to be a free and independent State, clothed with all the power to fix her own destiny and to secure her own rights and liberties." The convention then established a Provisional Government of Kentucky until such time as a permanent government could be organized free of the tyranny of the government in Frankfort. This simple government consisted of a governor and a council of ten members, one from each of the state's congressional districts; most necessary state offices were to be created by the governor and council. Bowling Green was designated as the capital, but with admirable prescience they were authorized "to meet at any other place they may consider appropriate." This government quickly applied for admission into the Confederate States of America, and on December 10, 1861, Kentucky became the thirteenth member of the Confederate States of America.

George W. Johnson, a wealthy Scott County farmer and Arkansas cotton planter, was elected governor. Strongly pro-Southern, he had been active in the events leading up to this drastic move. Johnson had hoped to avoid war by having Kentucky secede early and join the Confederacy. That, he believed, would probably bring Missouri out of the Union, and possibly Maryland would follow. The resultant balance of power would be so even as to preclude war. Johnson believed that two nations, bonded by a system of free trade, could coexist.[18]

Many of Governor Magoffin's detractors assumed that he would welcome the formation of a Confederate government of Kentucky. On the contrary, he denounced the "self-constituted" convention at Russellville because it did not represent the will of a majority of Kentuckians; the only legal government in the state was the one in Frankfort, which he headed. The General Assembly passed resolutions condemning the "effort to subvert and overthrow the civil government of the state, and substitute a military despotism in its stead, by an insignificant and factious minority in opposition to the often expressed and well known will of an overwhelming majority of its citizens."[19]

With the end of neutrality, Magoffin lost effective control of the state government. With large Unionist majorities in both houses of the General Assembly, his vetoes were quickly overturned. As early as September 30, 1861, a resolution demanding his resignation was introduced in the Senate. He was careful to execute all of the laws passed over his vetoes, no matter how distasteful they were to him. "My position has been and will continue to be, to abide by the will of the majority of the people of the State," Magoffin wrote the editor of the *Louisville Journal* on December 13, 1861.

Magoffin was not able to dispel the suspicions of the Unionists, and the General Assembly continued to hamper his use of constitutional powers and to hold him responsible for conditions within the state over which he had no control. When he issued the call on July 28 for a special legislative session to convene on August 14, 1862, the governor complained, "I am without a soldier or a dollar to protect the lives, property, and liberties of the people, or to enforce the laws." He could only appeal to the legislators to provide relief to the citizens who cried for help. In his August 15 message to the General Assembly, Magoffin declared that he believed that most of the state's Southern Rights advocates disapproved of John Hunt Morgan's recent raid into Kentucky, he condemned the anti-slavery policy of the federal government, and he charged Lincoln with changing the aim of the war from the preservation of the Union to ending slavery.[20]

By then Magoffin had let Union leaders know that he would resign if his replacement was a conservative, fair-minded man who would protect all law-abiding men. Linn Boyd, the lieutenant governor, had died in 1859, and the person next in line to become governor, John F. Fisk, Speaker of the Senate, was not acceptable to Magoffin. Almost anything is possible in Kentucky politics, and a deal was negotiated. On Saturday,

August 16, Speaker Fisk, "rising to perform what I consider a high patriotic duty," resigned as Speaker. Senator James F. Robinson was then elected to fill the position. Magoffin sent a message that he would resign on Monday morning, August 18, at ten o'clock. He did so, and after Robinson was sworn in as governor, Fisk was reelected Speaker of the Senate.[21] Beriah Magoffin, an honest man who was caught in an impossible position for one of his beliefs, was one of Kentucky's notable casualties of the war.

Lincoln had to be pleased with the change of governors in Kentucky. Although the summer 1861 elections had indicated the Unionism of a majority of Kentuckians, it was embarrassing to have a pro-Southern governor in a loyal state. Robinson and, after the 1863 election, Bramlette could and did disagree with some national policies, but their loyalty to the Union was not questioned.

10

Lincoln and Military Operations in Kentucky

President Lincoln paid considerable attention to the course of the Civil War in Kentucky, although it was only briefly, upon occasion, one of the major theaters in the conflict. He did so in part because of his acute and continuing interest in the state during its period of neutrality, but he continued his close attention because he seldom had confidence in the Union military commanders in the state. Indeed, one of Lincoln's major problems during much of the war was finding generals who were capable of waging successful campaigns instead of explaining why they could not accomplish what he wanted done. Many were tried and found wanting. The war was within a year of its close before the president finally had in place the leadership that finished the job. Although they had some able subordinates, Ulysses S. Grant, William T. Sherman, and Philip H. Sheridan were the trio who finally met Lincoln's hopes and expectations. George B. McClellan was probably Lincoln's greatest disappointment. An able organizer who had "the slows" and seemed to dislike fighting, McClellan was removed twice from command. But Henry W. Halleck would have come close to McClellan on the list of disappointments. Halleck won a good reputation in the West, largely on the basis of exploits by Grant and Sherman for which he took credit, and Lincoln brought him east in July 1862 to be general-in-chief of the Union land forces.

This assignment did not work as Lincoln had hoped. Asked

to give his professional opinion of Gen. Ambrose E. Burnside's proposed campaign, Halleck refused because "a General in command of an army in the field is the best judge of existing conditions." An exasperated Lincoln responded, "If in such a difficulty as this you do not help, you fail me precisely in the point for which I sought your assistance." He needed Halleck to confer with Burnside, look over the ground, and say whether he did or did not approve of Burnside's plan. "Your military skill is useless to me, if you will not do this." Highly offended, Halleck offered to resign, but he stayed on when the frustrated president withdrew his too harsh letter. Halleck became a sort of chief of staff; Grant ultimately performed the role that Halleck had refused to play. Forced into being his own advisor, the beleaguered president began studying works on military history and strategy from the Library of Congress.[1]

Lincoln also had trouble getting an effective secretary of war. Simon Cameron was appointed because of the strength of the party in Pennsylvania and in order to win that state's support at the nominating convention. Before long, Lincoln confided to Nicolay that Cameron was "utterly ignorant. . . . openly discourteous to the President. . . . incapable of either organizing details or conceiving and advising general plans." Cameron was also suspected of being dishonest in the awarding of contracts. In early 1862, after Cassius M. Clay, the minister to Russia, indicated that he wanted to return home, Lincoln surprised Cameron by informing him that since he had expressed a desire for a change of position, the President could "gratify your wish to quit the cabinet" by nominating him to succeed Clay at the court of the tsars. Russia was about as far from the United States as Cameron could be sent.[2]

Cameron was replaced by Edwin M. Stanton, a Pittsburgh lawyer who had once snubbed Lincoln in an 1855 case involving Cyrus Hall McCormick. Stanton was also a lifelong Democrat who had served as attorney general near the end of the Buchanan administration. Fiercely honest, intelligent, and indefatigable, Stanton revitalized the War Department. Persons often came to Lincoln to complain of the brusque treatment they had received from Stanton. To one complainant Lincoln explained: "We may have to treat Stanton as they are sometimes obliged to treat a Methodist minister I knew out West. He gets wrought up to so high a pitch of excitement in his prayers and exhortations that they put bricks in his pockets to keep him down. But I guess, we'll let him jump a while first."

Upon another occasion a group of westerners got an order from Lincoln for an exchange of prisoners. When they carried the order to Stanton, he refused to execute it, saying that the president was "a d——d fool." The confused party returned to Lincoln and told of their rebuff; they confirmed that Stanton had called him "a d——d fool." Lincoln reflected for a moment. "If Stanton said I was a d——d fool, then I must be one, for he is nearly always right and generally says what he means. I will step over and see him." The two often disagreed over the punishment of soldiers found guilty of major crimes. Stanton believed in the value of harsh punishments, including executions, as a means of enforcing discipline. More lenient, Lincoln sought reasons to grant a pardon or to ease sentences. Once when he looked over the record of a flagrant case of battlefield cowardliness, Lincoln commented to a visitor, "Well, I'll have to put that with my leg cases." What were his leg cases, he was asked. "Why, why, do you see those papers crowded into those pigeonholes? They are the cases that you call by that long title, 'cowardice in the face of the enemy,' but I call them for short, my 'leg cases.' But I put it to you to decide for yourself: If Almighty God gives a man a cowardly pair of legs, how can he help their running away with him?"[3] Though the secretary of war and the president often disagreed, Stanton knew that when it came to an important issue, he had to obey Lincoln. Stanton provided valuable service to the president and to the country.

Lincoln had trouble understanding why it took so long to get troops to take the offensive; his Black Hawk War experiences had not prepared him to understand large armies and the generals who commanded them. His lack of understanding was compounded by such generals as McClellan who would apparently never be ready to advance against the rebels. In early 1862, when no one seemed to be advancing, Lincoln resorted to General War Order No. 1. Issued on January 27, 1862, it set February 22 as "the day for a general movement of the Land and Naval forces of the United States against the insurgent forces." One of the armies receiving specific mention was "The Army near Munfordsville [*sic*], Ky."4

When the war started, Albert Sidney Johnston, born in Washington, Kentucky, on February 2, 1803, was in command of the department of the Pacific. He had hoped for some compromise to end the crisis, but he could not fight against his adopted state of Texas. Johnston signed his letter of resignation on April 9, then made a long and dangerous journey across the country to join the Confederacy. President Davis appointed him a full general and on September 10 gave him command of Confederate Department Number Two—a monstrosity that stretched all the way from the Appalachian Mountains to the Indian Territory. When he arrived in Nashville on September 14 to assume his command, one of his first decisions concerned Kentucky, in which Columbus had already been occupied. Should he move into Kentucky and attempt to win her for the Confederacy, or should he establish a defense line in Tennessee to ward off invasion?

Johnston decided to hold as much of Kentucky as he could with the inadequate forces he commanded. It would provide protection for Tennessee, particularly Nashville, and it would help the Confederacy in its efforts to gain the allegiance of the Bluegrass state. "If we could wrest this rich fringe from his [the U.S. government's] grasp the war could be carried across the border and the contest speedily decided upon our own terms," he wrote Gen. Samuel Cooper. Before arriving in Nashville, Johnston ordered Brig. Gen. Felix Zollicoffer to move his four thousand men from Knoxville to Cumberland Ford to guard the Cumberland Gap. The best defense line north of Nashville was the Barren River in southern Kentucky, and Johnston ordered Brig. Gen. Simon B. Buckner to occupy Bowling Green at once. Buckner used the Louisville and Nashville Railroad to move his troops, and they arrived in Bowling Green, a town of some twenty-five hundred inhabitants, on the morning of September 18.[5]

Josie Underwood, a young Unionist, reported in her diary, "The Philistines are upon us! Kentucky's neutrality is over! On the morning of the 17th [*sic*] Buckner with his host of disloyal Kentuckians and other Rebel troops—rushed up the rail from Camp Boone and took possession of the town." From the porch of her home outside town, she and her family watched the flag flying over the depot pulled down "and a new and strange one run up the pole—when again shout after shout rent the air." Some Unionists who had anticipated the occupation had fled the town before the Confederate troops arrived. A local woman wrote, "They have been moving the women and children out of town all the week, and some of them are frightened to death. . . . It seems evident that Bowling Green is a doomed city."[6]

On September 12 Buckner had denounced President Lincoln in an address "To the Freemen of Kentucky." Kentuckians, he said, had "been slow to oppose the usurpations of Abraham Lincoln," who had violated his pledge to observe Kentucky's neutrality. "We make no war upon the Union," Buckner declared. "We defend the principles of the Constitution against the fanatics who have disrupted the Union." Buckner issued another address to the people of Kentucky when he reached Bowling Green on September 18, and the same day he wrote a letter to Governor Magoffin. He asserted that the Confederate government was "ready to evacuate the military position already occupied whenever the Federal authorities will agree to respect the neutrality of the state."[7] But any chance of restoring neutrality had already vanished; whether it wanted it or not, Kentucky was engaged in the Civil War.

Before going to Bowling Green to establish his headquarters, Johnston visited Columbus and Forts Henry and Donelson.

He did not like the locations of the two forts, but they had been started while Kentucky was neutral and therefore had been located south of the Kentucky-Tennessee boundary. He decided that it was too late to start anew; construction on them was to continue. When he reached Bowling Green, he found some twelve thousand troops, many poorly armed if at all, which he organized into divisions commanded by Buckner and William J. Hardee. Buckner had frightened Unionists by advancing troops as far north as Elizabethtown; many Unionists feared that his next move would be to take Louisville. Governor Morton of Indiana was convinced that too little was being done to protect Louisville and Kentucky generally; he wanted the president to rush troops there from Washington. Lincoln tried to calm the governor. "As to Kentucky, you do not estimate that state as more important than I do; but I am compelled to watch all points. While I write this I am, if not in *range,* at least in *hearing* of cannon-shot, from an army of enemies more than a hundred thousand strong. I do not expect them to capture this city; but I *know* they would, if I were to send the men and arms from here, to defend Louisville, of which there is not a single hostile armed soldier within forty miles, nor any force known to be moving upon it from any direction."[8] Buckner's aim when he first advanced northward was to make the Unionists think that Louisville was in jeopardy and to burn bridges to impede a Union advance southward toward Munfordville on the Green River; Louisville was not his goal.

The "first shot of the war in Kentucky" was reliably reported to have been fired in several different places. None of the skirmishes fought in the state in 1861 was significant when compared to later engagements. The most important may have been the minor engagement at Camp Wildcat or Rockcastle Hills on October 21, 1861. Confederate general Zollicoffer was attempting to advance into central Kentucky beyond London when he was checked by Brig. Gen. Albin Schoepf. Casualties were light, but when Zollicoffer withdrew, Union newspapers described it as a major victory. Another small engagement at

Sacramento on December 28 featured the appearance of Col. Nathan B. Forrest.[9]

From the onset of the war President Lincoln was almost obsessed with the desire to open a route into eastern Tennessee from Kentucky. Aware of the strong Unionist sentiment in that area, he wanted to have an avenue through which they could be helped. On October 1, 1861, he drew up a memorandum for a "Plan of Campaign" for that area. On or about October 5 he wanted federal troops to advance and seize a point on the railroad connecting Virginia and Tennessee, somewhere near Cumberland Gap. Lincoln displayed his knowledge of the Kentucky situation by spelling out details as to the locations and numbers of troops in the state. Sherman was to hold his position at Muldraugh's Hill to protect Louisville, but the troops at Louisville and Cincinnati would move quickly by rail to join Brig. Gen. George H. Thomas and his troops at Camp Dick Robinson for a general advance into Confederate territory.[10] This planned move did not materialize as Lincoln envisioned it, but he did not abandon the idea. He never fully understood or accepted the difficulties of moving a large number of troops through a region sadly deficient in food, forage, and usable roads.

Lincoln also had to deal with command changes in Kentucky. General Anderson had never recovered from the strain placed upon him at Fort Sumter, and once he had moved to Louisville, he was sure that Johnston, with a much larger army, was about to overwhelm him at any moment. His health broken by "the mental tortures" of his responsibilities, Anderson gave up his command on October 5. He was replaced by Brig. Gen. William T. Sherman, who did not want the responsibility and tried to avoid it. "I am forced into the command of this department against my will," he wrote Garrett Davis on October 8. Newspaper correspondent Henry Villard, who saw Sherman daily, wrote that "he was simply appalled by the difficulties . . . and could not rid himself of the apprehension that he was due for defeat if the rebels attacked." Sherman gained the hostility of newspapermen when he forbade them to visit the Union camps. On October 17 Secretary of War Simon Cameron, Adj. Gen. Lorenzo Thomas, and their entourage visited Louisville, and Sherman poured out his concerns to them: recruits he needed were being sent elsewhere, Buckner could march into Louisville any time he decided to do so, Kentuckians were joining the Confederacy or just sitting at home, he had too few men and they were poorly armed. For defense, Sherman said, he needed sixty thousand men; for a successful offensive two hundred thousand would be required. Samuel Wilkinson, reporter for the *New York Tribune,* heard Sherman make his case, and when his paper published the story, it made Sherman seem mentally upset. Although there was dispute over just what Sherman had said, he was depicted as being irresponsible and possibly disloyal. The harassed general was greatly relieved when Gen. Don Carlos Buell arrived on November 15, 1861, to take command. Ordered to report to Gen. Henry W. Halleck in St. Louis, Sherman was soon sent home for a twenty-day rest leave. The attacks continued, and the *Cincinnati Commercial* on December 12 reported that Sherman was insane: "It appears that he was at the time while commanding in Kentucky stark mad." He was even accused of seeking permission to leave the state and retreat into Indiana.[11]

James Guthrie, George D. Prentice, and James Speed, three of Lincoln's most trusted confidants in Kentucky, alarmed him with a telegraphed warning on November 5, 1861, that Sherman might be overwhelmed by much larger Confederate forces. Another telegram the same day from Prentice asserted that Buckner's army was at least four times and possibly seven times as large as Sherman's command. The concerned president asked for specific information that showed he was following military affairs in Kentucky closely. "How near to Louisville is Buckner? Is he moving toward Louisville? Has he crossed Green River? Is the bridge over Green River repaired? Can he cross Green River in face of McCook? If he were on the North side of Green River, how long could McCook hold him out of

Louisville, holding the railroad with power to destroy it inch by inch?"[12] Lincoln was learning to be skeptical of unconfirmed reports and exaggerated numbers. Unfortunately, some of his generals never acquired his skepticism.

By the end of the year President Lincoln was concerned over the lack of cooperation between Buell in Louisville and Halleck in St. Louis and their inability to advance southward. Both generals replied on January 1, 1862, that there was no plan between them for a coordinated advance; Halleck even warned that "Too much haste will ruin everything." Lincoln pushed Buell into contacting Halleck, who replied that he hoped to be able to assist him in a few weeks. One of Lincoln's concerns was that when Buell moved on Bowling Green the Confederates would reinforce it from Columbus unless Halleck threatened that point. On January 4 Lincoln returned to the subject of East Tennessee. Had arms been sent there? What was the status of a move in that direction?[13]

Buell replied that arms could be sent only under the protection of an army. Despite the president's and his own sympathy for the Unionists in that region, he thought that an attack on Nashville would be a more profitable use of the army. Disappointed by that response, Lincoln argued that cutting the rebels' railroad south of Cumberland Gap would rally the Unionists in that region. "Our friends in East Tennessee are being hanged and driven to dispair," Lincoln lamented, "and even now I fear, are thinking of taking up rebel arms for the sake of personal protection." He was not giving Buell an order; he just wanted the general to understand "the grounds of my anxiety." On January 7, 1862, the impatient president told Buell and Halleck to name a day when they could begin a coordinated move against the enemy. "Delay is ruining us; and it is indispensable for me to have something definite."[14]

On January 13 Lincoln responded to Buell's statement that he would do the best he could with what he had. Lincoln explained his idea that they had to take advantage of greater numbers to threaten the rebels at several points, then attack where the enemy weakened his defense. In the present situation, "my idea is that Halleck shall menace Columbus, and 'down river' generally; while you menace Bowling Green, and East Tennessee. If the enemy shall concentrate at Bowling Green, do not retire from his front; yet do not fight him there, either, but seize Columbus and East Tennessee, one or both, exposed by the concentration at Bowling Green."[15]

Lincoln's desire to help the East Tennessee Unionists received a boost on January 19, 1862, when a Union army won the first engagement of any size in Kentucky. In late November Gen. Felix Zollicoffer had shifted some four thousand Confederate troops from Knoxville to Mill Springs on the south bank on the Cumberland River. Then he rashly moved part of his command to the north bank at Beech Grove. When Maj. Gen. George Crittenden assumed command on January 3, he decided that he could not withdraw the troops back across the flooded river. Instead, he decided to attack a Union force under Gen. George Thomas near Logan's Cross-Roads. In the confusion of the battle and poor weather conditions, Zollicoffer rode into the Union lines and was killed. The Confederates fled back to the flooded river, which they succeeded in crossing that night. Confederate losses were almost double those of the Union. But instead of moving into East Tennessee, Thomas began shifting westward toward Buell's army, which was finally probing southward toward Bowling Green.[16]

After considerable presidential prodding, Lincoln's reluctant generals in the west had finally moved. Halleck had directed Ulysses S. Grant toward Forts Henry and Donelson. Henry surrendered to Union gunboats on February 6 after only a token resistance, and Buckner surrendered Donelson on February 16. The Union had a new hero in "Unconditional Surrender" Grant. The Confederacy could have used the thousands of soldiers lost at Donelson a few weeks later when the Battle of Shiloh was fought. General Johnston's biographer concludes that it was doubtful that anyone could have defended Kentucky successfully with the resources in men and materials available to him. But he should have saved all of the army for later use. "Instead, Johnston lost both the line and a substantial portion of his army. He failed to act with the audacity and decision required by the crisis that he faced."[17]

When Lincoln issued his order for a forward move on February 22, Buell's army was located near Munfordville. Many followers of the course of the war in the West had expected the decisive battle for Kentucky to be fought at Bowling Green. The Confederates had strongly fortified the hills in and around the town, for the confluence of the L&N Railroad, the turnpike connecting those cities, and the river traffic of the Barren-Green-Ohio connections made the town an important transportation center. It had also been the capital of Confederate Kentucky after the formation of the Provisional Government at Russellville in November. The anticipated battle there never occurred. The Confederates were heavily outnumbered in the state, and after Johnston received word on February 7 of the fall of Fort Henry, he met with Generals William J. Hardee and P.G.T. Beauregard to decide what should be done. They agreed that Kentucky could not be held with the forces they had. Since Union gunboats could go far up the Cumberland and Tennessee Rivers, Johnston decided that he would withdraw to some undetermined point south of the Tennessee River. Bowling Green, Columbus, and Fort Donelson would all have to be abandoned. Somewhere in the South, the segments of the Confederate army in Kentucky would turn and fight their pursuers. The Confederates began to pull out of Bowling Green on February 11; all were gone by February 14. Despite cold rain and snow, they were near Nashville by February 15. The Barren River bridges at Bowling Green were destroyed to delay the Union advance, and much of the business section around the town square was burned, either as a result of fires started by the Confederates to destroy material they could not remove or by shelling from federal artillery north of the river. Federal troops occupied Bowling Green for the rest of the war. On

March 1, 1862, Bowling Green residents received the first U.S. mail since the Confederate occupation in September.

For some inexplicable reason, after he had decided to abandon Fort Donelson, Johnston poured reinforcements into that fort and allowed it to be captured. What should have been the Battle of Bowling Green was fought at Shiloh on April 6–7. What appeared to be a Confederate victory on the first day became a defeat on the second. Among the Confederate casualties were Gen. Albert Sidney Johnston and George W. Johnson, the governor of Confederate Kentucky.[18]

Lincoln was delighted with the victories in the West that cleared Kentucky of Confederate forces. Now he could focus his attention on the Army of the Potomac and attempt to get it moving southward. But he did not ignore the western theater. On the day that Fort Donelson fell, but before he had received the welcome news, he wrote Halleck about possible moves in the West. Again he returned to one of his pet projects. "Could a calvary force from Gen. Thomas on the upper Cumberland, dash across, almost unresisted, and cut the Railroad at or near Knoxville, Tenn.?" That was not done, but Clarksville, Tennessee, was occupied by a naval force on February 19. The president had suggested using a gunboat to destroy the bridge there. Several officers who had participated in the Donelson campaign were rewarded by promotions to brigadier or major general. On March 10 Lincoln warned Buell that some Confederate troops from the East might be headed in his direction. And on April 10 Lincoln issued a "Proclamation of Thanksgiving" that called for all the people of the United States to give thanks for the victories won and to invoke divine guidance for the restoration of peace and unity.[19]

John Hunt Morgan was responsible for keeping some of the president's attention fixed on Kentucky. A Lexington businessman, Morgan had led his elite Lexington Rifles to the Confederate army in Bowling Green. Soon noted for his dashing, hard-riding raids, he had become perhaps the most popular hero for Confederate Kentuckians. On July 4, 1862, he started on his first major Kentucky raid with 876 officers and men. They swept through Tompkinsville, Glasgow, Lebanon, Harrodsburg, Cynthiana, Richmond, Somerset, and many smaller places; they spread consternation across the common-wealth. Morgan was reliably reported to be in a dozen different places simultaneously; his command became several times larger than it was. Gen. Jeremiah T. Boyle, a native Kentuck-ian and the military commander in Kentucky, was frantic in his unsuccessful efforts to intercept the elusive raider. His temper was not improved by the taunting message he received from the magic fingers of George "Lightning" Ellsworth, Morgan's telegraph operator: "Good morning, Jerry. This telegraph is a great institution. You should destroy it as it keeps me posted too well. My friend Ellsworth has all your dispatches since July 10 on file. Do you want copies?"[20] Boyle's appeals for help left superiors concerned about his ability to handle what was obvi-ously no more than a raid.

General Boyle bombarded the president and the War De-partment for assistance. Lincoln told him on July 13 to call on General Halleck for help, that "We can not venture to order troops from Gen. Buell," who might himself be attacked. That same day Lincoln telegraphed Halleck in Corinth, Mississippi: "They are having a stampede in Kentucky. Please look to it." Halleck then ordered Buell, "Do all in your power to put down the Morgan raid even if the Chattanooga expedition should be delayed." Buell sent two cavalry regiments back to Kentucky, but before they got within shooting range, Morgan returned to Tennessee on July 28.[21]

The most important result of Morgan's raid was the exag-gerated hope that it gave the Confederacy of gaining Kentucky with a second invasion of the state. Morgan telegraphed Gen. E. Kirby Smith from Georgetown on July 16: "I am here with a force sufficient to hold all the country outside of Lexington and Frankfort. These places are garrisoned chiefly with Home Guards. The bridges between Cincinnati and Lexington have been destroyed. The whole country can be secured, and 25,000 or 30,000 men will join you at once."[22] Kirby Smith was already eager to move into Kentucky from his base at Knoxville. He was infected with the "independent command" virus that affected so many Confederate generals, but any move needed to be coordinated with Braxton Bragg, whose army was at Chattanooga. They conferred on July 31, 1862, but did not agree on a definite plan. Bragg wanted them to defeat Buell in central Tennessee, then move into Kentucky. Kirby Smith wanted to flush federal general George W. Morgan out of his Cumberland Gap defenses and destroy him when Humphrey Marshall brought his three thousand men from western Virginia to cut off his escape. Then he could either hold that position or advance into the Bluegrass.

Kirby Smith was in Barboursville on August 20 when he wrote Bragg that forage was so inadequate that he must either advance or retreat to Tennessee. Since the latter move would be "disastrous to our cause in Kentucky," he advanced. This move created a problem for Bragg, who did not feel strong enough to challenge Buell's army without Kirby Smith's help. If Bragg did nothing, Kirby Smith might be trapped between Buell and the Union forces being concentrated along the Ohio River. Bragg began moving out of Chattanooga on August 27. Bypassing heavily fortified Bowling Green, he moved into Kentucky through Glasgow to Munfordville, where he paused to capture more than four thousand men. Louisville was never Bragg's goal, though that city was panic-stricken until Buell passed by Bragg and moved into it. Bragg turned aside to the Bardstown area; surely he would be able to unite with Kirby Smith for a decisive battle.[23]

The Army of the Potomac was engaged in a critical campaign, as Robert E. Lee had led his army northward; the Battle of Antietam would be fought on September 17. Much of Lincoln's attention was focused on what was happening in the East, but the developments in the West were too important to be ignored. He was disturbed by the reports on the battle of Richmond, Kentucky. Poorly prepared Union troops had left the natural defenses along the Kentucky River and advanced south of Richmond. On August 30 they were almost destroyed by Kirby Smith's command. When "Bull" Nelson arrived and tried to rally the federal survivors, he walked along their line, saying, "If they can't hit me, they can't hit anything!" Then he received two wounds, and the line broke. Of some sixty-five hundred Union soldiers engaged at Richmond, one thousand were casualties and forty-three hundred were captured.[24]

On August 31 Lincoln inquired about the composition of Nelson's army. General Boyle thought that Nelson had had between seven and eight thousand before the debacle; he estimated the Confederates at fifteen to twenty thousand men.[25] Extensive use of the telegraph allowed Lincoln to keep in closer touch with commanders in the field than had ever been possible in earlier wars. He often received answers to his inquiries on the same day they were made. The president often ended long workdays by walking over to the War Department to read the telegrams that had arrived late that evening. A week later the anxious president was asking, "Where is Bragg?" Rumor had Bragg and his army on the way to join Lee in the eastern theater. Buell assured the president that Bragg was in Tennessee except for the troops with Kirby Smith. "His movements will probably depend on mine," Buell declared. "I expect that for the want of supplies I can neither follow him nor remain here. Think I must withdraw from Tennessee. I shall not abandon Tennessee while it is possible to hold on. Cut off effectively from supplies, it is impossible for me to operate in force where I am; but I shall endeavor to hold Nashville and at the same time drive Smith out of Kentucky and hold my communications."[26]

Kirby Smith, after capturing Lexington on September 1 and Frankfort two days later, had scattered his troops across the Bluegrass. The capture of Frankfort was a Confederate achievement; it was the only state capital captured by the Confederacy during the Civil War. The state government had hurriedly moved to Louisville and was prepared to cross the Ohio River if necessary.[27] Bragg and Kirby Smith still had not combined their forces.

Lincoln, concerned with the events in the eastern theater, had trouble learning just what was happening in the West. Where do you understand Buell to be? he demanded of General Boyle. And what is he doing? When Boyle responded on September 11 from Louisville, he complained that by sending troops from Louisville to Cincinnati, Gen. Horatio Wright "is creating a panic and will ruin the state." But the next day he admitted to the president that "I expect no enemy here soon." He had heard nothing directly from Buell, but Bowling Green had reported that part of his army had reached there. Lincoln asked Wright to provide him with a rational explanation for the governor and other Kentuckians why troops were being transferred from Louisville to Cincinnati. Wright replied on September 13 that he had sent only two regiments when it was in danger from Kirby Smith; after that move, Louisville had thirty regiments and more than thirty guns and was not in any immediate danger. "I have no intention of abandoning Louisville or of leaving it without adequate protection," he assured his anxious commander-in-chief.[28] The situation was complicated by the presence of Governor Robinson and other members of the government, who had fled from Frankfort.

During these tense days, Lincoln was besieged by requests for special favors. Thomas H. Clay, a son of Henry Clay, telegraphed on October 8 from Cincinnati that a committee of loyal Kentuckians, currently in Cincinnati, wanted Gen. George W. Morgan, who in Clay's opinion had fought a brilliant retreat from Cumberland Gap to the Ohio River, to be assigned to Kentucky. His record entitled him to preference, and the assignment would please all loyal Kentuckians. Lincoln replied somewhat tartly that Clay could not have reflected seriously on the request he had made; "The precedent established by it would instantly break up the whole army." Many other troops had also performed well. Morgan's assignment would depend largely upon what the enemy did.[29]

Anxious to ascertain the state of affairs in Kentucky, Lincoln questioned General Boyle again on October 1; what news did he have of General Buell? This request, repeated the next day, brought a report from Boyle that the battle had been fought at Perryville on October 8, 1862, by part of the Union army. Losses had been heavy, but the Confederate losses were believed to be even greater. Heavy fighting was reported to be under way near Harrodsburg; Buell was said to be pushing the enemy hard.[30] Actually, a confused battle had been fought at Perryville in which neither Buell nor Bragg used his entire force. The Confederate attack made progress on their right flank, but Bragg pulled back to Harrodsburg. The two Confederate armies finally came together in time to abandon Kentucky. Bragg decided that he could not run the risk of losing his entire army; it had to be preserved to protect the lower South. Bitterly disappointed that only some twenty-five hundred recruits had been gained, Bragg spoke harshly of cowardly Kentuckians. He became for most Kentuckians the most disliked Confederate general.[31]

The Confederates managed to escape through Cumberland Gap, along with the Provisional Government of Confederate Kentucky. Gov. Richard Hawes had been installed in Frankfort on October 4, but the festivities planned for that evening had to be abandoned as federal forces from Louisville came within shelling distance of the town. The Confederates were said to have departed in "deliberate haste," and the Provisional Government was a government in exile for the rest of the war.[32]

Lincoln was sorely disappointed with the failure of Buell to destroy the Confederate army as it struggled to get out of the state. He may not have trusted himself to address General Buell directly, for it was Halleck who wrote: "I am directed by the President to say to you that your army must enter into East Tennessee this fall, and that it ought to move there while the roads are passable. . . . He does not understand why we cannot march as the enemy marches, live as he lives, fight as he fights, unless we admit the inferiority of our troops and our generals." Even one of his soldiers wrote home that Buell "has shown himself to be either a coward or a Trator, for with such a force as ours, properly handled, old Bragg could never have escaped." By the end of the month Buell was replaced by Gen. William S. Rosecrans. A military commission conducted an exhaustive investigation of Buell's generalship but did not make a recommendation. Buell did not receive further orders, and after being dismissed as a major general of volunteers, he resigned his regular army commission on June 1, 1864.[33]

Morgan's second raid into Kentucky (the Christmas Raid) began on December 22, 1862, just eight days after his wedding to twenty-one-year-old Martha (Mattie) Ready of Murfreesboro, Tennessee. Morgan's main objective was destruction of the two massive railroad trestles on Muldraugh's Hill, about five miles north of Elizabethtown. They were burned on December 28, and the vital L&N supply line was closed there until February 1, 1863. General Rosecrans attempted to trap Morgan in Kentucky, but he used chiefly infantry instead of cavalry, and the detachments were not able to engage Morgan's main body of some thirty-nine hundred men. Then Rosecrans began to strengthen his cavalry units, and Morgan in the future encountered more resistance.[34] President Lincoln did not display as much interest in this raid as he had done in the first one, perhaps because his attention was focused on the Emancipation Proclamation, which was issued in its final form on January 1, 1863, and the Battle of Stones River, which was fought near Murfreesboro on December 31, 1862–January 2, 1863.

Morgan's most famous raid carried him across Kentucky and into Indiana and Ohio during the summer of 1863. He had permission to attack Louisville but not to cross the Ohio. He was in deliberate disobedience of orders when he crossed the Ohio River at Brandenburg on the night of July 8–9, just hours ahead of the pursuit. And he took about twenty-five hundred men, five hundred more than had been authorized. Gen. Ambrose E. Burnside was in Cincinnati preparing an army to invade eastern Tennessee, and the federals had a better chance to check Morgan than they had had on his previous raids. Gen. Henry M. Judah, commander of the Third Division, Twenty-third Army Corps, was one of the key chasers; Gen. Edward H. Hobson, in charge of Judah's second brigade, a native of Greensburg, Kentucky, played a major role in the pursuit, as did Col. Frank Wolford of Liberty, Kentucky, and his "Wild Riders" of the First Kentucky Cavalry Regiment, USA.[35]

Lincoln's first written concern about the chase came on July 24, when he queried Burnside: "What, if anything further, do you hear from John Morgan?" Once again, the president's main attention may have been focused on the eastern theater and the aftermath of the Battle of Gettysburg. Morgan was nearing the end of his run when Lincoln made his inquiry. Many of his men had been captured at Buffington Island on July 19. Burnside provided able direction of the pursuit, using gunboats to block fords at which the Confederates might have returned to Kentucky. Morgan ended the long run by surrendering at West Point, Ohio, on July 26, 1863. As Burnside explained to Halleck, he had not been able to start his expedition into East Tennessee as long as Morgan was free to disrupt his lines of supply and communications.[36]

After Morgan's famous escape from the Ohio penitentiary on November 27, 1863, he tried to rebuild his shattered command. His last Kentucky raid was designed in part to secure horses and equipment for many of his poorly supplied men. He left Abingdon, Virginia, on May 31, 1864, before he could be ordered not to make the raid. Morgan had enlisted some men whom he would never have tolerated in better days, and discipline broke down. A few men robbed banks in Mt. Sterling, Winchester, and Lexington, and a force left behind at Mt. Sterling was defeated by Gen. Stephen G. Burbridge. Morgan advanced to Cynthiana on June 11, where he captured Gen. Edward H. Hobson and his six hundred troops. Ignoring warnings of Burbridge's approach and with ammunition running low, Morgan camped for the night. Before daybreak the next morning, Burbridge's force smashed Morgan's raiders. Many were captured or killed, and only remnants, including Morgan, regained Confederate lines. Suspended from command and awaiting a court of inquiry, Morgan again ignored orders by continuing operations; he was killed by a Union soldier at Greeneville, Tennessee, on September 4, 1864.

Lincoln continued to follow Morgan's annoying exploits on his raids, and he wired congratulations to General Burbridge for his victory at Cynthiana. Charges against Hobson for surrendering to Morgan were dropped after the raider's death. When Lincoln was informed of Morgan's death, he was reported to have said, "Well. I wouldn't crow over anybody's death: but I can take this as *resignedly* as any dispensation of Providence."[37]

Morgan was not the only Confederate raider who invaded Kentucky during the war. Maj. Gen. Nathan B. Forrest drove into western Kentucky in March 1864 to find badly needed horses and supplies. He secured much of what he sought at Paducah, but when Union newspapers gleefully reported that he had missed some fine army mounts, Gen. Abraham Buford, a livestock producer in Woodword County, returned to Paducah. There he found 140 good horses hidden where the newspapers had said they were.[38] A number of smaller raids also occurred, as the Confederates sought to disrupt the Union rear lines, gather needed supplies, ease the demand on the Confederate resources, and, sometimes, allow Kentucky soldiers a brief visit with their home folks.

The apparent decline in Lincoln's level of interest in military affairs within Kentucky reflects the decreasing importance of the commonwealth in military operations. After 1862 Kentucky was no longer an important part of the military front in the western theater. The raids were an embarrassment and a nuisance, and they did considerable damage, but they did not threaten the Union control of the state. Before the war Lincoln had demonstrated his ability to master such academic fields as trigonometry and law. While he was searching for generals who could direct the war toward victory and unification, Lincoln demonstrated his ability to master the basic principles of warfare. He could not have matched maxims with the scholarly Halleck, but he saw what needed to be done and he tried to get it done. He was occasionally driven to sarcasm by such reluctant generals as McClellan. When that general once said that he could not advance because his cavalry was too tired, the exasperated president inquired, "Will you pardon me for asking what the horses of your army have done since the battle of Antietam to fatigue anything?" When Grant embarked upon a plan of attacking the Confederacy at all possible points, Lincoln was delighted: this was what he had sought for over two years. He put it in understandable frontier terms: "Those not skinning can hold a leg." Grant liked the expression so much that he used it in writing to Sherman.[39]

11

Wartime Politics
in Kentucky

Though lessened, Lincoln's concern with Kentucky affairs did not end when the state ceased to be a theater of major military operations. Much that happened in the state continued to be influenced by the war, and the president was frequently involved with issues that were referred to him. Given Kentucky's fondness for politics, it was evident that a mere war would not end partisan conflict on the political front. Indeed, the war created additional political turmoil for Kentuckians.

When James F. Robinson replaced Beriah Magoffin as governor, the Unionists were in control of the state government with large majorities in both houses of the General Assembly. But the State Rights party was not entirely without hope. In addition to a core of strong Southern sympathizers, it attracted some Unionists who were dissatisfied with policies of the Lincoln administration and actions of the military governors in the state. In an effort to enlist such support, they began to call themselves the Democratic Party, a change that the Unionists denied their right to make. Unionists who were proadministration were careful to avoid the use of *Republican;* that name would almost ensure defeat in Kentucky.

Statewide opposition to the Emancipation Proclamation encouraged the "Democrats" to make a bid for victory in the 1863 election. John Hunt Morgan's spectacular 1862 Christmas Raid and rumors that Humphrey Marshall was about to invade Kentucky from his mountain fastness convinced some apprehensive Unionists that another effort was under way to take Kentucky out of the Union. The *Tri-Weekly Commonwealth* of February 16, 1863, asserted that the unusually early call for a state party convention indicated that the party leaders believed that opposition to the Lincoln administration was "preparing the Kentucky Mind for revolt against the Union."

When the Democrats requested use of the hall of the House of Representatives for their convention, they were refused, for the first time in Kentucky's history, by a vote of 36–40.[1] They rented the Frankfort Metropolitan Hall, and at eleven o'clock on the morning of February 18, 1863, some two hundred delegates from forty counties were called to order. But before any business could be transacted, Col. E.A. Gilbert strode into the chamber as the troops of his Forty-fourth Ohio Infantry Regiment (USA) surrounded the building. Gilbert's adjutant took down the names of the delegates; that list, Gilbert remarked, could be of "great importance." Then the colonel informed the delegates that he would not allow them to hold a convention within the limits of his command. If nominations were made, the candidates would be arrested; if somehow elected, they would not be allowed to serve. He ordered the delegates "to return peaceably and quietly" to their homes and to refrain from "seditious and noisy conversation." Gilbert said that he might have taken a different approach had they not been denied the use of the legislative hall, but they had been repudiated as Democrats and were generally characterized as rebel sympathizers. Dr. A.B. Chambers, a delegate who was a member of the House from Gallatin County, was not allowed to read a previously prepared series of six resolutions that stated the views of those at the meeting. The delegates then adjourned sine die.[2]

The next day Dr. Chambers tried to get the Kentucky House of Representatives to vote to protect the civil rights of citizens against military violence. His motion lost on a 40–40 tie vote. On March 2 the Senate voted 14–12 to condemn the action taken by Colonel Gilbert; the party was capable of controlling such meetings; military interference was dangerous and should be rebuked. But that evening, in the absence of several senators who had voted for the rebuke, the resolution was reconsidered and sent to the committee on federal relations. Brig. Gen. Quincy Adams Gillmore upheld the actions of his subordinate. "The political status of Kentucky is by no means secure," he explained, "and I deem it sounder policy to arrest at once the organization of the rebel element, before it attained such impetus, strength, and character as would demand, six months hence, the exercise of force to retain the State in constitutional obedience." Sen. Lazarus W. Powell was unable to persuade the U.S. Senate to investigate Gilbert's action.[3]

The Unionists, calling themselves the Union Democracy, held a convention in Louisville on March 18–19, 1863, with 94 of 110 counties represented. James A. Cravens, recently a Democratic member of Congress from Illinois, created a storm of protest and was shouted down when he expressed hope that "they would inaugurate a policy which, while it would put down rebellion, would also preserve the constitution with all of its guarantees; Abraham Lincoln could not have organized the army without the aid of the Democratic party; the war could not have lasted twenty-four hours without their aid and assistance; they were the only party that could save the country, and yet they were denounced as traitors." After an hour of "violent confusion," he was allowed to proceed in relative peace. The convention then nominated Joshua F. Bell for governor and Richard T. Jacob for lieutenant governor. Bell, an old-line Whig, had been defeated by Magoffin in 1859. He had not sought the nomination in 1863, and he was greatly disturbed by the military presence in the state. After a month's consideration, he decided not to accept the nomination. The Union Democrat Central Committee then selected Thomas E. Bramlette. A lawyer and judge, Bramlette had resigned from the bench in 1861 to raise the Third Kentucky Volunteer Regiment and become its colonel. He resigned his commission in 1862 over a command dispute, and on January 23, 1863, President Lincoln appointed him U.S. district attorney for Kentucky. Bramlette resigned from that position on May 4, 1863, to raise a division that he would command as a major general.[4] Instead, he accepted the nomination for governor. As the party thought to be most supportive of Lincoln, the Union Democrats had to overcome that handicap. A correspondent wrote Joseph Holt that "the order of the day now in *Ky* is to denounce the measures of the administration. Lincoln is regarded as false to his pledges, his position and his country."[5]

In June a group of Union Democrat leaders who thought Bramlette too radical asked ex-governor Charles A. Wickliffe to run for governor on another Democratic ticket. Not willing to risk holding a convention, they in effect nominated him by writing letters. As they organized a campaign, they stressed the usurpation of power by the federal government, and they detailed the crimes committed in the state by the military governors. But they denounced secession in unequivocal terms: "We hold this rebellion utterly unjustifiable in its inception, and the dissolution of the Union the greatest of calamities." They suggested using "all just and constitutional means adopted to the suppression of the one and the restoration of the other." But what means were just and constitutional? Since the Peace Democrats, who opposed the strong Unionists, had some appeal to secessionists, to those who sought peace at almost any price, and to those who wanted to protest the Lincoln administration and the military rule within the state, they had the potential to gain a large number of voters. The Union Democrats sought to discredit their opponents by calling them traitors, rebels, even abolitionists. At the same time, the Union Democrats damned the Lincoln administration and its policies, especially the Emancipation Proclamation, the president's appeal for compensated emancipation, and the use of black troops. The *Tri-Weekly Commonwealth* of April 1, 1863, declared that "no administration man can be elected in Kentucky, in any congressional district, county, or precinct."[6]

John Hunt Morgan's raid across Kentucky and into Indiana and Ohio in July 1863 distracted attention from the election. Another distraction was the death on July 26, 1863, of John J. Crittenden, who was running for reelection to the U.S. House of Representatives. Honored for his futile efforts to avert the war, Crittenden was probably the most honored and respected politician in the state after the death of Henry Clay. The Union Democrats selected Brutus Clay, brother of Cassius Marcellus, as the replacement candidate. Brutus issued a statement on July 29 to inform the public of his views. He opposed secession, and if elected he would support the war to subdue the South. "At the same time, I am opposed to the policy of the Administration, as to the abolition of slavery, and the enlisting of slaves as soldiers. . . . Should the Union be restored, it would be for the courts of the slave states to decide upon the legal effects of the President's Proclamation of Emancipation. . . . I am not and have never been in favor of emancipation, either gradual, immediate or compensated." He would joyfully support all efforts to restore any state to its rightful allegiance. Clay's views apparently mirrored those of the voters in his district, for he was elected easily.[7]

On July 20, 1863, Governor Robinson issued a proclamation, accompanied by the Expatriation Act of March 11, 1862, that declared Confederates and their supporters expatriated from the state. It required a loyalty oath for voters. If the oath was violated, the offender could be punished by death or such other penalty as a military court might impose. On July 31, Gen. Ambrose Burnside, commander of the Department of the Ohio, which included Kentucky, imposed martial law in the state, "for the purpose only of protecting the rights of loyal citizens and *the freedom of elections.*" No disloyal person, he declared, would be allowed to vote. General Boyle's order of July 25 assumed that a vote for Wickliffe would be proof of disloyalty and would subject the voter's property to seizure. Anyone who attempted to vote and could not establish his right to do so would be arrested as a rebel. This oath was required:

I do solemnly swear that I have never entered the service of the so-called Confederate States; that I have not
been engaged in the service of the so-called "provisional
government of Kentucky," either in a civil or military
capacity; that I have never, either directly or in directly,
aided the rebellion against the United States or the
State of Kentucky; that I am unconditionally for the
Union and the suppression of the rebellion and am
willing to furnish men and money for the vigorous
prosecution of the war against the rebellious league
known as the "Confederate States"; so help me God.[8]

Wickliffe's name was not on the ballot in many counties.
In the First (Jackson Purchase) District, Judge Lawrence
Trimble, the Peace Democrat candidate, was arrested and held
until after the election. The military presence was so pervasive
that historian J.G. Randall wrote that Kentucky had "some of
the aspects of a region under military occupation." The results
were preordained. Bramlette received 67,586 votes to Wickliffe's
17,344. The 85,000 votes were a sharp drop from the 145,000
cast in 1860. Of course, thousands of Kentucky voters were in
Confederate armies and thus could not vote, but the remaining difference can be explained in large part by the military
interference with the elective process. Lincoln could not have
had much concern about the outcome. On August 8, 1863, he
wrote his wife that "the election in Kentucky has gone very
strongly right. Old Mr. Wickliffe got ugly, as you know, ran
for Governor, and is terribly beaten." Brutus Clay was elected,
and John Menzies, "who, as we thought, behaved very badly
last session of Congress, is largely beaten in the District opposite Cincinnati, by Green Clay Smith, Cassius Clay's nephew."
The president commented to Green Adams in a letter of August 22, 1863, that the newspapers reported that Bramlette had
a majority of 50,000 with returns still missing from some counties. He asked for the final count "to see whether it will be a
clear majority of the largest vote ever cast in Kentucky."[9]

Lincoln's speculation that it might have been the largest vote ever cast in Kentucky was far off the mark; the total was well under those of several previous elections.

If Lincoln believed that he had a strong ally in the new Kentucky governor, he was wrong. Bramlette started his administration with a strong Union declaration in his first message to the General Assembly in December 1863. "We have no cause of complaint against the Federal Government," the Governor asserted. The questions concerning slavery were insignificant in comparison to the preservation of the Union. "Neither the preservation nor the destruction of slavery is essential to our State or National existence."[10] This political honeymoon was of short duration, for Bramlette soon found many issues about which to complain.

Bramlette telegraphed Lincoln on January 5, 1864, after Maj. Gen. John G. Foster had ordered all organized military forces in Kentucky to move to Knoxville. This would remove the troops raised specifically for the defense of the state, as authorized by an act of Congress. That act gave the president power to move the troops, and Bramlette demanded that Lincoln rescind Foster's order. Lincoln responded the next day that nothing was known about the order except that he assumed that it came from General Grant, whose judgment "would be the highest incentive to me to make such order. Nor can I understand how doing so is bad faith or dishonor; nor yet how it exposed Kentucky to ruin." He was sure "Grant would not permit it, if it so appeared to him."

The governor responded that he had complete confidence in General Grant, whom "I regard . . . as the first Gen'l of the age." He had reason to think that Grant did not know of the proposed movement of troops when he made his protest, but the governor could not forbear from adding a note of rebuke to the president. "In all candor and with the kindest feelings I ask what reliance can our people place upon any pledge of the Government and its functionaries, if this be not observed. . . . Kentucky loyalty cannot be driven from its secure lodgment in the hearts of the people, by any bad faith of others. We are in and of the Union and will live and die there. Rebel outrages cannot drive us, nor federal injustice divert us from the true line of patriotism." In his response Lincoln again pointed out that the law allowed the president to send the troops out of state; if he did so on the judgment of General Grant, he assumed "it will be neither cruelty, bad faith or dishonor." When he had responded to Bramlette's protest, Lincoln explained, he had known that Grant was in Knoxville and knew of the order, but he was not free to divulge that information then.[11]

Bramlette and many other Kentuckians came close to rebellion over the Union decision to use black troops. Just the proposal to enroll military-age free blacks for possible future use aroused the state. Even Gen. J.T. Boyle protested to Gen. James B. Fry, the provost marshal general, against the policy. "You will revolutionize the State and would do infinite and inconceivable harm, and I am sure this is all wrong and there is not an honest loyal man in the State in favor of it, and it will meet with decided opposition." The order was temporarily suspended, but on February 29, 1864, Fry ordered "the enrollment, without delay, of all colored males of military age." Protests flowed from the governor's office and the General Assembly. The legislators denounced the policy and demanded that any camps for black soldiers be located outside the state. Lt. Gov. Richard T. Jacob wrote Lincoln that he had urged the governor to avoid bringing Kentucky into conflict with the federal government over that issue. He suggested that an offer of $300 for each slave taken would ease the situation, and he added that perhaps Col. Frank Wolford and his command could be sent outside the state.[12] Wolford, commanding the "Wild Riders" of the First Kentucky Cavalry, was bitterly opposed to the policy. On March 10, 1864, he voiced his opposition in intemperate speeches in Lexington and Danville. He declared that the first enrolling officer should be thrown into the state penitentiary, and he promised that his troops would help block implementation of the policy. Despite his early moderation,

Lieutenant Governor Jacob soon also attacked the policy in public speeches. Both of them were highly critical of the president. Wolford was placed under arrest and sent to Nashville and then Knoxville for a military trial. Authorities feared that a trial would give him a forum at which to restate his views; instead, he was given a dishonorable discharge from the army he had served well.[13]

Governor Bramlette also took a decided stand in a March 12 telegram to the provost marshal in Boyle County: "If the president does not, upon my demand, stop the negro enrollment, I will. I am awaiting his answer." The next day he asked Rev. Robert J. Breckinridge, who had two sons in each of the rival armies, "to come to Frankfort tomorrow . . . and go to Washington on an important mission." Breckinridge met in Frankfort with the governor and several other advisors. According to Breckinridge's later statement, which Bramlette denied, the governor had prepared a public proclamation that proposed "a general uprising in the state, strengthened by a contemporaneous invasion by a portion of the rebel army." A few days earlier Lieutenant Governor Jacob had written Lincoln that he feared the enrollment policy would produce "an outbreak of a portion of our loyal people, and I dreadfully fear a conflict between the Federal and State authorities." Either Bramlette was persuaded by cooler heads to rewrite his proclamation or, as he maintained, he never wrote the inflammatory one he was said to have revised. His proclamation of March 15, 1864, called upon Kentuckians to submit quietly to the enrollment plan. It provided only for the enrollment of names of those eligible for military service, not for actual enlistment; "Your indignation should not move you to commit crimes of violence, nor to unlawful resistance."[14]

Many Kentuckians did not agree with Bramlette's advice. Editor George Prentice charged that the federal government wanted a clash between the state and the nation; then Kentucky could be treated as if in insurrection, her officials deposed, her slaves freed, and a new government installed that would be dominated by radicals. Soon afterward Bramlette, Archibald Dixon, and editor A.G. Hodges went to Washington to repeat their protests and see what concessions, if any, the president would make. The results of their conference with Lincoln were contained in a March 28, 1864, letter from Lincoln to Secretary of War Stanton.

1. That the question of troops furnished, and to be furnished by Kentucky, may be adjusted on the basis as actually reduced by the able bodied men of hers having gone into rebel service; and that she be requested to furnish no more than her just quotas upon fair adjustment on such basis.
2. That to whatever extent the enlistment and drafting, one or both, of colored troops may be found necessary within the State, it may be conducted within the law of Congress; and, as far as practicable, free from collateral embarrassments, disorder, and provocation.

Lincoln added that he thought the Kentucky requests were reasonable; Stanton should give the delegation a full hearing and do the best he could to fulfill their requests. Attorney General Edward Bates recalled in his diary the results of the meeting with the president: "The Govr. says that the draft will not be opposed, if conducted in a simple and honest way—i.e. enlist the men and march them off, without making it a pretense to insult, and rob, and dominate every neighborhood—as in Maryland!" Two days later Lincoln told Bates that the arrangement "seemed to be satisfactory, all around."[15]

Whites did not rush to enlist, and the need for more troops became acute. On April 18, 1864, General Burbridge, the military commander, issued General Order No. 34, which opened the state to black enlistments, regardless of county. Those accepted were placed in squads and sent to Louisville; from there they went to camps of instruction out of state. Masters who could prove their loyalty were given certificates on which they could recover from the federal government not more than $300 per slave lost. When the number of slaves volunteering declined after an initial rush, federal troops impressed large numbers into service. The net result was that the army ultimately reported 23,703 black soldiers enlisted from Kentucky—more than from any slave state except for Louisiana. On May 12 Burbridge limited government contracts to "citizens of unquestionable loyalty," and two days later he halted the sale of *A Life of Stonewall Jackson* and other works that had a Confederate appeal. After his successes against John Hunt Morgan at Mt. Sterling on June 9, 1864, and at Cynthiana on June 12, he issued an order on June 18 prohibiting the circulation in Kentucky, "by sale or otherwise, of the Cincinnati *Enquirer*, a newspaper in the interest of the rebellion, and all other papers of like character." The general also decided that only persons who could prove their loyalty could recover horses that he had captured from Morgan.[16]

Opposition to the slave policy continued as masters saw much of their capital investment disappear and as crop production fell drastically because of a shortage of labor. Among the most vocal opponents were Lieutenant Governor Jacob, Paul R. Shipman of the *Louisville Journal*, and Frank Wolford, now out of the army. Wolford's fiery speeches were rallying support to the opposition, and on June 27, 1864, he was arrested at Lebanon and sent to Washington for trial. Lincoln paroled him so he would not have to be jailed and sent him to Louisville to await trial there. Wolford promised to stop his protest until his trial came up. Back in Louisville, he received an offer from Attorney General James Speed on behalf of Lincoln: all charges would be dropped if he would agree to cease his opposition to black enlistments. Wolford indignantly rejected freedom on such terms. "I have frankly to say that I cannot bargain for my liberty, and the exercise of my rights as a freeman, on any such terms. I have committed no crime. I have broken no law. . . . You, Mr. President, if you will excuse the bluntness of a soldier, by an exercise of arbitrary power caused me to be arrested and held in confinement contrary to law, not for the good of our common country, but to increase the chances of your reelection . . . and otherwise to serve the purposes of the political party whose candidate you are." He would not admit Lincoln's right to arrest him, which would deter others from being critical of his administration. "No Sir! much as I love liberty, I will fester in a prison, or die on a gibbet, before I will agree to any terms that do not abandon all charges against me, and fully acknowledge my innocence."[17]

Lincoln received another protest from Wolford on August 3, 1864. The judge advocate had ordered him to Washington to be tried before a military commission. He had carefully kept his promise to abstain from public speaking or doing anything to provoke public excitement until his trial, which the president had promised would be in Louisville. Lincoln's telegram the next day told Wolford to remain in Louisville until he heard more from him. With his fate undecided, Wolford, who was noted for his stump speaking, began to speak on behalf of ex-general George B. McClellan for president.[18] Soon after the election General Burbridge ordered Wolford and Jacob arrested, and Governor Bramlette telegraphed his protests to the president. Wolford, he said, was under arrest at Covington, and Jacob, "by order of the Secret Inquisition ordered into the rebel lines." Burbridge later explained that he had ordered the arrests, because "It is useless to attempt to keep Kentucky free from guerrillas and the people of the State true to their allegiance, if such men as Wolford and Jacob are permitted to make public speeches throughout the State reviling the administration, inducing the people to oppose the policy of the government, and thwarting the efforts of the military authorities in restoring law and order."

When Jacob wrote Lincoln from Richmond, Virginia, on December 26, 1864, he complained that he had to "accept the hospitality and protection of a people I had fought against. . . . It is difficult to defend ones self, when no charges are preferred. . . . True, Mr. President, I was opposed to your reelection, and it is the only charge that can with truth be brought against me." He had seen a newspaper report that he and Colonel Wolford were to be released. Can he now return to his duties as Kentucky's lieutenant governor? "As I have committed no crime, I ask not for pardon, but merely simple justice." Governor Bramlette entered the controversy by accusing men "afraid to avow their infamy in the face of an open tribunal, face to face with the men they accuse. . . . Mr. President, do stop these miserable, cowardly stay-at-home-every-body patriots from giving such aid and comfort to the rebellion. . . . Better send the accusers off; for they will not help us in the day of battle, and Jacob and Wolford will."

Lincoln had apparently not been aware of Burbridge's hasty expulsion of Jacob, for he ordered General Grant to pass him through the lines and return him to Washington, where he was pardoned. Jacob presided over the Kentucky Senate on February 4, 1865, nearly a month after the session started.[19] Wolford had not been expelled when Lincoln intervened, so he did not have to be returned to the Union. Burbridge had caused Lincoln problems several times with his overzealous attempts to stifle opposition to the war effort and to silence administrative critics. In February 1865 he was finally replaced by Gen. John Palmer as the military commander in Kentucky. The *Louisville Journal* of February 10 greeted the news with "Thank God and President Lincoln."[20]

Although Lincoln had some opposition in his own party, his nomination for reelection was certain before the 1864 convention met in Baltimore on June 6–7, 1864. To emphasize their unity, speakers insisted that it was the first convention of the National Union Party, not the third convention of the Republican Party. They hoped to avoid factional fights among Republicans and to win votes from the War Democrats. The Reverend Dr. Robert J. Breckinridge, who had become one of the president's trusted advisors in Kentucky, was the temporary president of the convention. "As a Union party I will follow you to the ends of the earth," he asserted. "But as an Abolition party—as a Republican party—as a Whig party—as a Democratic party—as an American party, I will not follow you a foot." The platform was strongly proadministration with demands for restoration of the Union, unconditional surrender of the Confederates, and a constitutional amendment abolishing slavery.

The Missouri delegates, acting on instructions from their state convention, cast 22 votes for General Grant. Lincoln received 484, and Missouri then moved that the nomination be made unanimous. Lincoln provided no guidance for the nomination of a vice president, and after some indecision the convention selected Andrew Johnson of Tennessee.

On their way to Baltimore the Kentucky delegates went through Washington to confer with the president. With Dr. Breckinridge as their spokesman, they protested the raising of troops in Kentucky for the protection of the Commonwealth, especially if such troops were placed under the command of Governor Bramlette or ex-colonel Wolford.[21]

Securing his nomination was easy, but during the summer of 1864 Lincoln believed that he would probably lose the election. Military affairs were not progressing well, with the major Union armies stalemated on nearly every front. In July Confederate general Jubal A. Early led a small army to the outskirts of the Washington defenses. Lincoln came under enemy fire when he stood on the rampart of Fort Stevens to witness the Confederates approach within 150 yards. He was being attacked within his party for not being harsh enough on plans for the ultimate reconstruction of the Southern states, and his acceptance of the abolition of slavery as a war aim antagonized many Northerners who saw restoration of the Union as the only legitimate object of the conflict. The Democrats seemed likely to nominate George B. McClellan, who had twice been removed from command of a major army by the president. Highly popular, McClellan was likely to be a formidable opponent. On August 23, 1864, Lincoln drafted a statement that he presented at the next cabinet meeting on a folded piece of paper; he had the cabinet members sign it on the outside without reading the contents. It reflected his belief that he was going to lose the election unless some great change occurred. "This morning, as for some days past, it seems exceedingly probable that this Administration will not be re-elected. Then it will be my duty to so cooperate with the President elect, as to save the Union between the election and the inauguration; as he will have secured his election on such grounds that he can not possibly save it afterward."[22]

At the Democratic convention in Chicago on August 29–31, letters were read from Kentucky delegates John W. Leathers and Dr. Joseph R. Buchanan, who had been arrested and were confined in Louisville as political prisoners. Ex-governor Charles A. Wickliffe contended in a convention speech that "many of the best and most loyal citizens in Ky.—among them 20 or 30 ladies—are now imprisoned by the military in Louisville, in damp and dirty cells, with only straw to lie on, and the coarsest fare; and the newspapers of Louisville are forbidden to make the slightest allusion to this terrible state of affairs. I proclaim it here and now—at the risk of my liberty, perhaps of my life." After McClellan received the nomination as expected, two Kentuckians received some support for the vice presidency. On the first ballot James Guthrie received 65½ votes and Lazarus W. Powell 32½. However, George H. Pendleton of Ohio won on the second ballot.[23]

Charges of military interference with the elective process continued through the 1864 campaign. In an August election Alvin Duvall was a candidate for reelection as a judge on the Kentucky Court of Appeals in the Second District. Three days before the election, General Burbridge ordered sheriffs in the district to keep Duvall's name off the poll books. The judge avoided arrest by fleeing the state. Union leaders decided on venerable Judge George Robertson as Duvall's replacement, then used the telegraph to spread the word to support him and thus avoid a public announcement that would have alerted the military authorities in time to block Robertson's election.

Burbridge deemed "it of the utmost importance that the state should be carried for Mr. Lincoln" in the presidential election, and he used his considerable powers to influence voters. He even thought that "with a judicious disposition of the troops the state may be carried for Mr. Lincoln."

Governor Bramlette denounced such tactics in a scathing letter to Lincoln on September 3, 1864, in which he detailed examples of illegal and intimidating acts by representatives of the national government. "We are dealt with, as though Kentucky was a rebellious and conquered province," he protested, "instead of being as they [*sic*] are, a brave and loyal people." The outraged governor left no doubt about the way he viewed the election. "I am opposed to your re-election and regard a change of policy as essential to the salvation of our country." He devoted most attention to the excesses of the military authorities in the state. "Extreme measures, by which they sought to break the just pride and subdue the free spirit of the people, and which would only have fitted them for enslavement, have aroused the determined opposition to your re-election of at least three-fourths of the people of Kentucky when a different and just policy might have made them friends."[24]

Bramlette took more direct action on October 17, 1864, to insure Lincoln's defeat in the state. In a lengthy proclamation he discussed the voting situation. Those who had the right to vote should do so, he insisted; qualifications were decided by law and not by military authorities. Any soldier who tried to interfere with the election should be arrested. "If you are unable to hold a free election, your duty is to hold none at all." A week later Wolford put it on a personal basis when he swore in a public speech that "*the man dies*" who would stand between him and the polling place on election day. Wolford was raising state troops, and some persons believed that he intended to carry out another of his threats: if Lincoln was elected by the bayonet, he could be displaced by the bayonet. Kentuckians witnessed a nasty campaign, in which Lincoln was referred to as "Abraham Africanus the First" because of his views on slavery and slaves.[25]

Bramlette's proclamation may have had significant effect in the state. McClellan received 61,478 votes to Lincoln's 26,592, and McClellan also came out ahead in the separate soldier vote, 3,068 to 1,205. The total vote was some 54,000 less than it had been in 1860.[26]

Nationally, the result was quite different. September saw a number of Union victories, such as Sherman's capture of Atlanta and Philip H. Sheridan's victories in the Shenandoah Valley. Robert E. Lee and the Army of Northern Virginia were under siege in Richmond, and suddenly the prospects for an end to the war appeared much brighter. Lincoln had been able to calm party differences, at least temporarily. McClellan carried only three states—Kentucky, Delaware, and New Jersey. Lincoln won by an electoral college landslide, 212 to 21, and in a popular vote of about 4,175,000, he enjoyed a majority of over 500,000. In sharp contrast to the outcome in Kentucky, the president won the national soldier vote, 116,887 to 33,748. Lincoln could view the results as approval for his leadership.[27]

Governor Bramlette addressed the significance of the election in a message to the General Assembly.

> He is as much the President of those who voted against him as those who voted for him; for he is the chosen President of the United States; and, as such, should receive the support of all in the discharge of his duties. Though a large majority of the people of Kentucky may differ with him in some proposed measures of policy, and may use all lawful measures to secure such means as they approve, and prevent the adoption of such as they disapprove, yet, when the question shall pass from a *proposition* to an *adopted* measure, their line of duty will be changed. . . . The good citizen will ever yield obedience to the adopted measures of government, however much he may have condemned the adoption.[28]

Yet Bramlette was involved in another controversy with the

administration before the final results of the election were known. His November 9, 1864, telegram to the president charged that General Burbridge had arrested Gen. John B. Houston, "a loyal man and prominent citizen," and intended to expel him through Union lines "for no other offense than opposition to your election. . . . You are doubtless reelected, but surely it cannot sanction this ostracizing of loyal men who honestly opposed you." Lincoln's reply the next day contained a touch of his humor. He could hardly believe that the arrest was "'for no other offense than opposition to my reelection,' for if that had been deemed sufficient cause of arrest, I would have heard of more than one arrest in Kentucky on election day." But if that were the case, General Burbridge was to release him at once. The president's telegraphed order went to Burbridge the same day. Burbridge replied that the governor was wrong. "Huston's influence & speeches have been of a treasonable character & he persisted in making the latter after several warnings of what the consequences would be. He has been allowed however to return from Covington under oath & bond not again to oppose his Govt. A vigorous policy against rebel sympathizers in this State must be pursued & if I have erred I fear I have made too few arrests instead of too many." Burbridge upset Bramlette by saying, "When the civil authorities make no efforts to suppress disloyalty, the military must and will." The angry governor castigated the general in a lengthy letter. He maintained that the civil authority had cooperated faithfully in all efforts to aid the war effort; the general was "attempting to cover up your failures under calumnious charges against state authorities." Burbridge refused to continue the controversy, but the animosity remained and continued to fester like an untreated wound.[29]

The 1864 presidential election was the last important election in Kentucky before the end of the war in the spring of 1865. The divisions of the war years and the treatment of the state during the era of reconstruction propelled Kentucky into the ranks of the Solid Democratic South during the postwar years.

12

Lincoln and Wartime Issues in Kentucky

The military governors were the focal point for much of the unrest in Kentucky and for the many disputes with the national government. They were in an almost impossible position. As army officers they had a duty to execute the orders that they were given, and most of them had a genuine interest in doing everything possible to insure a Union victory. In carrying out their functions, they were sure to antagonize the individuals whose activities they had to restrict or whose plans they had to foil. They knew that a sizable minority of Kentuckians were pro-Confederate, and they tended to assume that any opposition came from that source. In trying to suppress what they saw as treasonable activities, they often violated what their opponents saw as fundamental civil rights. Just how did one measure civil rights against wartime needs? To that question, the military governors found no ready answer. They provided President Lincoln with many of his problems in trying to deal with Kentuckians who protested the wrongs they said they had suffered.

Jeremiah Tilford Boyle was the first of the military governors to attract a great deal of opposition. Born in Mercer (now Boyle) County on May 22, 1818, he received an unusually good education at Centre College, Princeton College, and the law school of Transylvania University. He practiced law successfully in Harrodsburg and Danville. Although a slaveholder, he favored gradual emancipation in the constitutional convention of

1849. Boyle voted Constitutional Union in 1860, then raised troops after Kentucky's neutrality ended. He received a commission as brigadier general in early 1862, to date from November 9, 1861. Boyle was commended for bravery at Shiloh. Then on May 27, 1862, apparently at the request of Kentucky's congressmen, he was appointed state military governor. After November he commanded the Western District. Most of John Hunt Morgan's raids into Kentucky occurred during Boyle's tenure, and he was made to look foolish and inept by his failures to curb Morgan. Morgan and telegrapher Ellsworth enjoyed taunting "Jerry" with his inability to catch them.[1]

On June 9, 1862, Boyle issued lengthy "instructions for the guidance of provost marshals," which outlined his program in dealing with Kentucky citizens. Anyone who had joined the Confederate army or given aid and assistance to it, or had even gone within Confederate lines, must report to a provost marshal, take an oath of allegiance, and give bond for good conduct or be arrested and sent to a military prison to await action by the secretary of war. The required oath read:

> I do solemnly swear that I will bear true allegiance to the United States, and support and sustain the constitution and laws thereof; that I will maintain the *national sovereignty paramount to that of all state,* county, or Confederate powers; that I will discountenance, discourage, and forever oppose secession, rebellion, and disintegration of the Federal Union; that I disclaim and denounce all faith and fellowship with the so-called Confederate armies; and pledge my honor, my property, and my life to the sacred performance of this my solemn oath of allegiance to the government of the United States of America.

Beneath the oath was printed this warning: "The penalty for a violation of the oath is *death*."

In addition, anyone who assisted Confederate forces or were

guerrillas would be arrested and dealt with according to military law. "For any thing said or done with the intent to excite to rebellion, the offender must be arrested and his conduct reported, that he may be dealt with *according to law*." When guerrillas did damage to the person or property of a loyal citizen, "the disloyal of the neighborhood or county will *be held responsible*, and a *military commission appointed to assess damages and enforce compensation*."[2] Such edicts were certain to cause confusion and resentment, especially as the war wore on and guerrilla outrages became more common. Union authorities tended to assume that all guerrilla activities were pro-Confederate in intent.

Numerous arrests had been made before Boyle's appointment, but his zeal soon increased the number, as did the Confederate invasion of Kentucky by Braxton Bragg and Kirby Smith during the summer of 1862. An announcement from Henderson declared that arrests would continue "until the last Jeff Davis sympathizer is cleared out." The jails were soon so full that high bail had to be granted to some wealthy individuals in order to make room for other arrests. In September the Louisville newspapers were ordered to quit publishing the lists of prisoners. In August ninety-three political prisoners in Camp Chase, Ohio, petitioned Governor Magoffin to ask the legislature to help them get a trial. Boyle had a prison established at Newport for "disloyal females," who would be required to do sewing for Union troops. In many instances, the only charge was that the woman had some family member in the Confederate army.[3]

Protests began at once, and Lincoln received numerous complaints about General Boyle's high-handed methods. "The indiscriminate arrest making in the State is producing a dangerous state of things," John B. Temple, president of the Kentucky Military Board, wrote Lincoln on August 12, 1862. "Quiet, law abiding men holding state rights dogmas are required to take an oath repulsive to them or go to prison, [but] who are willing to take an oath substantially pledging allegiance to the State and United States." On August 13 Secretary of War Stanton ordered Boyle to be cautious and to make arrests "only when good cause exists or strong evidence of hostility to the Government." But subordinates continued to make arrests, and on September 15 Governor Robinson protested to the president. "I find great dissatisfaction and I fear injury to the Union cause in Kentucky from an irregular and changing system of military arrests, which as now organized and administered, does more harm than good." Stanton, acting before the governor's protest was received, ordered Boyle to make no arrests except on the order of the governor.[4] The situation improved briefly, but soon it reverted to its previous state of discontent. The Lincoln administration was blamed by many, perhaps most, Kentuckians, and the state became largely hostile toward the federal government. Garrett Davis exaggerated little when he declared in January 1863 that "fully one-third of the State of Kentucky are disloyal."[5]

Boyle fretted under the restrictions imposed upon him, and when he telegraphed President Lincoln at midnight on July 18, 1862, for permission to raise regiments of twelve-month Kentucky troops, he argued that "the rebel villains cannot be suppressed by leniency or considerations. . . . Give me the force and authority & I will rid the State of their presence." He was allowed to recruit three regiments of cavalry for one year and two regiments for two years. During the latter part of the summer, Boyle's attention was directed to military affairs as Kentucky was invaded by the armies of Kirby Smith and Braxton Bragg; the fright caused by that invasion led to more stringent measures. On October 23, 1862, General Buell ordered Boyle to arrest anyone who had actively abetted the invasion during the past three months and ship them to Vicksburg, forbidden to return to Kentucky. The next day Boyle issued "Order No. 18," which required an oath of allegiance and a military permit for anyone who wished to purchase and ship goods for retail trade. Persons who had given aid and comfort to the "late invaders" were prohibited from engaging in trade; if they somehow managed to get permits, their goods would be confiscated. Public carriers were prohibited from transshipping goods without a permit, and loyal citizens were asked to report violators to the military authorities. On October 25 contributions totaling $35,000 were levied by military authorities upon Southern sympathizers within ten miles of Caseyville, Union County, for depredations committed by guerrillas. On November 5 Boyle ordered all Confederate prisoners in Kentucky hospitals who could walk or ride to report to Louisville for shipment to Vicksburg. On November 6 provost marshal Gen. Henry Dent paroled two hundred arrested Southern sympathizers on condition that they go north of the Ohio River and remain there.[6]

Department commander Maj. Gen. Ambrose E. Burnside issued "Order No. 38" on April 13, 1863. It included still more restrictions on persons suspected of being in sympathy with the South. Underground routes had been discovered by which some Confederate soldiers managed to maintain contact with family and friends in the state. Henceforth, "carriers of secret mails and writers of letters sent by secret mails" were subject to death for their crime, without regard to the nature of the mail or its contents. In addition, "Persons declaring sympathy for the enemy will be at once arrested with a view to being tried as traitors, and if convicted suffer death, or sent beyond our lines into the lines of their friends."[7]

Occasional efforts were made to restrain General Boyle and his agents. General Buell wrote him on July 24, 1862, saying, "I approve of punishing the guilty, but it will not answer to announce the rule of no quarter even to guerrillas. Neither will it be judicious to levy contributions upon secessionists for opinions alone. But with those who have given aid and comfort to Morgan's raid it will be proper to deal in the strictest manner. I approve of your preventing any avowed secessionist from being run for an office." Lincoln intervened at the insistence of Sen. L.W. Powell, who wanted fines that had been levied upon citizens in Henderson, Union, Hopkins, and Webster Counties refunded. Boyle backed the assessments that had been made by military officers, but the president overruled him. "This course of procedure, though just and politic in some cases, is so liable to gross abuse, as to do great injustice in some others and give the government immense trouble."[8]

Burnside in June 1863 had prohibited circulation of two democratic papers, the *New York World* and the *Chicago Times*, in the Department of the Ohio, which included Kentucky, but Lincoln rescinded that order two days later. On June 3 a number of families considered dangerous to the national government were sent south. On June 6 Lexington merchants were restricted to importing only $34,000 worth of merchandise in a month; no merchant could purchase more than a two-month supply. Burnside in "Order No. 66," issued on May 13, ordered the wives and families of persons absent in the Confederate army to be sent south as soon as possible; his order was modified a few days later to make it less imperative. On July 1, 1863, Superintendent of Public Instruction Robert Richardson demanded repeal of the act of August 30, 1862, that required a stringent oath of loyalty from each school trustee and teacher. It was "visiting unmerited punishment on thousands of innocent and defenseless children" and was "a monument of misdirected patriotism and unfounded legislation." He added that wartime conditions made it impossible for many schools to remain open.

On July 20, 1863, Governor Robinson called for strict observance of the Expatriation Act of March 11, 1862, that had been passed over Magoffin's veto. It said that any Kentucky citizen who was in the Confederate army or civil service or who gave voluntary aid to the Confederacy "shall be deemed to have *expatriated* himself, and shall *no longer be a citizen of Kentucky*" unless restored to citizenship by the state legislature. On July 24, 1863, officers commanding in Lexington ordered that impressed property must be taken exclusively from rebels and rebel sympathizers as long as they had any property; men of "undoubted loyalty" would not be molested. Boyle had been quiet for a time, but on August 10, 1863, he ordered the impressment of six thousand male slaves in fourteen central counties to work on an extension of a railroad from Lebanon to Danville. Owners who did not deliver their quota as ordered would have all their male slaves of ages sixteen to forty-five taken into service. Then on October 30 he turned over to the army quartermaster the corn purchased by a number of Kentucky distilleries and ordered them to cease the purchase of corn. On January 4, 1864, Governor Bramlette issued a proclamation holding rebel sympathizers responsible for all guerrilla raids. Military commanders were to arrest five of the most prominent and active rebel sympathizers for each loyal man carried off by guerrillas. They would be held hostage for the safe return of the loyal Unionists.[9] This drastic measure, which Bramlette would have protested had it come from the national administration, shows the growing frustration of the state government as the number and severity of guerrilla raids increased.

During his tenure in Kentucky, General Boyle attracted much attention for the zeal with which he promoted the Union cause and the harsh methods he employed. He was often blamed for actions taken by others; for most Kentuckians, Boyle became the symbol of federal interference with their lives. A number of his actions were overturned when appealed to President Lincoln or other higher authorities, and his position in the state became untenable. His unsuccessful attempts in 1863 to be elected to Congress or as governor antagonized many Kentuckians, and his reluctance to use black troops cost him the support of his superiors. General Boyle became a liability to the administration, and he was relieved of his command on January 12, 1864. In a telegram to President Lincoln on January 10, Boyle complained, "My superior officers have shown distrust of me. I cannot therefore with proper regard to the public interest & my own character serve the public under this command. . . . I ask to be relieved & and that my resignation be accepted. I can take this course with true devotion to the government and consistently with good of the service."[10] He would probably have been removed had he not requested it.

Stephen Gano Burbridge, born in Scott County, Kentucky, on August 19, 1831, became the temporary commander of the District of Kentucky in February 1864. Educated at Georgetown College and the Kentucky Military Institute, he studied law but in 1861 was a large-scale planter in Logan County. He became colonel of the Twenty-sixth Kentucky Infantry Regiment, and after notable service at Shiloh, he was promoted to brigadier general on June 9, 1862. Burbridge fought in Kentucky during the 1862 Confederate invasion of the state. His work in the Vicksburg campaign and his defeat of John Hunt Morgan in June 1864 earned him a brevet promotion to major general of volunteers. On February 15, 1864, Burbridge was given temporary command of the Military District of Kentucky; that position was made permanent in August 1864. Governor Bramlette and other Kentucky leaders had petitioned for his appointment, and relationships between the civil and military authorities in the state appeared to be much improved.[11]

Burbridge sometimes appeared to be arbitrary and insensitive as he tried to carry out his orders to make Kentucky safe for the Union. In time, he encountered all of the problems that had plagued Boyle. Immediately, however, guerrillas, now more active than at any other time in the war, constituted Burbridge's most pressing problem. Sometimes in large numbers, they might strike in any part of the state. Champ Clark, who lived in Kentucky during the Civil War, described the conditions in his autobiography. "The land swarmed with cutthroats, robbers, thieves, firebugs, and malefactors of every degree and kind, who preyed upon the old, the infirm, the helpless, and committed thousands of brutal and heinous crimes in the name of the Union or the southern Confederacy." Another young Kentuckian, who later became a noted historian and scientist, wrote that conditions in Kentucky resembled the devastation of Germany during the Thirty Years War. Logan County Methodist minister–farmer George R. Browder was especially upset by what he considered the unfairness of the fines levied upon citizens to indemnify the victims of guerrilla raids. After visiting Russellville on September 2, 1864, to pick up the money from his tobacco crop and to pay some debts, he commented in his diary: "The best, & purest, most honorable, peaceable & quiet men in our country are by this act classed with horse thieves & barn burners & made to pay for what they never did, and as a general rule the damages assessed have been three or four times as much as was sustained. It is supposed that the military get a large share of the booty." His father and an uncle had each been assessed $100 after the most recent local claim. "N.H. Waters, whose negroes, house, provisions, & happiness were all destroyed in the war, was assessed $200 more and being unable to pay it has left the country." Of course some individuals who received benefits from the fines saw the program from a quite different perspective. W.F. Wickersham, of Mercer County, voiced the hatred felt by many Kentuckians toward the outlaws who disrupted life in many communities. "If you catch one of them," he instructed his family, "I want you to kill the infernal scamps of the earth, they are not fit for no place but hell."[12]

Burbridge's efforts to deal with the guerrillas were based on instructions received from Gen. William T. Sherman, who was well into his Georgia campaign. Sherman said that he had asked Governor Bramlette to organize a small, trustworthy band of loyal men in each county in the state, under authority of the sheriff. Then, at one dash, each group would arrest "every man in the county who was dangerous to it," as well as every fellow hanging around without an honest calling; they were "the material out of which guerrillas are made up." But the governor had rejected the proposal as being too arbitrary. Sherman told Burbridge to inform his commanders that "guerrillas are not soldiers, but wild beasts, unknown to the usages of war." Both men and women who had encouraged or harbored guerrillas and robbers were to be arrested and sent to Louisville. When some three hundred to four hundred had been collected there, Sherman would have them taken down the Mississippi River and sent "to a land where they may take their negroes and make a colony with laws and a future of their own." During June the government reported that 2,151 rebel prisoners were moved from military prisons in Louisville to prisons north of the Ohio River.[13]

On July 3, 1864, Burbridge ordered all prisoners who had been captured and paroled by Morgan's command to report immediately to their regiments for active duty; the paroles were invalid because they violated orders from the U.S. War Department. The guerrillas and Confederate raids into Kentucky had become so serious that President Lincoln suspended the writ of *habeas corpus* and imposed martial law in Kentucky on July 5. Burbridge then issued "General Order No. 59" on July 16 for "the suppression of guerrillas." Rebel sympathizers living within five miles of the scene of an outrage were subject to arrest and deportation from the United States. Their property could be seized and used to indemnify the government and loyal citizens for property lost. Then came the most drastic measure: "Whenever an unarmed Union citizen is murdered, four guerrillas will be selected from the prisoners in the hands of the military authorities, and publicly shot to death in the most convenient place near the scene of outrage."[14]

In late July and early August 1864, Burbridge ordered the arrests of a number of citizens across the state. Best known was Joshua F. Bullitt of Jefferson County, the state's chief justice. Judge Alvin Duvall and others escaped arrest by leaving the state. Duvall was running for reelection, but his name was kept off the ballot in a number of counties. In its August 8, 1864, issue the Louisville *Democrat* dared to raise a pertinent question about loyalty and disloyalty. Citizens were being declared disloyal because they were not providing active assistance against guerrillas. "It may be patriotic and heroic to take up arms or give information against them; but who is to protect the man who does this, when the guerrillas assail him the next day? If a citizen is to aid, let him be protected in it; otherwise any expectation of his active help is unreasonable."[15]

Burbridge's "General Order No. 63," issued August 13,

1864, prohibited the shipment of produce or goods within or through the state except by holders of permits, issued for four months, to persons whose loyalty was attested to by a board of five advisors. And this oath could also be required: "I do solemnly swear that I have not, by word or action, given the slightest aid and comfort to the present rebellion; and that by conversation and action I will do all I can to discourage, discountenance, and overthrow the rebellion, and will use my influence to restore the authority of the government of the United States over the states now in rebellion." Violators were to be arrested and their goods seized. Later that month, on August 24, Burbridge removed the Louisville restrictions on the marketing of goods.[16]

Despite all the restrictions and the numerous executions of guerrillas, outrages continued to occur in all parts of the state. Burbridge, becoming increasingly unpopular, was accused of not distinguishing between loyal and disloyal persons when making arrests. One of his few defenders was the Reverend Dr. Robert J. Breckinridge, who was said to have declared in a Lexington speech:

> As to these [illegal arrests], all the fault I have to find is, that more should not have been arrested than were; and many of those that were arrested, were set at liberty too soon. . . . When Simon De Montfort was slaughtering the Protestants in the south of France, he was appealed to by certain persons—declaring that his men were mistaken, that they were killing many who were good Catholics. To which he replied: 'Kill them *all*; God knows his own.' And this is the way we should deal with these fellows; treat them all alike; and if there are any among them who are not rebels at heart, God will take care of them and save them at least.

In a number of cases President Lincoln intervened to prevent punishments he considered too harsh.[17]

General Burbridge led a force of some four thousand troops against the important Confederate saltworks at Saltville in western Virginia in the early fall of 1864. Both Union and Confederate troops, the latter commanded by Gen. John S. Williams, included a number of Kentucky units. Ordered by General Sherman to return to Kentucky, Burbridge fought a series of skirmishes as he was hard pressed by Confederate troops. With the 1864 election rapidly approaching, Burbridge denied that the military was going to interfere with it. On October 26 he ordered officers to arrest anyone who violated his orders, and he asked citizens to report any violations they saw to military authorities. Then on the same day he issued his most drastic order concerning guerrillas. "Hereafter, no guerrillas will be received as prisoners; and any officer who may capture such, and extend to them the courtesies due to prisoners of war, will be held accountable for disobedience of orders."[18]

Burbridge and Bramlette became involved in a heated controversy over the arrest of Gen. John B. Houston, who was released from arrest by order of the president; Lincoln could "scarcely believe" that the arrest had been made because of opposition to his election. Burbridge charged that Houston, along with others, such as Wolford and Jacob, had not only been reviling the government but had been trying to discourage enlistments and therefore weakening "the power of the government in its efforts to suppress the rebellion. This has been done with the apparent sanction and approval of the state authorities." He attributed the presence of dangerous guerrillas to the lack of support from the state government. Governor Bramlette rejected the charges "made by innuendo and in apparent bullying tone." He charged the general with having threatened to take without compensation the property of those who dared to vote against Lincoln. As for the accusations against Houston and the others, they were "a shallow pretense, gotten up upon false accusations, to afford a pretext for wreaking political vengeance upon them." Kentucky had always cooperated with Burbridge; he was trying to conceal his failures by blaming state authorities for what he had failed to do. In a letter to Lincoln, Bramlette wrote, 'I regret that Gen. Burbridge is pursuing a course calculated to exasperate and infuriate, rather than pacify and conciliate." He had done what was "most calculated to inaugurate revolt and produce collisions . . . because of blindings of a weak intellect and an overwhelming vanity." Bramlette continued that "he and I can not hold personal converse, after his bad conduct within the past few weeks. . . . The system of arrests inaugurated by Burbridge outrages public judgment and ought to be restricted." He makes false charges "to sustain his outrages against public judgment." The governor closed with an appeal. "I beg of you, Mr. President to assist and give me such aid as you have in your power in preserving peace, order, and unity in Kentucky. Our people are right and true, though they have been much bedeviled by the course of subordinate officers. Burbridge will not correct these evils; for he has favorites to reward and enemies to punish, and will use his official station to carry out this favoritism and personal vengeance."[19]

Burbridge's reputation was hurt by the "Great Hog Swindle," which outraged many Kentuckians. On October 28, 1864, he issued a proclamation asking farmers to sell all their surplus hogs to Maj. H.C. Symonds for the use of the army. Symonds said that the army had fixed a fair price, but he paid a cent or two per pound less than what a farmer could have received at the Louisville and Cincinnati markets. Permits were required for hogs to be driven to market, and few were given to persons who did not sell to Symonds. Guards were stationed at crossing points on the Ohio River to prevent hogs from being sent north to better markets. Packers not involved in the deal were unable to get animals to slaughter, and farmers joined them in protesting what was being done to them. Bramlette fired another letter of protest to Lincoln and sent a committee to Washington to file a vocal protest over the steal. Burbridge denied any involvement in the swindle, and he acted promptly on November 27, 1864, when the president ordered him to revoke the proclamation. Bramlette estimated that state farmers had been cheated out of at least $300,000 during the period (nearly a month) of the "Great Hog Swindle." Despite his protests of innocence, many Kentuckians credited Burbridge with yet another crime against their state.[20]

Few Kentuckians were neutral in their estimate of General Burbridge; the majority saw him as the symbol of everything that was wrong with conditions in the state and relationships with the national administration. The Radical Unionists were the major exception. On January 4, 1865, when this group held a convention in Frankfort, Burbridge and his staff were invited to sit with the delegates. The convention voted to recommend that President Lincoln promote General Burbridge to brigadier general in the regular army "for his gallant services in the field, and for his able administration in the affairs of this military district." The Reverend Robert J. Breckinridge, a leader of the radicals, was suspected of exerting a great influence with the general.

Much of Governor Bramlette's message to the General Assembly on January 6, 1865, was an attack on Burbridge and his policies and a recital of the governor's efforts to block them. The cumulative effect of the criticisms of Burbridge was overwhelming. On January 14, 1865, the General Assembly selected a committee of two senators and three representatives to go to Washington and lay before President Lincoln the distressed state of affairs in Kentucky.

Maj. Gen. John M. Palmer, a Scott County native, relieved Burbridge on February 22 and ordered him to report to Gen. George H. Thomas in Nashville for assignment. Burbridge received a thirty-day leave, and when he returned to Louisville, the war was so near its end that no command was available for him. Out of power, he reconciled his differences with Governor Bramlette, and they resumed their earlier friendship. Burbridge resigned his commission in December 1865. Ostracized in Kentucky, he wrote in 1867 that he could not "live in safety or do business in Kentucky. . . . My services to my country have caused me to be exiled from my home, and made my wife and children wanderers."[21]

Burbridge was especially hated in the state for his execution of prisoners, not always clearly guerrillas, in retaliation for guerrilla activities. A devoted Union man, he did his best to carry out his orders to secure and maintain safe conditions in the state. A wiser and more diplomatic commander might have avoided some of his clashes with other Kentuckians, but under the conditions that existed in the state toward the end of the war, he faced an impossible task. Only the restoration of peace allowed the guerrilla scourge to be brought under control, and even then it was a slow process.

During much of the war the western part of the state was a military district separate from most of the commonwealth. The extreme western area, the Jackson Purchase, was the most pro-Southern portion of the state; in the 1861 election it had elected the only pro-Confederate representative to Congress, and Union enlistments had been slow in most of its counties. Although there had been some clashes with Union authorities, the military-civilian relationships had been reasonably good until the summer of 1864. On July 19, 1864, Brig. Gen. Eleazer Arthur Paine assumed command at Paducah.

Born in Parkman, Ohio, on September 10, 1815, Paine graduated from West Point in 1839. After a brief period of service in the Seminole War, he resigned his commission in 1840 and became a lawyer. He moved to Monmouth, Illinois, in 1848 and became well acquainted with Abraham Lincoln in the 1850s. At the start of the war he organized the Ninth Illinois Volunteer Regiment and became its colonel. On September 2, 1861, President Lincoln nominated Paine and eight others for promotion to brigadier general. After spending a few months in Paducah, Paine commanded a division in the Army of the Mississippi, then was assigned to help protect the L&N Railroad in Tennessee from Confederate attacks.[22] His conduct there, which foreshadowed his later antics in Kentucky, prompted General Grant to ask General Thomas if he could not order Paine to the command of a brigade in the field. "He is entirely unfit to command a post," Grant complained. If that could not be done, "I advise that you send a staff officer to investigate fully and report upon his administration." Thomas did not think it advisable to assign Paine to a field command: "His rank will entitle him to a division, and if not placed in command according to rank, I should have constant troubles with him."

The army's solution was to assign him to the command of the District of Western Kentucky in July 1864 after the Union League of America at Paducah requested his appointment. There he began what Richard H. Collins, a Kentucky historian of that era, called "a fifty-one days' reign of violence, terror, rapine, extortion, oppression, bribery, and military murders." The Unionists had hoped that he would punish the rebel sympathizers who had been dominant in the district, but Paine "assumed a violent and abusive attitude toward everyone, loyal and disloyal alike; in his mad career he took no time to draw distinctions."[23]

Almost immediately he levied a $100,000 tax upon the citizens in the First District. He said it was to benefit the families of Union soldiers, but little if any of the money ever reached them. Deciding that disloyalty was especially prevalent in McCracken County, he imposed an additional tax of $95,000 upon its citizens. On August 10 he banished a number of men, women, and children to Canada. Some of those expelled had considerable wealth; Paine ordered their property seized and placed under guard. Alarmed citizens who feared that their turn would soon come fled across the Ohio River into Illinois. He taxed each hogshead of tobacco $10 and levied an ad valorem tax of 25 percent on cotton shipped by anyone who was not an unquestioned Union supporter—as defined by Paine. Trade permits were sold for large sums; confiscated property could be recovered upon the payment of heavy bribes; bank checks could not be cashed until a 50-cent tax was paid. No mail could be sent out of town until stiff duties were paid; special taxes of 10 to 50 cents were placed on each letter addressed to a Union soldier. Business and trade was almost paralyzed across the district unless an adequate bribe was passed along to General Paine. He aroused bitter hatred, but his "reign of terror" made it dangerous for anyone who opposed him. Some forty-three persons were shot by his orders during his tenure of fifty-one days.[24]

One of the victims was seventeen-year-old Harry Hicks, whose crime was having two brothers in the Confederate army. He was delivered in irons to the post commander at Mayfield at noon on August 30, 1864, and informed that he would be executed at two o'clock. Placed in front of his designated grave, the lad said, "I have got enough nerve to face the music; do not tie my hands; do not blindfold me." But he was blindfolded, then shot. His body was put in the grave, his hat placed over his face, and the grave filled in.[25]

As word of Paine's outrages seeped out, Governor Bramlette requested President Lincoln to appoint a military commission to investigate the actions of Paine and his associates. (On June 18, 1864, Lincoln had written Secretary Stanton: "I personally know Gen. Paine to be a good true man, having a West Point education; but I do not know much as to his Military ability.") The president may have given an order to General Burbridge, for on September 9 he sent Gen. Speed Smith Fry and Col. John Mason Brown to the western district to investigate conditions there. The commissioners rendered a devastating report on what they found. In addition to Paine, they pinpointed a number of military and civilian men who had cooperated with him and shared in the spoils.

One of Paine's most notorious schemes concerned "fort building" in the town square at Mayfield. Hundreds of men and boys from Graves and surrounding counties were conscripted under guard by black soldiers to build a useless fort. Few were excused for reasons of health or age, but those with money could buy exemptions from the labor. It was one of the extortionists' most profitable enterprises.[26]

Paine and his principal accomplices fled to Illinois during the inquiry, but the findings were so damaging that Burbridge, acting in accordance with orders from General Grant, replaced Paine with Brig. Gen. Solomon Meredith. A court-martial was held in March 1865, but, apparently at the order of Joseph Holt, advocate general of the United States, the "most startling, terrible, and easily proved outrages" were omitted. In early November 1865 Secretary Stanton finally revealed that Paine had been found guilty of some of the charges but had been sentenced only to a reprimand, which was later remitted. Paine's legend lived on the hatred he engendered among his victims in the First District.[27]

When Maj. Gen. John McCauley Palmer replaced Burbridge, he enjoyed the approval of most Kentuckians, who contrasted him favorably with his predecessor. Born in Scott County on September 13, 1817, he moved to Illinois with his family in 1831. Palmer practiced law and was active in the Democratic party, but he broke with Stephen A. Douglas in 1854. Encouraged by Lincoln, he became a Republican who helped secure Lincoln's nomination and election in 1860. First colonel of the Fourteenth Illinois Volunteer Regiment, Palmer was promoted to brigadier general in December 1861 and to major general in March 1863 after commendable service in several campaigns in the western theater. As a corps commander during the Atlanta campaign, he became involved in a controversy over rank with Generals John M. Schofield and William T. Sherman. Palmer asked to be relieved and was assigned to the Department of Kentucky on February 22, 1865.[28]

The *Lexington Observer and Reporter* of March 11 welcomed Palmer's appointment. "The fact that he regards Kentucky as a loyal State, and her people who yield obedience to the Constitution and laws as entitled to the same treatment that the people of the other loyal states receive, is enough in itself to give assurance that Kentuckians are not to be subjected to the system of arrogance and wrongs which has hitherto oppressed them." When Palmer visited Frankfort, Governor

Bramlette introduced him to each member of the General Assembly, and that body voted a resolution of welcome. But it soon became apparent that Palmer's policies did not differ greatly from those of his predecessor. He may have been somewhat more tactful than Burbridge, and he did not have to deal with the accumulated animosity that made Burbridge so unpopular with most Kentuckians. During the brief time that Palmer served in Kentucky while Lincoln was still alive, the president was not as bombarded with protests as he had been during the administration of General Burbridge. The *Tri-Weekly Commonwealth* came close to the truth in its February 24, 1865, issue: "Mr. Lincoln either had to change his commander here, or give the whole of his time to the management of Kentucky affairs."[29] The approaching end of the war eased the possibilities of disagreement with Palmer, although his continued efforts to free slaves as rapidly as possible antagonized many Kentuckians, who refused to admit that slavery would soon end in Kentucky as it would elsewhere.

Palmer issued orders on April 29, 1865, that "the power of arrest will hereafter be sparingly exercised, and directed against real offenders. There is no dignity or justice in pursuing foolish people for foolish words. The bands now prowling through the country are simply guerrillas and robbers, and are to be treated as such, they will be allowed to surrender for trial." Gradually, the worst of the outlaws were eliminated, and the state recovered some degree of normalcy. In his detailed study of Kentucky during the Civil War era, historian E.M. Coulter concluded that "the military authorities throughout the war failed to evaluate and understand Kentucky, the character of her people and their sentiments, the peculiar position of the state, its history immediate and remote. Any regime that could have been devised would have had troubles enough; but it seems the Federal commanders sent to Kentucky were particularly unfortunate in their understanding of the best way to perform their work."[30] The situation would have been much worse had it not been for the frequent intervention of President Lincoln to change orders and policies calculated to cause discontent. With all of the other burdens that he bore as the wartime leader of the nation, Lincoln had to devote considerable attention to affairs in his native state. He understood prickly Kentuckians better than did most of the military commanders who were assigned there.

In his study *Lincoln and the South*, J.G. Randall commented that "his Kentucky policy was such a balancing of delicacy with firmness, of delay with watchfulness, of Unionism with self determination, that he, as much as any man, must be given the credit for keeping Kentucky in the Union." Though federal acts such as the ones of July 31, 1861, and July 17, 1862, provided punitive punishment for treason and other crimes against the United States, Lincoln made less drastic use of them in Kentucky than he could have. Many of the Kentuckians swept up by overzealous authorities were innocent of the charges made against them, and others were willing to repent of their actions and declare loyalty to the Union if allowed to do so. On February 14, 1862, Lincoln ordered the release of "all political or state prisoners" who promised "to render no aid or comfort to the enemies of the United States." Those who made the promise were considered pardoned. Bonds for good behavior of an individual ranged from $500 to as much as $20,000, but his surety was not required to post the designated sum with any authority; they agreed that the amount fixed could be levied against the surety's property if the parole was violated. The chances of obtaining a pardon were greatly enhanced if the case was recommended by a Kentuckian in whom Lincoln had confidence. Joshua Speed, James Speed, Robert J. Breckinridge, and James Guthrie were among those in whom the president had such confidence. His pardons were done on an individual basis; the terms were set to fit a particular case.[31]

A number of Kentuckians benefitted from President Lincoln's amnesty proclamation of December 8, 1863, although its main purpose was to encourage the formation of loyal governments in the seceded states. It excluded most Confederate civil officials and military officers above the rank of colonel or naval lieutenant, as well as those who treated "colored persons, or white persons in charge of such, otherwise than lawfully as prisoners of war." On March 26, 1864, he also excluded from amnesty benefits persons who were in confinement. However, Lincoln indicated that anyone could apply to him for a special pardon. The Richmond, Kentucky, law firm of Curtis F. Burman and James W. Caperton secured the release of thirty-four prisoners from Union prison camps for a fee of $100 per person. The number of Kentuckians imprisoned increased after the Emancipation Proclamation of January 1, 1863. It angered many Kentuckians, who believed that Lincoln had broken his promise not to interfere with slavery in the states that had it.[32]

Louisville Journal editor George D. Prentice was involved in one of Lincoln's special clemency cases. His son Clarence had entered Confederate service and was a major when he was captured in Louisville in April 1863; he had slipped into town to visit his family. Sent to Camp Chase, he was to be tried as a spy. The parents' other son had been killed while fighting with John Hunt Morgan, and the parents were distraught at the thought of losing Clarence as well. On April 28, 1863, Prentice implored the president "to let him go on his taking that simple oath anywhere outside of the United States and of the rebel Confederacy. I know his plans. His mother will go with him and he will never bear arms against us again. I will be surety for this with fortune and life." Judge Advocate Joseph Holt recommended that Clarence be exchanged instead; Clarence had not indicated a willingness to take the oath of allegiance, and no one could be sure that he would not take up arms again if an opportunity presented itself. Lincoln issued a parole order to Secretary Stanton on May 16, 1863, but it was apparently not used. Major Prentice was exchanged, and he ended the war as a Confederate colonel.

In 1864 Clarence was charged with the murder of a man named White in Virginia. Once again his father appealed to President Lincoln for help. Confederate captain R.H. Baptist, a prisoner of war at Johnson's Island, had informed Prentice that he could give valuable testimony on Clarence's behalf. Prentice asked Lincoln to parole Baptist and allow him to go south to testify. Lincoln issued the requested document on February 16, 1865, "at the special request to Mr. George D. Prentice." Clarence was tried at Abingdon, Virginia, and acquitted of the charge.[33]

The Reverend Robert J. Breckinridge, who believed in harsh treatment of disloyal persons, relented somewhat when members of his family were involved. In February 1865 Col. Robert J. Breckinridge Jr. was captured near Versailles. He carried orders from Maj. Gen. John C. Breckinridge designed to get Confederates then in Kentucky back to their units or run the risk of having Union authorities in the state told that they did not have to be treated as prisoners of war if captured. His father intervened with federal authorities, and his son was kept in the Columbus penitentiary rather than being sent to one of the prison camps. He was released at the war's end. The Reverend Breckinridge also intervened when his son-in-law Theophilus Steele was captured and accused of being a guerrilla. The reverend asked that Steele be kept in prison but not hanged, and that was done.[34]

Another example of Lincoln's clemency toward a Kentuckian involved Capt. John Breckinridge Castleman of Fayette County. Castleman was captured near Sullivan, Indiana, on October 1, 1864, while using an assumed name. He was accused of being a spy who was trying to incite insurrection in the Old Northwest and to free Confederate prisoners of war. When his mother brought him a Bible in Indianapolis, it included three small saws and $3,000 thoughtfully included by Capt. Thomas H. Hines, who had experience in prison escapes. These assets failed to get him out of prison, but Judge Samuel M. Breckinridge employed an Indianapolis law firm to defend him. Then in late November the judge went to Washington to plead the case with President Lincoln. On the evening of November 29, 1864, Lincoln wrote out a note: "Whenever John

B. Castleman shall be tried, if convicted and sentenced, suspend execution until further order from me and send me the record." An exchange was arranged, but Lincoln was assassinated before it was completed. Castleman was in danger of being tried, but instead he was banished from the country after the war was over. Not until August 27, 1866, did President Andrew Johnson revoke the order and allow Castleman to return home upon taking the oath of allegiance.

According to a story in the *Louisville Post* of September 4, 1916, Lincoln said when he handed the requested note to Judge Breckinridge, whose wife Virginia was the sister of John B. Castleman: "Sam, this is for you and Virginia, entrusted in confidence, with the condition that its existence shall not be known unless the emergency arises for which the letter provides." Castleman did not know of the letter until fifteen years later when his brother-in-law gave it to him.[35]

After his marriage to Mary Todd, Lincoln had closer connections with the Todds than with any other Kentucky family. The relationship was generally good, perhaps because Lincoln did not see much of the family with the exception of the ones who also lived in Springfield. When he visited in Lexington in 1847 for three weeks on his way to Washington to take his seat in the House of Representatives, he met a number of in-laws for the first time. Joseph Humphreys, a nephew of Mrs. Robert S. Todd, arrived at the Todd house on West Main Street before the Lincolns. He had ridden the train with the Lincolns from Frankfort to Lexington without knowing who they were. "Aunt Betsy," he said, "I was never so glad to get off a train in my life. There were two lively youngsters on board who kept the whole train in a turmoil, and their long-legged father, instead of spanking the brats, looked pleased as Punch and sided with and abetted the older one in mischief." Joseph looked out of the window at the sound of carriage wheels. "Good Lord, there they are now!" and he disappeared out the back door.[36]

Mary and the boys returned to Lexington in the spring while Lincoln remained in Washington until the end of the session. He and his family visited Lexington again in 1849 following the death of Mary's father. This visit was also for a few weeks. Lincoln represented the four heirs who lived in Springfield (Mrs. Ninian W. Edwards, Mrs. William Walker, Mrs. Clark M. Smith, and Mary) after George Todd objected to the probate of the will. Robert S. Todd had also left a lawsuit in progress that Lincoln investigated.[37]

Lincoln enjoyed a good relationship with his father-in-law after the initial family shock over Mary's marriage to an unknown. The first Lincoln son was named Robert, and in December 1843 Todd visited Springfield to see his grandson and the members of the family who lived there. Soon aware of the Lincolns' financial straits, he arranged for a considerable amount of help to them. The settlement of his estate revealed that he had advanced $1,157.50 to the Lincoln family. Todd had also entrusted some legal matters to Lincoln.[38]

Levi Todd, one of Mary's brothers, was responsible for one of Abraham Lincoln's most troublesome legal experiences. Prompted by Levi, the remaining partners in Robert S. Todd's old firm of Oldham and Hemingway sued Lincoln in May 1853, claiming that he had collected some Illinois debts for the firm but had kept the money for his own use. Lincoln, realizing that the false accusation could hurt his reputation, took swift action. When the plaintiffs had to file particulars of the case, he presented proof that the allegations against him were completely false. His proof was so overwhelming that the plaintiffs moved to dismiss the case on February 10, 1854.[39]

The Civil War brought additional complications, for the Todds, like so many other Kentucky families, were divided over the conflict. Because Mary was from a Kentucky slaveholding family, and because she had a brother, three half-brothers, and three brothers-in-law fighting for the Confederacy, she was the target of persistent rumors that she was pro-Confederate and even that she spied for the South. Such tales were false. Mary Lincoln was totally loyal, both to her country and to her husband. In April 1862, when the Battle of Shiloh was being fought, she told the Reverend N.W. Niner, a Springfield neighbor who was visiting the Lincolns, that she hoped her brothers fighting for the Confederacy would be killed or captured: "They would kill my husband if they could, and destroy our government—the dearest of all things to us." The legend that President Lincoln once appeared before a congressional committee to vouch for his wife's loyalty is only a legend; it did not happen.[40]

Ben Hardin Helm was one of Lincoln's favorite in-laws. Born in Bardstown on June 2, 1831, he graduated from West Point in 1851. He resigned his commission in 1852, studied law at the University of Louisville and Harvard Law School, then practiced in Elizabethtown and Louisville. Helm served a term in the General Assembly and from 1856 until 1858 was the commonwealth attorney in the Third District. He married Emelie (Emily) Todd on March 20, 1856. Lincoln asked Helm to come to Washington in April 1861 and offered him a commission as major in the paymaster division of the regular army. With the army beginning a rapid expansion, the position offered a splendid career possibility. But his sentiments were Confederate, and Helm soon entered the Confederate army. Promoted to brigadier general after Shiloh, he was commanding the famed Orphan Brigade when he was killed at Chickamauga on September 20, 1863. When Lincoln learned of Helm's death, he said to David Davis, "I feel as David did of old when he was told of the death of Absalom. 'Would to God that I had died for thee! Oh, Absalom, my son, my son'"[41]

Emelie (Little Sister) Helm was left in the South with three young children. She wanted to join her mother in Lexington, but her request for a pass through the lines was not answered by General Grant. She started home anyway but was halted at Fort Monroe, Virginia, when she refused to take an oath of allegiance. When the perplexed officers there wired President Lincoln for instructions, he replied, "Send her to me." The Lincolns welcomed her at the White House. Mary was still mourning the death of son Willie on February 12, 1862, and she and Emelie shared their grief. Concerned over Mary's mental and physical health, Lincoln told "Little Sister" that he hoped she would come back to Washington and spend the summer with them. The Lincolns were criticized for harboring a rebel, and Gen. Daniel E. Sickles, who had lost a leg at Gettysburg, told the president bluntly, "You should not have that rebel in your house." Lincoln replied with great dignity and a touch of warmth: "Excuse me, General Sickles, my wife and I are in the habit of choosing our own guests. We do not need from our friends either advice or assistance in that matter." Youngsters Tad Lincoln and Katherine Helm got into a shouting match when Tad showed her a photograph of his father and said proudly, "This is the President." Katherine disputed his assertion: "No, that is not the President. Mr. Davis is President." Emelie refused to sign the oath that Lincoln wrote out for her on December 14, 1863, but she was allowed to go to Lexington on the pass that he provided.

During the summer of 1864 Lincoln heard rumors that Burbridge had refrained from arresting Emelie because of Lincoln's pass. "I do not intend to protect her against the consequences of disloyal words or acts spoken or done by her since her return to Kentucky," Lincoln wrote the general, "and if the paper given her by me can be construed to give her protection from such words or acts, it is hereby revoked *pro tanto*. Deal with her for current conduct, just as you would with *any other*." Emelie returned to Washington in the fall of 1864 with a demand for a license to sell six hundred bales of cotton. She still refused to sign an oath of allegiance, and Lincoln refused to grant the permission.

When she got home, she found that brother Levi Todd, a Unionist, had died. He had asked Lincoln for $150 to $200 in September: It would be used "to your advantage and my own as I stand in great need of things." Levi's wife had divorced him because of habitual drunkenness, cruel and inhuman treatment, and failure to support his family. Lincoln, perhaps remembering that Levi had instigated the suit against him in 1853, refused the request. Emelie, bitter over being refused the cotton permit, penned a savage letter to the Lincolns. She blamed them for the death of Levi, and she concluded by saying, "I also remind you that your minie bullets have made us what we are." Mary Lincoln never saw or corresponded with Emelie again.[42]

Martha Todd White, another of Mary's half-sisters whom she hardly knew, also became an embarrassment to the White House. The wife of Confederate major Clement C. White of Selma, Alabama, Martha was in the Union in December 1863. She wanted permission to carry articles of clothing back to Selma that could not be obtained in the South. After she went home in the spring of 1864, some newspapers reported that she had used the presidential pass to carry trunkloads of medicine and a Confederate uniform with solid gold buttons through the lines without inspection. The Lincolns refused to see her while she was in Washington, and the president rejected her demand that her baggage not be inspected. Her presence became so obnoxious that Lincoln warned her of possible arrest if she did not leave at once. Back in Washington again in March 1865, Martha sought a permit to ship her cotton out of the South. Lincoln refused the request but gave her a pass that allowed her to return South.[43]

President Lincoln bore the burden of many problems during the war, and most historians have decided that he was a great wartime president whose management of men and events did much to determine the outcome of the conflict. A considerable part of his burden came from the members of the Todd family, including Mary Todd Lincoln.

13

Lincoln, Slavery,
and Kentucky

Although Lincoln hoped for the ultimate end of slavery, his primary object in 1861 was the preservation of the Union. Four slave states had remained in the Union, and they seemed to the president to offer a way to move toward voluntary emancipation within the framework of states' rights but with federal encouragement. Viewing Kentucky as the bellwether of the loyal slave states, Lincoln tried repeatedly to persuade Kentucky to adopt a program of gradual emancipation with compensation provided by the federal government. After Kentucky's refusal to accept emancipation and under increased pressure from abolitionists to destroy slavery, Lincoln turned to what James M. McPherson called "a revolutionary new war aim—the overthrow of slavery by force of arms if and when Union armies conquered the South." The Emancipation Proclamation was followed by an effort to secure a constitutional amendment that would resolve any doubts about the legality of the measure. Events had moved Abraham Lincoln into the role of a somewhat reluctant revolutionary leader.

Lincoln's attitude toward slavery had hardened since the Kansas-Nebraska Bill, but he had not become an abolitionist. As a result, by the time he became president he was attacked by the two most opposed parties on the slavery issue. Proslavery advocates believed that he was a distinct threat to their peculiar institution; abolitionists feared that he would never move to eradicate the infamous practice. His racial views were mixed.

He never used the virulent racial epithets that were common in that period; his comparisons between blacks and whites were always tentative. The Negro *might* not be his equal; the Negro was not his equal *in certain respects*. Lincoln did not believe that blacks had the same civil rights as whites, but he insisted that they did have the natural rights stated in the Declaration of Independence. As president he met and worked with black leaders without a trace of condescension. Sojourner Truth said she "never was treated by any one with more kindness and cordiality. . . . I felt I was in the presence of a friend," and Frederick Douglass, who often thought that Lincoln moved too slowly on the slavery question, came to admire the man who treated him as an equal. Douglass saw the president as "a progressive man; he never took any step backwards. His last days were better than his first." Lincoln was "the first great man that I talked with in the United States freely who in no single instance reminded me of the difference between himself and myself, of the difference of color." In an 1876 speech Douglass admitted that Lincoln was correct in his order of priorities. "Had he put the abolition of slavery before the salvation of the Union, he would have inevitably driven from him a powerful class of the American people and rendered resistance to rebellion impossible. . . . He knew the American people better than they knew themselves, and his truth was based upon that knowledge."[1]

When he became president, Lincoln believed strongly in gradual emancipation, followed by colonization. Recognizing how much slavery was a part of the Southern way of life, he was willing to leave it untouched in the states that had it. He would even accept adding an amendment to the Constitution that would be specific on that point. But he also believed that slavery would ultimately die out if it was prevented from expanding, and on that point Lincoln and the Republican party were unyielding. His paramount object was to preserve the Union. He made that clear in a letter of August 22, 1862, to Horace Greeley, editor of the *New York Tribune*. In a letter to

Lincoln printed as "The Prayer of Twenty Millions" in the August 20 issue, Greeley had charged the president with being remiss in not using existing laws to free the slaves. Lincoln's reply was designed to leave no one in any doubt about his objective.

> I would save the Union. I would save it the shortest way under the Constitution. . . . If there be those who would not save the Union, unless they could at the same time *save* slavery, I do not agree with them. If there be those who would not save the Union unless they could at the same time *destroy* slavery, I do not agree with them. My paramount object in this struggle *is* to save the Union, and it is *not* either to save or destroy slavery. If I could save the Union without freeing *any* slave I would do it, and if I could save it by freeing *all* the slaves I would do it; and if I could save it by freeing some and leaving others alone I would also do that. What I do about slavery, and the colored race, I do because I believe it helps to save the Union; and what I forebear, I forebear because I do *not* believe it would help to save the Union. I shall do *less* whenever I shall believe what I am doing hurts the cause, and I shall do *more* whenever I shall believe doing more will help the cause.[2]

What Lincoln did not say in his letter was that on July 22, a month earlier, he had read to his cabinet members his draft of a preliminary emancipation proclamation. On January 1, 1863, acting as the nation's commander-in-chief, he would free the slaves in the rebel states or in the portions of states still in rebellion. Secretary Seward argued that the proclamation should not be issued until the Union had won an important victory, preferably in the East.[3] Lincoln agreed, and he waited for an appropriate battle.

Slavery and its future had been a major issue in American

politics for years before the Civil War; its importance increased once the war began. Opinion in the North was not unanimous. Abolitionists insisted that the slaves should be free at once; the secession of Southern states made it possible. But Lincoln knew that many people in the North did not favor abolition, he did not believe that the national government could interfere with the rights of the states in regard to slavery, and he was very much aware of the embarrassment of having slavery exist in the four loyal slave states. He was convinced that the Confederates continued to hope that the common bond of slavery would detach those states from the Union and bring them into the Confederate States of America. With the four border states, the Union had a 5–2 population advantage; if they were in the Confederacy, the advantage became only 3–2.[4] Lincoln's acceptance of Kentucky's unique neutrality had proved how important he considered the status of his native state to be; the attitude of Kentucky toward emancipation would probably be decisive in determining the attitudes of Delaware, Maryland, and Missouri. If something could be done to end slavery in the loyal slave states, it would allay some of the abolitionists' criticism and discourage the Confederates.

The president's solution was to try to persuade the loyal slave states to accept some plan of gradual, compensated emancipation. In his 1861 inaugural address Lincoln had stressed the Republican acceptance of the right of each state "to order and control its own domestic institutions," and he reaffirmed that pledge whenever possible. Yet there were doubters in Kentucky from the start of his administration. William Mobley reported to the American Missionary Association headquarters in July 1861 that "it is the common and general opinion of both pro and anti people that the present conflict will somehow or other bring about the extinction of slavery." Many Kentuckians howled in outrage when Lincoln accepted the First Confiscation Act of August 6, 1861, which provided for the freeing of slaves who were used in direct support of Confederate military forces. Three Kentucky congressmen, Robert Mallory, John J.

Crittenden, and James S. Jackson, saw the president on Sunday, August 14, in an unsuccessful effort to get him to veto the bill. Despite some misgivings about the effect it might have on Kentucky's neutrality, Lincoln signed it.[5]

Much more serious was a proclamation issued on August 30, 1861, by Maj. Gen. John C. Fremont, the "Pathfinder of the West" and the Republicans' first presidential candidate. Commanding the Department of the West from St. Louis, Fremont declared martial law in Missouri, announced that civilians bearing arms would be tried by court-martial and executed if found guilty, and stated that slaves belonging to rebel owners in Missouri would be freed. Kentuckians reacted promptly and generally adversely to Fremont's proclamation. Editor Prentice called it "dangerous and odious, and should, we trust will be, promptly repudiated by the Government." Unionist E.T. Bainbridge implored Joseph Holt to use his influence to get the proclamation rescinded, for with it "the hopes of our best, most talented and sanguine Union men seems now almost destroyed." The pro-Southern *Louisville Courier* warned that the proclamation would be only the first of acts that would be taken to destroy slavery: "Remember Missouri, Kentuckians, and be ready."

Lincoln received a number of urgent protests and demands for repudiation of the offensive order. Joshua Speed reminded him, "Our Constitution and laws prohibit the emancipation of slaves among us—even in small numbers. If a military commander can turn them loose by the threat of a mere proclamation—it will be a most difficult matter to get our people to submit to it." Two days later Speed repeated his warning: "So fixed is public sentiment in this state against freeing Negroes . . . that you had as well attack the freedom of worship in the North or the right of a parent to teach his child to read as to wage war in the state on such principles." James Speed, Joshua's brother, warned that Fremont's foolish proclamation "will crush out every vistage of a union party in the state," and similar warnings came from other Unionists, such as Garrett Davis and Robert Anderson, in whom Lincoln had confidence.[6]

Fully aware of the dangers involved, the president moved swiftly to contain the damage. He sent by special messenger a "Private and Confidential" message of September 2, 1861, to Fremont. The general was ordered to shoot no one without the president's consent. Since the confiscation of property and the freeing of slaves "will alarm our Southern Union friends, and turn them against us—perhaps ruin our rather fair prospect for Kentucky," Lincoln asked "that you will as your own notion" modify your proclamation to conform with the congressional act of August 6 for the confiscation of property. "This letter is written in a spirit of caution and not of censure," the president added. A reasonable subordinate would have welcomed the opportunity to save face by modifying the objectionable order, but Fremont was too arrogant and self-righteous to take that course.[7]

Instead, in his reply of September 8 he asserted that his was the best policy. If the president still insisted that Fremont was wrong, "I have to ask that you will openly direct me to make the correction." His wife, the capable Jessica Benton Fremont, carried his reply to Washington. She arrived in Washington on the evening of September 10 and sent a message asking for an appointment to see the president. "Now, at once," he responded, and she hurried to the White House in a futile effort to change Lincoln's mind. He refused. The war was for "a great national idea, the Union, and . . . General Fremont should not have dragged the Negro into it." The next day Lincoln wrote Fremont. After reviewing their exchange, including his futile request that Fremont modify his proclamation, the President "very cheerfully" ordered the changes to be made. Although his action placated the Kentucky Unionists, it hurt Lincoln's relationship with antislavery groups that saw Fremont as a heroic martyr. Antislavery groups also blamed the state of Kentucky for insisting on the modification of the proclamation.

In a December 3, 1861, message to Congress, Lincoln indicated that arrangements should be made to provide for the slaves who would be freed under terms of the Confiscation Act of August 6. The problem would increase if some states passed similar enactments for themselves. To encourage such state action, he suggested that the states and the federal government might agree upon some plan for compensation for the slaves freed—perhaps a credit against taxes. Freeing slaves might be encouraged if freedom was followed by colonization "at some place or places in a climate congenial to them." Blacks already free might also be colonized outside the country. By late November Lincoln had drafted a bill for gradual, compensated emancipation in Delaware, but it was not introduced. James Speed introduced a bill in the Kentucky General Assembly in December 1861 that would allow the army to confiscate the slaves of Kentucky Confederates but then turn them over to the state for disposal. His bill met with strong opposition, and the Senate tabled it.[8]

By March 1862 Lincoln was ready to offer a more detailed scheme. On March 6 he sent Congress a draft resolution proposing that the United States cooperate with any state that agreed to the gradual emancipation of slaves by providing financial assistance. Then the president spelled out some of his ideas, though leaving states free to adopt different plans. If a state set a specific date for ending slavery—say, January 1, 1882—he would recommend a payment of $400 per person. The payments might be made in twenty annual installments of 6 percent government bonds. He calculated that 432,622 slaves in the four loyal slave states could be freed for $173 million, the approximate cost of eighty-seven days of the war.[9]

Few Kentuckians were convinced by Lincoln's figures. Loyal Kentuckians generally viewed the preservation of the Union as the paramount purpose of the war, and they resented any effort to bring about the end of slavery. The state's newspapers led the attack on Lincoln's proposal. The editor of the *Covington Journal* denied that slavery was the cause of the war: "Upon this same reasoning the timber of a house is the cause of the fire, and not the incendiary who fired it." The *Louisville Daily Democrat* concluded that "the radical Abolitionists are as good friends of the Constitution as the Secessionists.... We have long held the opinion that the anti-slavery leaders in this country are at heart Disunionists." After some consideration, the *Covington Journal* decided that Lincoln was being prodded into an anti-slavery position: "The extreme men of the Republican party are advancing step by step to the accomplishment of their long cherished purpose. The more moderate men of the party follow on, feebly protesting as they advance, but occupying today the ground that the radicals left yesterday." A correspondent to the *Frankfort Weekly Yeoman* of March 28, 1862, challenged Lincoln's estimate of the costs; a realistic price for Kentucky's slaves would make the program cost prohibitive. But the real point, he warned abolitionists, was that Kentuckians were opposed to emancipation, "that whenever they attempt this outrage upon humanity, the Kentucky soldiery, who are now fighting in the Federal army, will lay down their arms, or use them in defense of all they hold dear on earth, their wives, their mothers and their sisters." In December 1861, before emancipation became a major issue, a Louisville editor asserted that if the Kentucky slaves were freed, an army of two hundred thousand would be required "to retain Kentucky in the Union" and to help exterminate the black race. For if the slaves were freed, "they must be wiped out—totally obliterated. It must be a merciless, savage extermination.... The two races ... cannot exist in the same country, unless the black race is in slavery."[10]

Many Kentuckians echoed the editorial comments—or the editors echoed the sentiments of many Kentuckians, including ones who had never owned a slave and had no prospect of ever achieving that status. Lunsford Yandell Jr., who made an early decision to join the Confederacy, told family members in April 1861, "We are fighting for our liberty against tyrants of the North.... who are determined to destroy slavery." Methodist minister George Browder's diary contained frequent references to the slavery issue. "The people of Ky. if left to themselves will not vote for compensated or any other emancipation," he wrote on July 23, 1862. Later that year he revealed that he did not fear a slave insurrection in Kentucky as did some people in the neighborhood, but he predicted that the pending Emancipation Proclamation "will create division in the army & probably be the cause [of] many resignations and desertions." Before the end of 1863, Browder noted that thousands of slaves were deserting their masters and joining the Union army. "Our Governor," he complained, "offers no protection to the right of property & the president is opposed to any peace that does not destroy slavery. Times now look like slavery is doomed. If such be the will of God I say Amen—but I cannot so understand the Bible." Earlier in the war, Alfred Pirtle had threatened to resign his commission if President Lincoln moved against slavery despite his promises not to do so. But by the late summer of 1863 he seemed somewhat surprised that his opinion was changing. "The 'inexorable logic of events' is rapidly making practical abolitionists of every soldier," he wrote his sister. "I am afraid that I am getting to be an abolitionist. All right! better that than a Secessionist." Benjamin Jones, a private in the Twenty-first Kentucky Infantry Regiment, also saw the purpose of the war changing, but he could not accept it. "This is nothing but an abolition war," he complained to his brother. "I am a strait out Union and Constitution man, I am not for freeing the negroes."[11]

Kentuckians in Congress also attacked Lincoln's proposal. Crittenden asked why Kentuckians should be asked to give up their "domestic institution" when they had already done so much for the Union. No other state, he asserted, had made the sacrifice of friends and relatives to the rebel cause that Kentucky had made. Crittenden conceded that the president meant well and that he often agreed with him, "but I regret that in this my conscience and judgment will not permit it." Sen. Lazarus W. Powell called the plan "a pill of arsenic, sugar-coated" that hoped "to inaugurate abolition parties in the border slave states." He did not believe that the Northern states would ever pay adequate compensation for the slaves that were to be freed. Sen. Garrett Davis introduced an amendment to

Lincoln's proposal on March 24. It declared that a state had complete jurisdiction over slavery within its borders, but it pledged the United States to pay reasonable costs for emancipation and colonization in any state that chose to free its slaves. He declared that subsequent colonization was essential; Kentucky would not free slaves unless they were then removed from the state. His amendment was defeated in the Senate on March 26 by a vote of 4–34; Powell voted against it. On April 2, 1862, the Senate passed a joint resolution saying that the nation should provide unspecified financial assistance to states that adopted a plan for gradual emancipation. Davis voted for it; Powell opposed it.[12]

Several federal actions during the spring and summer of 1862 alarmed proslavery Kentuckians. On April 16 the president signed a bill providing for immediate compensated emancipation in the District of Columbia. Masters could apply to the federal government for as much as $300 for each slave freed, and $100,000 was appropriated for the colonization of slaves who desired to emigrate. Lincoln would have preferred gradual emancipation, and in an uncharacteristic act he was reputed to have delayed signing the bill until Rep. Charles A. Wickliffe of Kentucky had time to move two slave families out of the District so that they would not be freed. An act of June 19 abolished slavery in the territories without providing any compensation. Passage of the Second Confiscation Act and the Militia Act of July 17, 1862, also alarmed conservatives. The Confiscation Act defined rebels as traitors and ordered confiscation of their property, including the freeing of slaves. Lincoln considered vetoing the act. "It is startling to say that Congress can free a slave within a state," he protested; it violated the pledge made by the Republican party not to interfere with slavery in the states that had it. "Congress has no power over slavery in the states, and so much of it as remains after the war is over . . . must be left to the exclusive control of the state where it may exist." The Militia Act allowed harsh and sometimes illegal enforcement of the acts for the enlistment of soldiers.[13]

On July 12, 1862, President Lincoln made a major effort to secure support for compensated emancipation in the border states when he met at the White House with the members of Congress from those states and some from Tennessee and West Virginia, which was seeking admission as a state. There he read to them his appeal for cooperation. They had power to help determine how much longer the war would last. In his opinion, "if you all had voted for the resolution in the general emancipation message of last March, the war would now be substantially ended." Divest the rebel states of any hope that you will ever join them, and they will not be able to maintain the contest much longer. "You and I know what the lever of their power is. Break that lever before their faces, and they can shake you no more forever." Lincoln argued that he was not trying to invade states' rights; his proposal was simply the best course for the entire nation. Then Lincoln warned his audience of the results in their states if they rejected his proposal. "If this war continues long, as it must, if the object be not sooner attained, the institution in your states will be extinguished by mere friction and abrasion—by the mere incidents of the war. It will be gone, and you will have nothing valuable in lieu of it. Much of its value is already gone. How much better for you, and for your people, to take the step which, at once, shortens the war, and secures substantial compensation for that which is sure to be wholly lost in any other event." He assured them that he was not speaking of immediate emancipation; he was proposing "a *decision* at once to emancipate *gradually*." South America could provide room for cheap colonization, and he believed that freed blacks would choose to go there in large numbers.

Lincoln reminded the group that he had recently voided Gen. David Hunter's attempt to free and arm slaves in the South Atlantic states. By doing so, Lincoln asserted, he had lost the support of many persons whose support the country could not afford to lose. Pressure was increasing for him to do something about slavery. The "patriots and statesmen" to whom he was appealing could help by considering and discussing his

231

proposal and at least submitting it to their states and their people. They had an opportunity to help preserve popular government "for the best people in the world."[14]

His audience was not convinced by his arguments. The majority response, signed by twenty members of Congress, which reached him on July 14, rejected his appeal. His plan would entail more expense than the government could bear; it would consolidate the spirit of rebellion in the seceded states; it would encourage secession among loyal slaveholders in the border states; it would not lessen the pressure for the emancipation of 3 million slaves by proclamation, a step which they adamantly opposed. Although they pledged support of the war, they asked the president to restrict himself to his proper constitutional area—which did not include interfering with slavery in the states. The next day seven members of the group submitted a minority report; Samuel L. Casey was the only Kentucky member who signed it. They promised to "ask the people of the Border States, calmly, deliberately, and fairly to consider your recommendations." They pointed out that some Confederates had advocated abolishing slavery in return for foreign recognition. "If they can give up slavery to *destroy* the Union, we can surely ask our people to consider the question of emancipation to *save* the Union." On July 16 Horace Maynard of Tennessee sent the president an individual pledge of support for his plan.[15]

On July 22, when Lincoln presented his emancipation proclamation draft to his cabinet members for their consideration, his Kentucky friends Joshua and James Speed were in Washington. The president read them the draft and asked for their reaction; both of them advised against issuing it. Cassius M. Clay, back from Russia, advised Lincoln to issue it. Sent to Kentucky to ascertain the state's sentiment, Clay reported to the president that there would be no problem in Kentucky. He was wrong, for the reaction in Kentucky was largely adverse. Such generals as McClellan, Buell, and Halleck had been careful not to interfere with the rights of slaveholders, but before the end of 1862 many of the officers and soldiers stationed in the state were actively assisting slaves to escape from slavery. Kentucky was not covered by the Emancipation Proclamation, but after January 1, 1863, Lincoln was committed to the abolition of slavery as a major Union objective. He called upon all members of the army and navy to assist in carrying out the aims of a new article of war (March 13, 1862) and the Confiscation Act (July 17, 1862), which prohibited the return to their owners of slaves who had escaped and those who belonged to rebel owners.[16] One Kentucky soldier described the Emancipation Proclamation as "a most abominable, infamous document," which voided all of the president's pledges regarding slavery. "We find ourselves in arms to maintain doctrines, which, if announced 12 months ago, would have driven us all, not withstanding our loyalty to the Constitution & the Union, into the ranks of the Southern army." The editor of the *Frankfort Tri-Weekly Commonwealth* asserted that "the President's nigger proclamation ought to be crammed down his throat, if he will not withdraw it, as a flagrant violation of his official oath, according to his own declaration. We ought not to allow such a move to be made with impunity." The editor of the *Louisville Daily Democrat* declared that "if this rebellion is not put down, the fault will be at the door of a party that has abandoned the idea of doing that work, and gives its sole attention to abolishing slavery."[17]

Clashes were inevitable between Kentucky slaveholders who wanted to retain their slaves and Union officers and soldiers who wanted to see the slaves freed as soon as possible. Perhaps the most public of the encounters was between George Robertson, one of the state's most distinguished judges and political figures, and Col. William L. Utley, commander of the Twenty-second Wisconsin Infantry Regiment, stationed at Nicholasville, Kentucky. Utley said that Judge Robertson came to his camp and demanded the return of a Negro boy who was found with the regiment. Utley disclaimed any knowledge of how the boy came to be there, and he did not forbid Judge

Robertson from taking the boy with him. But Utley refused to deliver the youth beyond the regimental lines, and he would not order his soldiers not to interfere with the Judge's effort to recover the boy. The boy asked for protection from the cruel treatment he said he had received as a slave, and the Union soldiers refused to let him be carried away.[18]

Judge Robertson had Utley indicted in a Lexington court for violation of Kentucky laws concerning fugitive slaves. Then on November 19, 1862, Robertson telegraphed an appeal to President Lincoln. In a reply that was apparently drafted but not sent, Lincoln described the counterpressure that was growing in the North: "Do you not know that I may as well surrender this contest, directly, as to make any order, the obvious purpose of which would be to return fugitive slaves?" Utley had already written the president on November 17 in an appeal for protection from the Kentucky courts; he was being persecuted because he was obeying the laws of the United States. In a letter to a friend, the harassed colonel expressed some of the dislike that many Unionists had toward the commonwealth of Kentucky. "There is no such thing as unionism in Kentucky. . . . I wish Abraham Lincoln could hear what the professed union men call him. I told the Governor (Robinson) that all Kentuckeyans were either d——d traitors or cowards, that there was no loyalty in the state, that you might put it all in one end of the scales, and a niger baby in the other end, and Loyalty and unionism would go up with a rush. I have given them hell, and now they intend to give me h——l." Utley charged that the general officers in the state were in agreement to ignore the proclamation about not returning fugitive slaves to their alleged owners.

When Lincoln responded to Judge Robertson on November 26, he said that he understood that Colonel Utley had five slaves in his camp, four belonging to rebels and one to the Judge. In an unusual personal effort to resolve the dispute, Lincoln suggested that Robertson convey his slave to Utley, who would free him and "I will pay you any sum not exceeding five hundred dollars." The judge was not appeased by the president's personal offer. In his reply of December 1, 1862, he said that Lincoln had been misinformed and thus misunderstood Robertson's motives in the affair. "I had put Col. Utley in the position which I preferred, and I had neither intended nor desired to seek any. . . . intervention in . . . my own case. . . . The citation in my civil suit against him having been served, I can certainly obtain a judgment for $1,000 and perhaps more. . . . My object in that suit was far from mercenary—it was solely to try the question whether the civil or the military power is Constitutionally supreme in Kentucky." In addition to opposing Lincoln's Emancipation Proclamation of September 22, 1862, Judge Robertson objected to Lincoln's proclamation of September 24, which suspended the writ of habeas corpus for persons arrested by military authorities and made those who gave aid and comfort to the rebels subject to martial law and military courts. Judge Robertson pressed his case against Colonel Utley, and on October 6, 1871, the U.S. Circuit Court for the Eastern District of Wisconsin gave the determined plaintiff a judgment for $908.06 and court costs of $26.40. An act of Congress on February 14, 1873, authorized the secretary of the treasury to pay those sums, plus interest, for the relief of Colonel Utley.[19] This was only one of several cases that involved the status of Kentucky blacks who were trying to escape slavery.

From September 1861, when Kentucky became involved in the war, blacks had been used extensively in the Civil War for the support of military units and for labor on military projects. Many blacks went to Union camps to earn money, and some antislavery soldiers and officers encouraged them to leave their masters and protected them from efforts to secure their return. During the first two years of the war, the Union did not have a consistent policy concerning such fugitives who entered the Union lines. The way they were handled depended largely upon the local situation and the sentiments of the officers and men with whom they associated. When large numbers of laborers were needed, the army impressed slaves. The first recourse was to take slaves from rebels and Confederate sympathizers; but as the need increased, slaves were impressed from Unionists as well. Wages were paid to Union owners; the impressed slaves who belonged to pro-Confederates received wages and subsistence for themselves. Given this taste of freedom, many never returned to their masters. Among the major projects were the erection of fortifications, the construction of military roads, and the building of railroads. On August 10, 1863, General Boyle, who had used some slave labor previously, ordered the impressment of six thousand men from the central counties to work on a railroad between Lebanon and Danville. Owners who disobeyed the order were liable to lose all their male slaves between the ages of sixteen and forty-five. On Sunday evening, December 13, 1863, soldiers seized all of the male worshipers as they left a black church in Lexington and sent them off to work on military roads.[20]

The growing demand for manpower in the Union army and navy finally convinced Lincoln that use must be made of blacks. The Emancipation Proclamation provided for the use of blacks in somewhat restricted noncombat roles, and the president pushed the use of such troops in the spring of 1863. "The bare sight of fifty thousand armed and drilled black soldiers on the banks of the Mississippi," Lincoln predicted, "would end the rebellion at once." When Frederick Douglass had his first interview with Lincoln on August 10, 1863, he protested the pay discrimination against black soldiers. Lincoln explained that there was still so much opposition to the use of black troops that "the fact that they were not to receive the same pay as white soldiers, seemed a necessary concession to smooth the way to the employment at all of soldiers; but ultimately they would all receive the same."[21]

When Lincoln authorized the use of black troops in December 1862, he exempted Kentucky from the order, but during the next several months a number of Kentucky slaves enlisted in the Union army at points outside the state. Kentucky protested this practice, but Governor Bramlette, when he ordered a recruiting agent to cease his activities in the state, asserted, "I am well assured that in deference to our public position, and to avoid unnecessarily aggravating the troubles of loyal men of Kentucky, the authorities at Washington do not contemplate recruiting 'colored men' in Kentucky." The General Assembly warned the federal government against using black soldiers and demanded that no camps be set up in the state that would entice slaves to leave their masters.

But by March 1864 the demand for troops was so acute that Kentucky lost some of the favoritism that Lincoln had shown toward that commonwealth. Bramlette accepted the recruitment of blacks to make up the portion of the state's quota that had been left unfilled by whites. However, the federal government at first promised to enroll only free blacks and slaves who applied for inclusion. Loyal owners received certificates for payments of $300 for each slave received, and enlistees were taken to training camps outside the state. Some owners with prescience saw the end of slavery and enrolled their slaves who were qualified for military duty; some masters even claimed a bounty payment for them. After July 1864 the government paid the bounty to a slave who volunteered. A number of white Kentuckians and Northerners from nearby states used Kentucky blacks as substitutes to avoid military service.[22]

The enrollment and enlistment of blacks met intense opposition within the state. Governor Bramlette came close to rebellion before finally advising Kentuckians to accept what was being done. Col. Frank Wolford became a commonwealth hero in the eyes of many Kentuckians by his outspoken opposition to the use of black troops. Arrested and denied a trial, he was dishonorably discharged from the army he had served well. When Governor Bramlette, ex-senator Archibald Dixon, and editor Albert G. Hodges went to Washington in March 1864, they asked the president to halt the enlistment of blacks in the state, for it would practically end the enlistment of white Kentuckians. They received some concessions: Kentucky's quota of soldiers would be adjusted to take into account the large number of men who had joined the Confederate army, and when black troops were enlisted in the state, it would be done with as much circumspection as possible.[23]

This meeting had an interesting by-product: it produced one of Lincoln's most comprehensive statements about the way he saw his role in the war and his views on slavery and the war. After he and the three Kentucky emissaries reached an amicable agreement, Lincoln asked if he could make a little speech. Hodges, editor of the *Frankfort Commonwealth*, returned that afternoon and asked the president for a copy of his remarks to take back to Kentucky. Lincoln had not written out his remarks, and he did not have time to do so then, but he promised to send them to Hodges as soon as he could write them out. True to his promise, he wrote the editor on April 4, 1864. His letter gave Kentuckians one of the president's clearest explanations on several important issues.

> I am naturally anti-slavery. If slavery is not wrong, nothing is wrong. I can not remember when I did not so think, and feel. And yet I have never understood that the Presidency conferred upon me an unrestrained right to act officially upon this judgment and feeling. It was in the oath I took that I would, to the best of my ability, preserve, protect, and defend the Constitution of the United States. I could not take the office without taking the oath. Nor was it my view that I might take the oath to get power, and break the oath in using the power. I understood, too, that in ordinary civil administration this oath even forbade me to practically indulge my primary abstract judgment on the moral question of slavery. I had publicly declared this many times, and in many ways. And I aver that, to this day, I have done no official act in mere deference to my abstract judgment and feeling on slavery. I did understand, however, that my oath to preserve the constitu-

tion to the best of my ability, imposed on me the duty of preserving, by every indispensable means, that government—that nation—of which that constitution was the organic law. Was it possible to lose the nation, and yet preserve the constitution? By general law life *and* limb must be protected; yet often a limb must be amputated to save a life; but a life is never wisely given to save a limb. I felt that measures, otherwise unconstitutional, might become lawful, by being indispensable to the preservation of the constitution, through the preservation of the nation. Right or wrong, I assumed this ground, and now avow it. I could not feel that, to the best of my ability, I had even tried to preserve the constitution, if, to save slavery, or any minor matter, I would permit the wreck of government, country, and Constitution all together. When, early in the war, Gen. Fremont attempted military emancipation, I forbade it, because I did not then think it an indispensable necessity. When a little later, Gen. Cameron, then Secretary of War, suggested the arming of the blacks, I objected, because I did not yet think it an indispensable necessity. When, still later, Gen. Hunter attempted military emancipation, I again forbade it, because I did not yet think the indispensable necessity had come. When, in March, and May, and July 1862 I made earnest and successive appeals to the border states to favor compensated emancipation, I believed the indispensable necessity for military emancipation, and arming the blacks would come, unless averted by that move. They declined the proposition; and I was, in my best judgment, driven to the alternative of either surrendering the Union and with it, the Constitution, or of laying strong hand upon the colored element. I chose the latter. In choosing it, I hoped for greater gain than loss; but of this, I was not entirely confident. More than a year of trial now shows no loss by it in our foreign relations,

nor in our home popular sentiment, none in our white
military force,—no loss by it any how or any where. On
the contrary, it shows a gain of quite a hundred and
thirty thousand soldiers, seamen, and laborers. These
are palpable facts, about which, as facts, there can be
no caviling. We have the men; and we could not have
had them without the measure.

And now let any Union man who complains of the
measure, test himself by writing down in one line that
he is for subduing the rebellion by force of arms; and
in the next, that he is for taking these hundred and
thirty thousand men from the Union side, and placing
them where they would be but for the measure he con-
demns. If he can not face his case so stated, it is only
because he can not face the truth.

I add a word which was not in the verbal conversation. In telling this tale I attempt no compliment to
my own sagacity. I claim not to have controlled events,
but confess plainly that events have controlled me. Now,
at the end of three years struggle the nation's condition is not what either party, or any man, devised, or
expected. God alone can claim it. Whither it is tend-
ing seems plain. If God now wills the removal of a great
wrong, and wills also that we of the North as well as
you of the South, shall pay dearly for our complicity
in that wrong, impartial history will find therein new
cause to attest and revere the justice and goodness of
God.[24]

In his acknowledgment of the receipt of Lincoln's letter,
Hodges promised to give it to the people of Kentucky at the
proper time. He had shown it to a number of prominent Union
men, "and I have met but one as yet who dissents from your
reasoning upon the subject of slavery." Hodges reported "receiving information of your steady gain upon the gratitude and
confidence of the People of Kentucky," and he predicted that

Lincoln would *"flax them out handsomely."*[25] That prediction was wrong, for in the presidential election later that year McClellan defeated Lincoln in Kentucky by a wide margin. Most Kentuckians were not converted to acceptance of Lincoln's scheme of compensated emancipation. Nor did they enlist in sufficient numbers to fill the state's quota from the white population.

The initial rush of Kentucky blacks to join the Union army declined after the first few months, and by early 1864 army units, often consisting largely of black soldiers, were used to impress slaves to get the number needed. This process worked much like the infamous British naval press gangs in the Napoleonic era. The departure of many farm laborers resulted in drastic declines in state crops. Tobacco production decreased 57 percent, wheat 63 percent, barley 15 percent, hemp 80 percent. The assessed value of Kentucky slaves in 1860 was $107,494,527; by 1864 it was $34,179,466; and in 1865 it was only $7,224,851 and falling. Some owners complained that the slaves who remained were becoming intractable and more insubordinate. In early March 1865 the federal government ruled that the wives and children of black soldiers were also free, and soon the government estimated that 71 percent of Kentucky's slaves of 1860 were free. President Lincoln had been correct when he warned the representatives of the loyal slave states that unless they accepted his plan for compensated emancipation, the abrasion of war would bring an end to the institution and leave them with nothing to show for it. Editor George Prentice was honest enough to admit that slavery was practically dead. "Kentucky slavery is now worth less than nothing," he wrote in the spring of 1865. "While we have it nominally, there is really no involuntary servitude among us, there is no earthly hope of our having genuine slavery in our State again."[26] But some Kentuckians, citing the Constitution and the laws of the state and the promises made by President Lincoln during the early days of the war, stubbornly refused to accept the inevitable.

The army later reported that Kentucky supplied 23,703

black troops, more than any other state except Louisiana. That number was 56.5 percent of the eligible male slaves and free-men between the ages of eighteen and forty-five in the state. Of that number, 97 percent listed their occupation as farmer or laborer. The medical enlistment examinations found the black soldiers to be remarkably healthy—in many respects healthier and stronger than the white recruits in the state. A Covington doctor, E.P. Bucknor, who examined approximately sixteen hundred black recruits, disqualified only 10 percent; he con-cluded that the blacks had fewer disabilities than the men of other races. Their teeth were nearly always perfect, but their eyesight was generally inferior to that of whites, and they were more afflicted by rheumatism than whites.[27]

Lincoln doubted that the Emancipation Proclamation would provide permanent freedom for the slaves in the Con-federacy. Its legal justification was that it was a war measure; when peace came, the courts might declare it unconstitutional or a new administration might revoke it. And it did not apply to the slaves in the loyal border states. In his annual message to Congress on December 1, 1862, Lincoln proposed adding three amendments to the Constitution. The first would pay states in U.S. bonds if they abolished slavery by January 1, 1900. The second guaranteed freedom to slaves who achieved it "by the chances of the war," but it authorized payment to loyal owners. The third authorized Congress to provide appropria-tions for the colonization of "free colored persons with their own consent, at any place or places within the United States." The president argued strongly for his proposals. If it was to work, it needed to be started before he issued his Emancipa-tion Proclamation in final form on January 1, 1863. His propos-als were not accepted by Congress or by the individual states, and during the next two years Congress refused to accept by the required two-thirds vote the proposed Thirteenth Amendment to abolish slavery. Lincoln undertook intensive personal lobby-ing to secure passage. A joint resolution was introduced in the Senate on January 11, 1864, debated, amended, and passed on

April 11, 1864. After the House refused to give it the necessary two-thirds majority, Lincoln insisted that passage of the amendment be included in the 1864 platform of the Union Party, which nominated him for a second term. The House of Representatives finally passed the joint resolution January 31, 1865, by a vote of 119 to 56 with eight members not voting. Although his signature was not required, the relieved president signed the resolution and forwarded copies to the state governors.

In Kentucky Governor Bramlette sent the proposed amendment to the General Assembly without a direct recommendation. Instead, he sought to link approval with the compensation that the state would have received had it accepted Lincoln's earlier proposal. Pointing out that England had appropriated some $100 million in 1833 when slavery was abolished in the British Empire, Bramlette insisted, "It cannot be that *our* government will be less just." He suggested that Kentucky might ratify the amendment upon condition that the 1864 assessed value of slaves be paid to the state to compensate owners. The assessed value of $107,494,527 in 1860 had declined to only $34,179,246 in 1864. On February 20, 1865, Sen. Henry D. McHenry made an unfavorable report from the Judiciary Committee, to which the proposal had been assigned. John F. Fisk made a substitute motion that the amendment be ratified but that Kentucky's members of Congress urge that compensation for the loss of slaves be made to loyal men who had neither participated in the rebellion nor had given aid and comfort to it. Ex-governor James F. Robinson presented a minority report from the committee. It called for ratification upon payment of $36,530,496 as compensation for all slaves enlisted or drafted in the army and for all other claims growing out of the labor and services of the slaves. All slavery laws in the state were to be repealed, and the freed blacks should thereafter "have all of the rights, responsibilities, and privileges of free-born colored persons," but they had to leave the state within ten years of their emancipation. The Senate accepted the majority report to reject the amendment by a vote of 21–13.[28]

In the House of Representatives, E.C. Smith moved on February 11 that the issue of ratification be submitted to the voters in the August election. William R. Kinney submitted the same motion for ratification, contingent upon payment of the 1864 value of slaves, that Fisk had made in the Senate. On February 17 James F. Lacur proposed that the amendment be rejected, and that was done on February 23 by a 56–28 vote. The governor sent the General Assembly a message on March 1; in his opinion, the rejection simply remitted the question to the next and succeeding legislatures until the amendment was ratified.[29]

During the debates in the legislature, its members were bombarded with demands from citizens across the state. Editor Prentice tried vainly to get his fellow Kentuckians to accept reality. He saw an "irresistible current of popular opinion sweeping on to the overthrow of slavery," and only a foolish person would get in its way. The death of slavery, he predicted, would end "the most fruitful source of political strife in America." For practical purposes, slavery had already ceased to exist in Kentucky. But Prentice did not convince the majority of his Kentucky readers. The many protests against ratification that reached the members of the General Assembly helped defeat the amendment. Efforts in the May session to reopen the issue failed. Even after the amendment was ratified by the required three-fourths of the states on December 18, 1865, Kentucky still refused to add her endorsement. Nevertheless, slavery in the state was dying; in May 1865 the Boone County tax assessors listed the number of remaining slaves but did not indicate a value for them.[30] When tax collectors give up, not much remains.

Even as he sent the Thirteenth Amendment to the states for ratification, Lincoln continued to think in terms of using compensation to lure the rebellious states back into the Union and to get their acceptance of the end of slavery. On February 5, 1865, the president showed his cabinet the draft of a joint resolution that would allow the president to pay $400 million to the sixteen states that had slavery, provided that all resistance to the national authority ceased by April 1. Half of that sum (in 6 percent government bonds) would be paid if the Thirteenth Amendment was ratified by July 1. The president would pardon all political offenses, and property, except for slaves, that was liable to confiscation and forfeiture would be released, unless a third party had interests. In a wry endorsement to the document, Lincoln wrote: "To-day these papers, which explain themselves, were drawn up and submitted to the Cabinet & unanimously disapproved by them."[31]

Lincoln was disappointed by the refusal of Kentucky to accept a scheme of voluntary, compensated emancipation and by the state's rejection of the Thirteenth Amendment to the Constitution. He had also been disappointed in 1861 when his birth state was hesitant in declaring her stand with the Union. His acceptance of Kentucky's neutrality until the Unionists were able to establish firm control in the state had succeeded in holding Kentucky in the Union. He would have liked stronger support from Kentuckians during the course of the war, especially in regard to freeing slaves and the use of black soldiers, and he would have liked to have carried the state in the 1864 presidential election. The continued opposition in Kentucky to many of his policies caused him to devote attention there that could have been well spent elsewhere. But Lincoln understood Kentucky and Kentuckians, and the state had made significant contributions to the winning of the war.

With the end of the war and the end of slavery at last in sight, the president directed more of his attention to plans for the reconstruction of the Union when the Southern states would regain their proper relationship. His policy would be a mild one, aimed at completing the process as easily and quickly as possible, although it was evident that some members of his own party would demand a harsher and slower reconstruction policy. That battle remained to be fought.

On April 4 Lincoln and his son Tad visited Richmond, so recently abandoned by the Confederate army and government.

The president was acclaimed by crowds of happy blacks, now free from slavery. "Bless the Lord, there is the great Messiah! . . . Glory Hallelujah!" a black workman shouted, and he and others fell to their knees in an effort to kiss the president's feet. As Lincoln walked through the Richmond streets, crowds of happy blacks shouted, "Bless the Lord, Father Abraham's Come!" In the Confederate White House he sat in Jefferson Davis's chair, then visited the statehouse where the Confederate Congress had met and Libby Prison, which had housed many Union prisoners. During his visit Lincoln spoke about reconstruction with John A. Campbell, once a member of the Supreme Court, more recently the Confederate assistant secretary of war.[32] Back in Washington, Lincoln learned on the evening of April 9 that Lee had surrendered to Grant at Appomattox. Two nights later he spoke from a White House window to a celebrating crowd about his desire for a quick and easy reconstruction of the South.

President Lincoln did not live to see the end of slavery or the surrender of the last of the Confederate armies, although both goals were clearly in sight. On the evening of April 14, 1865, he and his wife went to Ford's Theatre to see *Our American Cousin*.

Notes

Abbreviations

Collected Works   Roy B. Basler, ed., *The Collected Works of Abraham Lincoln,* 9 vols., 2 supplements (1953–90).

FCHQ   Filson Club History Quarterly.

OR   War of the Rebellion: A Compilation of the Official Records of the Union and Confederate Armies, 128 vols. (1880–1901).

Register   *Register of the Kentucky Historical Society*

1. Lincoln in Kentucky's Memory

1. David Herbert Donald, *Lincoln* (1995), 592.

2. Both Lincoln quotations in ibid., 593. Nasby was the pseudonym for David L. Locke. *The Nasby Papers* had been published in 1864.

3. Donald, *Lincoln,* 594; Stephen B. Oates, *With Malice toward None; The Life of Abraham Lincoln* (1977), 427–29.

4. Donald, *Lincoln,* 595. Much that has been written about Lincoln's assassination deals with the conspiracy. Among the best of the modern studies that focus on Lincoln's last day are W. Emerson Reck, *A. Lincoln: His Last 24 Hours* (1987); Jim Bishop, *The Day Lincoln Was Shot* (1955); and Ralph Borreson, *When Lincoln Died* (1965). The reason accounts differ in detail may be understood by reading Timothy S. Good, *We Saw Lincoln Shot: One Hundred Eyewitness Accounts* (1995). One account was taken as late as 1954.

5. Donald, *Lincoln,* 585–88; quotation on 588.

6. Ibid., 596–97.

7. Reck, *Last 24 Hours,* 116–31, Rathborn quoted on 112, Booth quoted on 107–8, Leale quoted on 120; Donald, *Lincoln,* 597–99, Mary Lincoln quoted on 597.

8. Reck, *Last 24 Hours,* 81–92, 132. Rathbone and Clara Harris married in 1867. He never recovered from the shock of Lincoln's death

and his own injury; on December 25, 1883, he killed his wife when they were in Hanover, Germany.

9. Ibid., 136–53.

10. Ibid., 148, 157.

11. Ibid., 157, 159.

12. *Collected Works,* 4:190–91. There are several slightly different versions of this speech. This one was written on the train after it left the station, partly by Lincoln, partly by John Nicolay.

13. Donald, *Lincoln,* 272.

14. Ibid., 38–60.

15. Ibid., 23–36.

16. William Moody Pratt Diaries, Special Collections, Univ. of Kentucky.

17. Quoted in Willard Rouse Jillson, *Lincoln Back Home* (1932), 85–86.

18. Copy in Governor Bramlette's Correspondence, State Library and Archives, Frankfort, Ky.

19. Jillson, *Lincoln Back Home,* 111, 113, 114.

20. Ibid., 89, 103–4.

21. Ibid., 139, 156.

22. William H. Townsend, *Lincoln and the Bluegrass: Slavery and Civil War in Kentucky* (1955), 356. This is an expanded and revised version of his *Lincoln and His Wife's Home Town* (1929).

23. "Give me a child for the first seven years, and you may do what you like with him afterwards," quoted in Angela Partington, ed., *The Oxford Dictionary of Quotations,* 4th ed. (1992).

24. Merrill D. Peterson, *Lincoln in American Memory* (1994), 177–79. The bizarre story of the logs of the Lincoln Memorial cabin has been traced in Roy Hays, "Is the Lincoln Birthplace Cabin Authentic?" *Abraham Lincoln Quarterly* 5 (September 1948): 127–63; Louis A. Warren, "The Authenticity of Lincoln's Birthplace Cabin: The Jacob S. Brothers Tradition," *Lincoln Lore* 1016 (September 27, 1948): 1; and Louis A. Warren, "The Authenticity of Lincoln's Birthplace Cabin: The John A. Davenport Tradition," *Lincoln Lore* 1019 (October 18, 1948): 1.

25. Peterson, *Lincoln in American Memory,* 179–83.

26. *Louisville Courier-Journal,* November 20, 1997.

2. A Kentucky Boyhood

1. Anthony Gross, comp., *Wit and Wisdom of Abraham Lincoln* (1994), 11; Donald, *Lincoln,* 19. Lincoln's reference was to Thomas Gray, "Elegy Written in a Country Churchyard."

2. "The Scripp's 'Campaign Life,'" *Lincoln Lore* 1532 (October 1965): 1–2.

3. Louis A. Warren, "Lincoln's Autobiographies," *Lincoln Lore* 2 (August 26, 1929): 1.

4. W.H. Herndon and J.W. Weik, *Life of Lincoln* (1936), 2–3, xl.

5. William E. Barton, *The Women Lincoln Loved* (1927), 3–32; Donald, *Lincoln*, 23; Benjamin P. Thomas, *Abraham Lincoln, A Biography* (1952), 6. However, Adin Baber, *Nancy Hanks, the Destined Mother of a President* (1963), vii, 73, believed that Nancy was the legitimate daughter of Abraham and Sarah Hanks, both of whom died in Virginia while she was a child.

6. Oates, *With Malice toward None*, 5; W.H. Herndon and J.W. Weik, *Abraham Lincoln, The True Story of a Great Life* (1924), 13–14.

7. Louis A. Warren, "Abraham Lincoln, Senior, Grandfather of the President," *FCHQ* 5 (July 1931): 136–52.

8. Ibid.; Donald, *Lincoln*, 20–21. President Lincoln said that his father repeated this story so often it "more strongly than all others imprinted upon my mind and memory." The president erred in citing 1784 as the year of his grandfather's death.

9. Lincoln to Solomon Lincoln, March 6, 1848, *Collected Works*, 1:455–56; Lincoln to Jesse W. Fell, December 20, 1859, "Enclosing Autobiography," *Collected Works*, 3:511–12; "Autobiography Written for John L. Scripps," June 1860, *Collected Works*, 4:60–61.

10. Woodrow Wilson, *Division and Reunion, 1829–1889* (1893), 216.

11. John Y. Simon, *House Divided: Lincoln and His Father* (1987), 3–16; Donald, *Lincoln*, 21–22; Oates, *With Malice toward None*, 36.

12. Louis A. Warren, "Thomas Lincoln–Nancy Hanks Nuptials, Date and Place," *Lincoln Lore* 1418 (June 11, 1956): 1; C.W. Hackensmith, "Lincoln's Family and His Teachers," *Register* 67 (October 1969): 323–24.

13. Louis A. Warren, "Mr. and Mrs. Thomas Lincoln at Home," *Lincoln Lore* 1105 (June 12, 1950): 1.

14. "Autobiography for Scripps," *Collected Works*, 4:61–62; Donald, *Lincoln*, 22.

15. Statistics are from Lowell H. Harrison and James C. Klotter, *A New History of Kentucky* (1997), 99, 100; Louis A. Warren, "The Religious Background of the Lincoln Family," *FCHQ* 6 (April 1932): 79–85.

16. "Autobiography for Scripps," *Collected Works*, 4:61; Louis A. Warren, "The Knob Creek Farm—Playground of Lincoln," *Lincoln Lore* 411 (February 22, 1937): 1.

17. Louis A. Warren, "Pike's Arithmetic," *Lincoln Lore* 67 (July 21, 1930): l; Lincoln on the aggregate of his schooling quoted in Louis A. Warren, "Abraham Lincoln's School Days," *Lincoln Lore* 283 (September 30, 1934): 1; Louis A. Warren, "Lincoln's Primary Education," *Lincoln Lore* 1116 (August 28, 1950): 1; Donald, *Lincoln*, 23; Hackensmith, "Lincoln's Family and Teachers," 325–26.

3. Kentuckians in Indiana

1. Thomas, *Lincoln*, 8–10.
2. "Autobiography for Scripps," *Collected Works*, 4:62.
3. Ibid.
4. Joseph E. Suppiger, "The Intimate Lincoln: Part II: Growing Up in Indiana," *Lincoln Herald* 83 (summer 1981): 671.
5. Donald, *Lincoln*, 25–26.
6. Ibid., 26.
7. Ibid.; Oates, *With Malice toward None*, 8–9.
8. Thomas, *Lincoln*, 11–12; Charles H. Coleman, "Sarah Bush Lincoln, the Mother Who Survived Him," *Lincoln Herald* 54 (summer 1952): 13–18; Barton, *Women Lincoln Loved*, 98–194; R. Gerald McMurtry, "The Patton House, Elizabethtown, Kentucky," *Lincoln Lore* 1952 (October 1970): 1–3.
9. Coleman, "Sarah Bush Lincoln," 14; "Mrs. Thomas Lincoln's Statement to William Herndon, September 8, 1865," in Emanuel Hertz, *The Hidden Lincoln: From the Letters and Papers of William H. Herndon* (1938), 351; Coleman, "Sarah Bush Lincoln," 19.
10. Simon, *House Divided*, 10–11; Deed to John D. Johnston, August 12, 1851, and Lincoln to John D. Johnston, November 9, 1851, *Collected Works*, 2:108–9, 111–12.
11. Simon, *House Divided*, 12–13; Lincoln to John D. Johnston, November 25, 1851, *Collected Works*, 2:113.
12. Simon, *House Divided*, 14–15; Lincoln to John D. Johnston, January 12, 1851, *Collected Works*, 2:96–97.
13. Simon, *House Divided*, 17–18.
14. Ibid., 18, 21, 20.
15. "Autobiography for Scripps," *Collected Works*, 4:62; Donald, *Lincoln*, 29–30; Lincoln to Jesse B. Fall, "Enclosing Autobiography," December 20, 1859, *Collected Works*, 3:511. The "Rule of Three" was a method of finding the fourth term of a proportion when the other three are given, the numbers being so arranged that the first is to the second as the third is to the unknown fourth. Lincoln multiplied the second and third numbers together and divided the result by the third. Warren, "Pike's Arithmetic," 1.
16. Donald, *Lincoln*, 28–32, Sally Lincoln on Lincoln's memory quoted on 29, Sally Lincoln on Lincoln's reading quoted on 33; Warren, "Abraham Lincoln's School Days," 1; Louis A. Warren, "Lincoln's Background of Borrowed Books," *Lincoln Lore* 1073 (October 31, 1949): 1; Hackensmith, "Lincoln's Family and Teachers," 330–34; Hartz, *Hidden Lincoln*, 346-51, Hanks quoted on 346, 351; Lincoln's doggerel quoted in Thomas, *Lincoln*, 15.
17. Oates, *With Malice toward None*, 10, 13; Donald, *Lincoln*, 32–33.

18. "Autobiography for Scripps," *Collected Works*, 4:62; Suppiger, "Growing Up in Indiana," 676; Thomas, *Lincoln*, 17–18.

19. "Autobiography for Scripps," *Collected Works*, 4:63; Thomas, *Lincoln*, 19–21.

20. Donald, *Lincoln*, 36–37.

21. Ibid., 37, 39.

4. Kentuckians in Illinois

1. Joseph G. Suppiger, "The Intimate Lincoln: Part III: On the Illinois Frontier," *Lincoln Herald* 83 (fall 1981): 740–44; Abraham Lincoln, "Communication to the People of Sangamo County," *Collected Works*, 1:5–9; Donald, *Lincoln*, 38–46.

2. Suppiger, "Illinois Frontier," 744–46; Thomas, *Lincoln*, 30–34.

3. Joseph G. Suppiger, "The Intimate Lincoln: Part IV: From New Salem to Vandalia," *Lincoln Herald* 83 (winter 1981): 775–80; Donald, *Lincoln*, 46–53, 53; Lincoln on his position as postmaster quoted in "Autobiography for Scripps," *Collected Works*, 4:65; Betty Carolyn Congleton, "George D. Prentice: Nineteenth Century Southern Editor," *Register* 65 (April 1967): 94–119; Thomas, *Lincoln*, 35–42.

4. Donald, *Lincoln*, 53; Thomas, *Lincoln*, 42–43.

5. Robert L. Kincaid, "Joshua Fry Speed, 1814–1882: Abraham Lincoln's Most Intimate Friend," *FCHQ* 17 (April 1943): 63–68.

6. Thomas, *Lincoln*, 45–49, 52–56, 58–64; Suppiger, "From New Salem to Vandalia," 781–85. The career of Douglas is well described in Robert W. Johannsen, *Stephen A. Douglas* (1973).

7. Louis A. Warren, "Lincoln Stumps Kentucky," *Register* 27 (May 1929): 545–47; George B. Simpson, "Abe Lincoln's 1840 Kentucky Political Speech and the Whig Presidential Campaign of 1840 in Southern Illinois," 1989, Kentucky Library, Western Kentucky Univ., typed manuscript.

8. Donald, *Lincoln*, 70–74, 86; Joseph G. Suppiger, "The Intimate Lincoln: Part V: Life in Springfield, 1837–1840," *Lincoln Herald* 84 (spring 1982): 27–36; Thomas, *Lincoln*, 54–55, 67, 92–95.

9. Joseph G. Suppiger, "The Intimate Lincoln: Part VI: Life in Springfield, 1840–1847," *Lincoln Herald* 84 (summer 1982): 118–19, 121; Thomas, *Lincoln*, 95–96, 110; Donald, *Lincoln*, 88, 96–100; Oates, *With Malice toward None*, 58–59, 69, 71. The quotations are from Donald, *Lincoln*, 98, 99.

10. Paul M. Angle, ed., *Herndon's Life of Lincoln*, (1965), vii–xlvi; Don Davenport, *In Lincoln's Footsteps: A Historical Guide to the Lincoln Sites in Illinois, Indiana & Kentucky* (1991); Donald, *Lincoln*, 101–2, 103, 100–106, 142–46, 159–60, 160, 401; Thomas, *Lincoln*, 96–100, 156; Benjamin P. Thomas, *Portrait for Posterity: Lincoln and His Biographers* (1947), 9–14, 132–59.

11. Donald, *Lincoln,* 103–4; Oates, *With Malice toward None,* 101–2.

12. Lincoln to Richard S. Thomas, February 14, 1843, *Collected Works,* 1:307.

13. Donald, *Lincoln,* 109–15; Handbill, "To the Voters of the Seventh Congressional District," July 31, 1846, *Collected Works,* 1:382; Lincoln to Allen N. Ford, editor of the *Lacon, Illinois Gazette,* August 11, 1846, *Collected Works,* 1:383–84; Suppiger, "Life in Springfield, 1840–1847," 121–23.

14. Quoted in Donald, *Lincoln,* 123.

15. Townsend, *Lincoln and the Bluegrass,* 123–40; Lincoln to Jesse Lynch, April 10, 1848, *Collected Works,* 1:463–64: Donald, *Lincoln,* 118–30.

16. Quoted in Glyndon G. Van Deusen, *The Life of Henry Clay* (1937), 391.

17. Quoted in "What General Taylor Ought to Say," [March ?] 1848, *Collected Works,* 1:454; "Speech in the U.S. House of Representatives on the Presidential Question," July 27, 1848, *Collected Works,* 1:501–16; Donald, *Lincoln,* 127–30.

18. Donald, *Lincoln,* 131–32; Joseph G. Suppiger, "The Intimate Lincoln: Part VII: Congressman and Family Man," *Lincoln Herald* 84 (fall 1982): 159–60.

19. "Remarks and Resolution Introduced in the United States House of Representatives concerning Abolition of Slavery in the District of Columbia," January 10, 1849, *Collected Works,* 2:20–22.

20. Lincoln to Joshua F. Speed, February 20, 1849, *Collected Works,* 2:28–29; Lincoln to Zachary Taylor, February 27, 1849, *Collected Works,* 2:30; Lincoln to William M. Meredith, March 9, 1849, *Collected Works,* 2:32; and numerous other requests to members of the Taylor administration; Donald, *Lincoln,* 137–40, 138.

21. Donald, *Lincoln,* 139–41; Lincoln to Joseph Gillespie, July 13, 1849 (two letters), *Collected Works,* 2:57–59; Lincoln to John M. Clayton, secretary of state, August 21, 1849, *Collected Works,* 2:61; Lincoln to Thomas Ewing, September 27, 1849, *Collected Works,* 2:65; Thomas, *Lincoln,* 128–29; Oates, *With Malice toward None,* 87–89.

5. Lincoln and Romance

1. Barton, *Women Lincoln Loved,* 172–78; Herndon and Weik, *Lincoln,* 106–8; Ida Tarbell, *The Early Life of Abraham Lincoln* (1896, 1974), 209–12.

2. Roy P. Basler, *The Lincoln Legend* (1935, 1980), 148–61; Herndon and Weik, *Lincoln,* 112–14; Carl Sandburg, *Abraham Lincoln, The Prairie Years,* 2 vols. (1926), 1:140–41, 185–190. Herndon said that McNamar returned to New Salem in the fall of 1835, accompanied by his mother and siblings.

3. Don E. Fehrenbacher and Virginia Fehrenbacher, comps., *Recollected Words of Abraham Lincoln* (1996), William G. Greene and Elizabeth Abell, 184, Isaac Cogdal, 111.

4. After a careful study of Herndon's sources relating to Ann Rutledge, Douglas L. Wilson found substantial agreement among them in support of the love affair. Twenty-two of the twenty-four agreed that Lincoln had loved or courted Ann Rutledge; two of them had no opinion. Did Lincoln grieve excessively after her death? Seventeen said yes, and seven had no opinion; none denied the statement. Did they have a marriage understanding? Fifteen said that they did, two said that they did not, and seven had no opinion on that question. Wilson wrote that several of the authors who had denied the validity of the relationship had not had access to the Herndon notes or his interviews or had failed to do a thorough job of researching the issue. David Donald, Lincoln's most recent and one of his best biographers, accepts the truth of the relationship but without the sentimentality that colored many of the early accounts. Douglas L. Wilson, "Abraham Lincoln, Ann Rutledge, and the Evidence of Herndon's Informants," *Civil War History* 36 (December 1990): 301–24; Donald, *Lincoln,* 55–58.

5. Herndon and Weik, *Lincoln,* 116–18, Lincoln quoted on 118; Barton, *Women Lincoln Loved,* 187–204; Davenport, *In Lincoln's Footsteps,* 85; Oates, *With Malice toward None,* 32, 43–44; Ward H. Lamon, *Life of Abraham Lincoln, from His Birth to His Inauguration as President* (1872), 172–76.

6. Lincoln to Mary Owens, December 13, 1836; May 7, 1837; August 16, 1837, all in *Collected Works,* 1:54–55, 78–79, 94–95; Davenport, *In Lincoln's Footsteps,* 85.

7. Lincoln to Mrs. Orville H. Browning, April 1, 1838, *Collected Works,* 1:117–19.

8. Herndon and Weik, *Lincoln,* 129.

9. Townsend, *Lincoln and the Bluegrass,* 50–52; Jean H. Baker, *Mary Todd Lincoln* (1987), 4–40; Justin G. Turner and Linda Levitt Turner, *Mary Todd Lincoln: Her Life and Letters* (1987), 6–8.

10. Townsend, *Lincoln and the Bluegrass,* 57–60, 63–64, 66–69, 67; Turner and Turner, *Mary Todd Lincoln,* 9–10; Baker, *Mary Todd Lincoln,* 40–47, 51–52; Katherine Helm, *True Story of Mary, Wife of Lincoln* (1928), 58–69, 73.

11. Herndon and Weik, *Lincoln,* 165, 165–68; Keith W. Jennison, *The Humorous Mr. Lincoln* (1965), 30; Donald, *Lincoln,* 84–87, 85; Ruth Painter Randall, *Mary Lincoln: Biography of a Marriage* (1953), 4–6, 14–15, 28–41.

12. Donald, *Lincoln,* 86.

13. Lincoln to John T. Stuart, January 20, 1841, *Collected Works,* 1:228–29; Oates, *With Malice toward None,* 56–57; Douglas L. Wilson, *Honor's Voice: The Transformation of Abraham Lincoln* (1998), 215–81. After

a careful examination of evidence, Wilson concluded that Lincoln did not almost abandon Mary at the alter on January 1, 1842. Lincoln was most concerned with his honor and his ability, which he seemed to have lost, to remain consistent in his resolves once they were made. His reference to the fatal first of January referred more to problems in the life of Joshua Speed than to Lincoln's own problem with Mary. Douglas L. Wilson, "Abraham Lincoln and 'That Fatal First of January,'" *Civil War History* 38 (June 1992): 101–30. Ida M. Tarbell, *The Life of Abraham Lincoln,* 2 vols. (1900), 1:198–208, was one of the first challenges to the story that Lincoln had almost literally left Mary standing at the alter by breaking their engagement at the last moment. Martin McKee to John J. Hardin, January 22, 1841, quoted in *Collected Works,* 1:229 n.

14. Lincoln to John T. Stuart, January 20, 23, 1841, *Collected Works,* 1:228–29, 229–30; Lincoln to Joshua Speed, June 19, 1841, *Collected Works,* 1:254–58, 258; Donald, *Lincoln,* 86, 88.

15. Lincoln seldom revealed as much of his thoughts as he did in a series of letters in 1841–42. Lincoln to Mary Speed, September 27, 1841, *Collected Works,* 1:259–61; Lincoln to Joshua F. Speed, January 3[?], 1842; February 3, 1842; February 13, 1842; February 25, 1842 (two letters that day); March 27, 1842; July 4, 1842; October 5, 1842, all in *Collected Works,* 1:265–66, 267–68, 269–70, 280–81, 282–83, 288–90, 302–3; Gross, *Wit and Wisdom of Lincoln,* 142. See also Suppiger, "Life in Springfield, 1840–1847," 115–17, 119–22.

16. Lincoln to Joshua Speed, July 4, 1842, *Collected Works,* 1:288–90.

17. Thomas, *Lincoln,* 89; Donald, *Lincoln,* 90; Randall, *Mary Lincoln,* 64–72; Helm, *Mary, Wife of Lincoln,* 92–95; Wilson, *Honor's Voice,* 282.

18. Donald, *Lincoln,* 90–93; Oates, *With Malice toward None,* 61–62. But Wilson, *Honor's Voice,* 265, maintains that the ladies did not make their contributions to the newspaper until after Shields had demanded the name of the author. Wilson does not believe that Mary and Lincoln had resumed meeting before the aborted duel.

19. Oates, *With Malice toward None,* 62–63; Baker, *Mary Todd Lincoln,* 97–98; Barton, *Women Lincoln Loved,* 264–65; Helm, *Mary, Wife of Lincoln,* 92–95; Randall, *Mary Lincoln,* 69–72.

20. Donald, *Lincoln,* 94–96; Oates, *With Malice toward None,* 63–66; Thomas, *Lincoln,* 90–91; Baker, *Mary Todd Lincoln,* chap. 5, "Domestic Portrait: The Springfield Years," 99–130. Interesting descriptions of the Lincoln domestic life by two women who worked for Mary Lincoln are Elizabeth Keckley, *Behind the Scenes* (1868), and Lloyd Ostendorf and Walter Olesky, eds., *Lincoln's Unknown Private Life: An Oral History by His Black Housekeeper, Mariah Vance, 1850–1860* (1995). The Vance account has been rejected by most historians; the Keckley book must be used with considerable skepticism.

21. Oates, *With Malice toward None,* 66; Wilson, *Honor's Voice,* esp. the last chapter.

6. Lincoln and Slavery to 1854

1. Donald, *Lincoln,* 151–52; Joseph E. Suppiger, "The Intimate Lincoln: Part VIII: Lawyer and Politician," *Lincoln Herald* 84 (winter 1982): 222–26. A good account of Lincoln's legal career is John J. Duff, *A. Lincoln: Prairie Lawyer* (1960).

2. "Eulogy on Zachary Taylor," July 25, 1850, *Collected Works,* 2:83–90, 83, 85; Suppiger, "Congressman and Family Man," 162–63.

3. "Eulogy on Henry Clay," July 6, 1852, *Collected Works,* 2:121–32.

4. *Collected Works,* 3:29; Don C. Seitz, *Lincoln the Politician* (1931), 47, 74, 98; Lincoln's endorsements of the Thomas H. Clay nominations in *Collected Works,* 4:557; Louis A. Warren, "Clay's Influence on Lincoln," *Lincoln Lore* 519 (March 20, 1939): 1; Louis A. Warren, "Lincoln's Campaign for Clay," *Lincoln Lore* 530 (October 23, 1939): 1.

5. "Eulogy on Henry Clay," *Collected Works,* 2:121–32, 123, 124, 126.

6. Ibid., 130–32.

7. Lincoln, "Speech at Peoria, Illinois," October 16, 1854, *Collected Works,* 2:260; "Autobiography for Scripps," *Collected Works,* 4:62; Donald, *Lincoln,* 88–89; Quarles, *Lincoln and the Negro,* 18; Lincoln to Mary Speed, September 27, 1841, *Collected Works,* 1:260; *Aggregate Amount of Each Description of Persons in the United States of America . . . 1810* (1811), 3:72a.

8. Townsend, *Lincoln and the Bluegrass,* 60–61, 72–73.

9. Cassius Marcellus Clay, *The Life of Cassius Marcellus Clay, Memoirs, Writings and Speeches* (1886), 232–38. David L. Smiley, *Lion of White Hall: The Life of Cassius M. Clay* (1962, 1969), and H. Edward Richardson, *Cassius Marcellus Clay: Firebrand of Freedom* (1976), are the best biographies of this colorful character. See also Lowell H. Harrison, "Cassius M. Clay and the *True American,*" *FCHQ* 22 (January 1948): 30–48. The head of the Committee of Sixty, which closed down the *True American,* was George W. Johnson, the first governor of Confederate Kentucky in 1861–62.

10. Lincoln, "Speech at Springfield, Illinois," July 17, 1858, *Collected Works,* 2:514; Speech at Bloomington, May 29, 1856, in Arthur Brooks Lapsley, ed., *Writings of Abraham Lincoln,* 8 vols. (1905), 2:259. The editors of Lincoln's *Collected Works* question the accuracy of this version of Lincoln's speech. Richardson, *C.M. Clay,* 72.

11. Some of the best accounts of the political developments of the 1850s are David M. Potter and Don E. Fehrenbacher, *The Impending Crisis, 1848–1861* (1976); Michael F. Holt, *The Political Crisis of the 1850s*

(1978); Don E. Fehrenbacher, *Prelude to Greatness: Lincoln in the 1850s* (1962); William E. Gienapp, *The Origins of the Republican Party, 1852–1856* (1987). The roles of Henry Clay and Stephen A. Douglas in shaping the Compromise of 1850 are well described in Robert V. Remini, *Henry Clay: Statesman for the Union* (1991); and Johannsen, *Douglas.* Lincoln's views on colonization are discussed in Michael Vorenberg, "Abraham Lincoln and the Politics of Black Colonization," *Journal of the Abraham Lincoln Association* 14 (summer 1993): 23–45. Among the many studies of Lincoln and slavery, see Robert W. Johannsen, *Lincoln, the South, and Slavery: The Political Dimension* (1991); and Benjamin Quarles, *Lincoln and the Negro* (1962). The Cassius M. Clay quotation is from his *Life,* 232–33.

12. Lincoln, "Speech at Winchester, Illinois," August 26, 1854, *Collected Works,* 2:226–27; Lincoln, "Speech at Springfield, Illinois," July 17, 1858, *Collected Works,* 2:514; Donald, *Lincoln,* 170–78; Thomas, *Lincoln,* 146–52.

13. Lincoln, "Speech at Peoria, Illinois," October 16, 1854, *Collected Works,* 2:255–56; Suppiger, "Lawyer and Politician," 226–227. This speech is often considered to be one of Lincoln's best efforts. It was also one of his longest.

14. Lincoln, "Speech at Springfield, Illinois," October 4, 1854, *Collected Works,* 2:240–47. The quotation is from the Peoria Speech, *Collected Works,* 2:260; the Springfield speech was not reported fully.

15. Oates, *With Malice toward None,* 112–13, 118–19; Donald, *Lincoln,* 189–202. Two good accounts of the origins of the Republican party are Gienapp, *Origins of the Republican Party,* and Michael F. Holt, *Political Parties and American Political Development from the Age of Jackson to the Age of Lincoln* (1992).

16. Quoted in Donald, *Lincoln,* 181.

17. Ibid., 180–85; Thomas, *Lincoln,* 152–55.

18. Robert M. Ireland, "George Robertson," in John E. Kleber, ed. *The Kentucky Encyclopedia* (1992), 776; Townsend, *Lincoln and the Bluegrass,* 176–83, 190, 216–19; Lincoln to George Robertson, August 15, 1855, *Collected Works,* 2:317–18.

7. The Gathering Storm

1. Lincoln to Joshua F. Speed, August 24, 1855, *Collected Works,* 2:320–23.

2. Lincoln, "Speech at Bloomington, Illinois," May 28, 1856, *Collected Works,* 2:340–41; Donald, *Lincoln,* 190–91; Suppiger, "Lawyer and Politician," 229–30. Fehrenbacher, *Prelude to Greatness,* and Johannsen, *Lincoln, the South and Slavery,* give good accounts of Lincoln's role as a party leader in the 1850s.

3. Oates, *With Malice toward None*, 128–29; Mary's letter is quoted in Townsend, *Lincoln and the Bluegrass*, 223–24. His determination to make a good appearance is from Herndon and Weik, *Lincoln*, 118.

4. Lewis Collins and Richard H. Collins, *History of Kentucky*, 2 vols (1874), 1:77; Donald, *Lincoln*, 197–99.

5. The best single volume on the Dred Scott case is Don E. Fehrenbacher, *The Dred Scott Case* (1978), but Paul Finkelman, *An Imperfect Vision* (1991), and his *Dred Scott v Sanford: A Brief History with Documents* (1997) are also useful. A good older short account is Allan Nevins, *The Emergence of Lincoln*, 2 vols. (1950), 1:90–118.

6. Lincoln, "Speech at Springfield, Illinois," June 26, 1857, *Collected Works*, 2:398–410.

7. Lowell H. Harrison, *The Antislavery Movement in Kentucky* (1978), 61–78, 76.

8. Johannsen, *Douglas*, chap. 23, "This Flagrant Violation of Peoples' Rights," 591; Donald, *Lincoln*, 204–9; Lincoln, "'A House Divided' speech," Springfield, Illinois, June 16, 1858, *Collected Works*, 2:461–69, quotation on pages 461-62.

9. Johannsen, *Douglas*, 640–41.

10. Ibid., 641–44, Douglas quoted on 642, Lincoln quoted on 143 and 642; Lincoln, "Speech at Chicago, Illinois," July 10, 1858, *Collected Works*, 2:484–502.

11. A good general account of the Lincoln-Douglas debates is Richard Allen Heckman, *Lincoln vs. Douglas: The Great Debate Campaign* (1967), but there are lengthy accounts also in Donald, *Lincoln*, 209–29; and Johannsen, *Douglas*, 645–79. Perhaps best of the several editions of the debates are Paul M. Angle, ed., *Created Equal? The Complete Lincoln-Douglas Debates of 1858* (1958); and Don E. Fehrenbacher, ed., *Abraham Lincoln: Speeches and Writings, 1832–1858* (1989). The *Collected Works*, vol. 3, also contains a version of the debates.

12. Lincoln, "The Freeport Debate," August 27, 1858, *Collected Works*, 3:38–76. Lincoln's four questions are on 43, Douglas's answers on 51–53.

13. Lincoln, "The Quincy Debate," October 13, 1858, *Collected Works*, 3:245–283.

14. Lincoln, "The Alton Debate," October 15, 1858, *Collected Works*, 3:283–325.

15. Thomas, *Lincoln*, 192–93: Donald, *Lincoln*, 224–27; Suppiger, "Lawyer and Politician," 235–36; Nevins, *Emergence of Lincoln*, 1:394–99.

16. Lincoln to Dr. Anson G. Henry, November 19, 1858, *Collected Works*, 3:339–40.

17. Lincoln to Crittenden, July 7, 1858, *Collected Works*, 2:483–84; Crittenden to Lincoln, July 29, 1858, in Mrs. Chapman Coleman, *The Life of John J. Crittenden*, 2 vols. (1871, 1970), 2:162–64; Lincoln to

Crittenden, November 4, 1858, in Coleman, *Crittenden*, 2:164. The last Lincoln letter is not in the *Collected Works*. In it Lincoln commented that even in the mood that accompanied his defeat, "I cannot for a moment suspect you of anything dishonorable." See also Albert D. Kirwan, *John J. Crittenden: The Struggle for the Union* (1962), 337–38.

18. Donald, *Lincoln*, 231–38, Lincoln quoted on 235; Oates, *With Malice toward None*, 167–71.

19. Lincoln, "Address at Cooper Institute," February 27, 1860, *Collected Works*, 3:522–50.

20. Ibid., 547, for the modern use of "cool."

21. New England speeches at Providence, Manchester, Dover, *Collected Works*, 3:550–54, and at Hartford and New Haven, *Collected Works*, 4:1–30. Lincoln declined invitations to make a number of other speeches. Lincoln to Mary Todd Lincoln, March 4, 1860, *Collected Works*, 3:555.

22. Lincoln to Lyman Trumbull, April 29, 1860, *Collected Works*, 4:45–46.

8. An Election, a War, and Kentucky's Neutrality

1. Lincoln to Mark W. Delahay, March 16, April 14, 1860, *Collected Works*, 4:31–32, 44; Lincoln to E. Stafford, March 17, 1860, *Collected Works*, 4:33; Donald, *Lincoln*, 241–44.

2. Donald, *Lincoln*, 244–46.

3. Ibid., 246–50, message quoted on 249.

4. Smiley, *Lion of White Hall*, 144–47, 149–59.

5. Ibid., 162–65, Clay quoted on 163, 165; Reinhard H. Luthin, *The First Lincoln Campaign* (1944), 114–16.

6. *Lexington Observer and Reporter*, May 5, 1860; Luthin, *First Lincoln Campaign*, 166–67.

7. Smiley, *Lion of White Hall*, 166; Luthin, *First Lincoln Campaign*, 166–67.

8. Nevins, *Emergence of Lincoln*, 2:254–60; Oates, *With Malice toward None*, 177–79; Joseph E. Suppiger, "The Intimate Lincoln: Part IX: The Making of a New President," *Lincoln Herald* 85 (spring 1983): 12–13.

9. Suppiger, "Making of a New President," 13–14, Lincoln quoted on 12; "Lincoln's Reply to the Republican National Committee," May 19, 23, 26, 1860, *Collected Works*, 4:51–53.

10. Thomas, *Lincoln*, 220–21; Donald, *Lincoln*, 251–55.

11. Nevins, *Emergence of Lincoln*, 2:203–28; Johannsen, *Douglas*, 732–73; Maury Klein, *History of the Louisville and Nashville Railroad* (1972), 28–32, 37–40. Guthrie was president of the L & N until June 11, 1868.

12. Johannsen, *Douglas*, 786–94, Douglas quoted on 788; William C. Davis, *Breckinridge: Statesman, Soldier, Symbol* (1974), 206–27. Breckinridge, who had been a childhood playmate of Mary Todd, had met

Lincoln in Lexington in 1849. They had been friendly but not intimates (45, 513–14); Townsend, *Lincoln and the Bluegrass,* 127, 183; William C. Davis, *Jefferson Davis: The Man and His Hour* (1991), 282–84.

13. *Kentucky Statesman,* August 17, 1860, in E. Merton Coulter, *The Civil War and Readjustment in Kentucky* (1926, 1966), 22. The anti-Lincoln stance of state newspapers has been examined in David L. Porter, "The Kentucky Press and the Election of 1860," *FCHQ* 46 (January 1972): 49–52.

14. Townsend, *Lincoln and the Bluegrass,* 252; Coulter, *Civil War and Readjustment,* 23, 24; Breckinridge quoted in Davis, *Breckinridge,* 234.

15. Donald, *Lincoln,* 255–56.

16. Horace Buckner to John J. Frost, November 26, 1860; letter to Charles Hedden, December 28, 1860, both quoted in Townsend, *Lincoln and the Bluegrass,* 252–53.

17. Speed to Lincoln, November 14, 1860, *Collected Works,* 4:141; Herndon and Weik, *Abraham Lincoln,* 2:187.

18. Donald, *Lincoln,* 258–59.

19. Lincoln to John A. Gilmer, December 15, 1860, *Collected Works,* 4:151–53.

20. Lincoln to Francis P. Blair Sr., December 21, 1860, *Collected Works,* 6:157–58; Lincoln to Elihu B. Washburne, December 21, 1860, *Collected Works,* 6:159.

21. Quoted in Coulter, *Civil War and Readjustment,* 5.

22. Quoted in ibid., 12.

23. Ollinger Crenshaw, *The Slave States in the Presidential Election of 1860* (1945), 159.

24. Lowell H. Harrison, "Governor Magoffin and the Secession Crisis," *Register* 72 (April 1974): 91–110; Michael T. Dues, "Governor Beriah Magoffin of Kentucky," *FCHQ* 40 (January 1966): 22–28.

25. *House Journal,* called session, January–April, 1861, 20–28.

26. Ibid., 28–32.

27. Ibid., 6–11, quotations on 6, 7.

28. Collins and Collins, *History of Kentucky,* 1:86.

29. Coulter, *Civil War and Readjustment,* 27–29, quotations on 28.

30. Ibid., 29, 30–34, 37, 51–52.

31. Donald, *Lincoln,* 270–84.

32. Lincoln, "First Inaugural Address—First Edition and Revision," *Collected Works,* 4:249–62; Lincoln, "First Inaugural Address—Final Text," *Collected Works,* 4:262–71, quotations on 268, 271.

33. Lincoln to Robert Anderson, April 4, 1861, *Collected Works,* 4:321–22. Many studies have been made of the events that led to the beginning of the war. Among the best are Richard N. Current, *Lincoln and the First Shot* (1963); David M. Porter, *Lincoln and His Party in the Secession Crisis* (1942, 1962); J.G. Randall, *Lincoln the President: Springfield to Gettysburg* (1945); Kenneth M. Stampp, *And the War Came: The*

North and the Secession Crisis, 1860–1861 (1950); Phillip Shaw Paludan, *The Presidency of Abraham Lincoln* (1994). But see also Charles W. Ramsdell, "Lincoln and Fort Sumter," *Journal of Southern History* 3 (August 1937), 259–88; and Kenneth M. Stampp, "Lincoln and the Strategy of Defense in the Crisis of 1861," *Journal of Southern History* 11 (August 1945): 297–323.

34. Collins and Collins, *History of Kentucky*, 1:87.

35. Donald, *Lincoln*, 298–99; C.M. Clay, *Life*, 252–64; Smiley, *Lion of White Hall*, 169–77. Clay said that Lincoln "presented me with a Colt's revolver, as a testimony of his regard." *Life*, 264.

36. Kirwan, *Crittenden*, 434; Coulter, *Civil War and Readjustment*, 40.

37. *OR*, ser. 1, vol. 52, pt. 2, pp. 26, 43–44, 46, Morgan quoted on 49. Morgan's telegram was sent on April 16, 1861.

38. Collins and Collins, *History of Kentucky*, 1:88.

39. Coulter, *Civil War and Readjustment*, 50–53.

40. G. Davis to George D. Prentice, April 28, 1861, in Fehrenbacher and Fehrenbacher, comps., *Recollected Words of Lincoln*, 133–34; Collins and Collins, *History of Kentucky*, 1:88–89.

41. Thomas Speed, *The Union Cause in Kentucky, 1860–1865* (1907), 47–49; Resolution and vote quoted in Collins and Collins, *History of Kentucky*, 1:90–91.

42. Lincoln to Browning, September 22, 1861, *Collected Works*, 4:531–33.

43. Coulter, *Civil War and Readjustment*, 53. This statement has sometimes been attributed to an anonymous minister, who was reported to have said, "Mr. Lincoln would like to have God on his side; he has to have Kentucky."

44. U.S. Census Office, *Eighth Census* (1860), vol. 2, *Agriculture*, 62–63, 184–86; vol. 3, *Manufacturing*, 729.

45. A good description of the economic policies in 1861 is Coulter, *Civil War and Readjustment*, chap. 4, "Neutrality and the Southern Trade," 59–80. Miscellaneous information is also found in Collins and Collins, *History of Kentucky*, 1:85–94.

9. The War Enters Kentucky

1. "Addresses of the Convention of the Border States: To the people of the United States; To the people of Kentucky," in Frank Moore, ed., *The Rebellion Record: A Diary of American Events. . .*, 11 vols. (1861–1869), 1:350–53.

2. Richard G. Stone Jr., *A Brittle Sword: The Kentucky Militia, 1776–1912* (1977), 54–73, Morehead quoted on 59.

3. Coulter, *Civil War and Readjustment*, 86–88, 90–91, 98–101; Collins and Collins, *History of Kentucky*, 1:91–92; Stone, *Brittle Sword*, 64–65; Lincoln to Buckner, July 10, 1861, *Collected Works*, 4:444.

4. Lincoln to Simon Cameron, August 17, 1861, *Collected Works,* 4:489; Lincoln to Robert Anderson, May 14, 1861, *Collected Works,* 4:368–69; Anderson to Lincoln, May 19, 1861, Robert Todd Lincoln Papers, Library of Congress, Washington, D.C.; Lincoln to the Kentucky Delegation in Congress, July 29, 1861, *Collected Works,* 4:464; John T. Hubbell and James W. Geary, eds., *Biographical Dictionary of the Union: Northern Leaders of the Civil War* (1995), 8–9.

5. Lincoln's endorsement, William Nelson to William H. Seward, June 9, 1861, *Collected Works,* 4:398; Coulter, *Civil War and Readjustment,* 88–89; Daniel Stevenson, "General Nelson, Kentucky, and the Lincoln Guns," *Magazine of American History* 10 (August 1883): 115–39. Nelson was commissioned a brigadier general of volunteers in September 1861. Lincoln to Anderson, May 14, 1861, *Collected Works,* 4:368–69.

6. Coulter, *Civil War and Readjustment,* 89–91; *Louisville Journal,* June 5, 1861; *OR,* ser. 1, vol. 52, pt. 1, p. 141.

7. Edward Conrad Smith, *The Borderland in the Civil War* (1927), 283–85; Collins and Collins, *History of Kentucky,* 1:92; *Frankfort, Kentucky Yeoman,* June 25, 1861; Coulter, *Civil War and Readjustment,* 95–98.

8. Collins and Collins, *History of Kentucky,* 1:92.

9. Blanton Duncan to Leroy Pope Walker, March 29, 1861, *OR,* ser. 1, vol. 52, pt. 2, p. 32; Joshua Speed to Joseph Holt, May 24, 1861, in Coulter, *Civil War and Readjustment,* 93.

10. Coulter, *Civil War and Readjustment,* 93–94, 96–97, Holt quoted on 97; Donald, *Lincoln,* 299–301.

11. E.F. Drake to Chase, August 29, 1861, in "Letters to Secretary Chase from the South, 1861," *American Historical Review* 4 (October 1898): 343; S.M. Starling to Mary S. Payne, May 6, 1861, Lewis-Starling Papers, Library Special Collections, Western Kentucky Univ.; Christopher Dell, *Lincoln and the War Democrats* (1975), 107.

12. Adj. Gen. L. Thomas to Nelson, July 1, 1861; Nelson to Thomas, July 16, 1861, both in *OR,* ser. 1, 4:251–53; Kirwan, *Crittenden,* 444; Collins and Collins, *History of Kentucky,* 1:92; Prentice and Shipman quoted in Coulter, *Civil War and Readjustment,* 103.

13. Lincoln to Magoffin, August 24, 1861, *Collected Works,* 4:497.

14. Magoffin to Davis, August 24[?], 1861, *OR,* ser. 1, 4:378; Davis to Magoffin, August 28, *OR,* ser. 1, 4:396–97; Collins and Collins, *History of Kentucky,* 1:92; Confederate Congress recruitment law quoted in Coulter, *Civil War and Readjustment,* 106.

15. Polk to Magoffin, September 1, 1861, *OR,* ser. 1, 4:179; Polk to Harris, September 4, 1861, *OR,* ser. 1, 4:180; Collins and Collins, *History of Kentucky,* 1:93–94; Coulter, *Civil War and Readjustment,* 106–10.

16. Walker to Polk, September 4, 1861, *OR,* ser. 1, 4:180; Polk to Kentucky senator John M. Johnston, September 9, 1861, *OR,* ser. 1, 4:186–87; Jefferson Davis to Polk, September 15, 1861, *OR,* ser. 1, 4:188;

Buckner to Samuel Cooper, September 13, 1861, *OR,* ser. 1, 4:189–90; Harris to Davis and Davis to Harris, both September 13, 1861, *OR,* ser. 1, 4:190; Davis message to the Congress of the Confederate States, March 18, 1862, in James D. Richardson, comp., *A Compilation of the Messages and Papers of the Confederacy,* 2 vols. (1906), 1:137–38; Collins and Collins, *History of Kentucky,* 1:93.

17. Collins and Collins, *History of Kentucky,* 1:93.

18. Lowell H. Harrison, "George W. Johnson and Richard Hawes: The Governors of Confederate Kentucky," *Register* 79 (winter 1981): 6–15, convention members quoted on 12; Lowell H. Harrison, "Confederate Kentucky: The State That Almost Was," *Civil War Times Illustrated* 12 (April 1973): 12–21; "Proceedings of the Convention held at Russellville, November 18, 19, and 20, 1861," *OR,* ser. 4, 1:740–43, vote quoted on 741, authorization quoted on 743; Davis, *Breckinridge,* 296–97; G.W. Johnson to Davis, November 21, 1861, *OR,* ser. 4, 1:743–47.

19. Magoffin to Prentice, December 13, 1861, in Collins and Collins, *History of Kentucky,* 1:98.

20. Magoffin to House of Representatives, September 30, 1861, *House Journal,* 262–63; *Senate Journal,* September 30, 1861, 203; governor's complaint quoted in Collins and Collins, *History of Kentucky,* 1:105–6; Magoffin to O.P. Hogan, July 1, 1862, Governors' Correspondence: Magoffin, Kentucky State Library and Archives, Frankfort, Kentucky. For general discussions of Magoffin's problems during this period, see Dues, "Governor Beriah Magoffin of Kentucky," 22–28; and Harrison, "Governor Magoffin and the Secession Crisis," 91–110.

21. Collins and Collins, *History of Kentucky,* 1:108–9; John David Smith, "James F. Robinson," in Lowell H. Harrison, ed., *Kentucky's Governors, 1792-1985* (1985), 74. Magoffin defended his record in his message to the Senate and the House of Representatives, August 15, 1862, *House Journal,* 901–15. Letters leading to his resignation are on 927–30.

10. Lincoln and Military Operations in Kentucky

1. Burnside to Lincoln, January 1, 1863, *OR,* ser. 1, 21:941–42; Lincoln to Halleck, January 1, 1863, *Collected Works,* 6:31; Halleck to Stanton, January 1, 1863, *OR,* ser. 1, 21:940–41; Oates, *With Malice toward None,* 284, 300. Halleck's status is in Donald, *Lincoln,* 410. Lincoln's problem in finding a fighting team of generals is discussed in Kenneth P. Williams, *Lincoln Finds a General,* 5 vols. (1949–1959); and T. Harry Williams, *Lincoln and His Generals* 2 vols. (1952).

2. Donald, *Lincoln,* 325–26; Lincoln to Cameron, January 11, 1862, *Collected Works,* 5:96–97; Cameron to Lincoln, January 11, 1862, Robert Todd Lincoln Papers.

3. Anthony Gross, *Lincoln's Own Stories* (1912), 78, 198–99; Allen Thorndike Rice, ed., *Reminiscences of Abraham Lincoln by Distinguished*

Men of His Time (1888), 56–57. See Benjamin P. Thomas and Harold M. Hyman, *Stanton: The Life and Times of Lincoln's Secretary of War* (1962), chaps. 6, "From Critic to Colleague," 119–42, and 7, "Secretary of a War," 143–68, for an excellent description of the Lincoln-Stanton relationship.

4. "President's General War Order No. 1," January 27, 1862, *Collected Works*, 5:111–12; Donald, *Lincoln*, 334–35.

5. Charles P. Roland, *Albert Sidney Johnston: Soldier of Three Republics* (1964), 259–63, Albert Johnston letter of October 17, 1861, quoted on 263; Charles P. Roland, "Albert Sidney Johnston," in William C. Davis, ed., *The Confederate General*, 6 vols. (1991), 3:188–89.

6. "Johanna Louisa Underwood Nazro Civil War Diary," September 20, 1861, Library Special Collections, Western Kentucky Univ.; Martha Lucas Graham to C. Fontaine Alexander, September 15, 1861, Alexander Collection, Library Special Collections, Western Kentucky Univ.

7. "To the Freemen of Kentucky," September 12, 1861, in Moore, *Rebellion Record*, 3:127–29; "To the People of Kentucky," September 18, 1861, *OR*, ser. 1, 4:413–14; Buckner to Magoffin, September 18, 1861, *OR*, ser. 1, 4:414.

8. Roland, *Johnston*, 266–73; Lincoln to Morton, September 29, 1861, *Collected Works*, 4:541–42.

9. Collins and Collins, *History of Kentucky*, 1:96, 98; Brian Steelwills, *A Battle from the Start: The Life of Nathan Bedford Forrest* (1992), 53–56.

10. "Memorandum for a Plan of Campaign," October 1, 1861, *Collected Works*, 4:544–45.

11. Sherman is quoted in Charles Edmund Vetter, *Sherman: Mercenary of Terror, Advocate of Peace* (1992), 91; Lloyd Lewis, *Sherman: Fighting Prophet* (1932), 189–203, Villard quoted on 192, *Cincinnati Commercial* quoted on 201; William T. Sherman, *Memoirs of General William T. Sherman* (1957), 197–218.

12. Guthrie, Prentice, and Speed to Lincoln, November 5, 1861, Robert Todd Lincoln Papers; Lincoln to Guthrie, Prentice, and Speed, November 5, 1861; Prentice to Lincoln, November 5 1861, both in *Collected Works*, 5:14–15. No reply has been found to the president's specific questions.

13. Lincoln to Halleck and Buell, December 31, 1861, *Collected Works*, 5:84, 84 n; Lincoln to Halleck and Buell, January 1, 1862, *Collected Works*, 5:86, 87; Halleck to Lincoln, January 1, 1862; Buell to Lincoln, January 7, 1862, both in *OR*, ser. 1, 7:526.

14. Lincoln to Buell, January 4, 1862, *OR*, ser. 1, 7:530; Buell to Lincoln, January 5, 1862, Robert Todd Lincoln Papers; Lincoln to Buell, January 6, 1862, *Collected Works*, 5:91; Lincoln to Buell, January 7, 1862, *Collected Works*, 5:91–92.

15. Lincoln to Buell (copy to Halleck), January 13, 1862, *Collected Works*, 5:98–99.

16. Raymond E. Meyers, *The Zollie Tree* (1964, 1998), passim; C. David Dalton, "Zollicoffer, Crittenden, and the Mill Springs Campaign: Some Persistent Questions," *FCHQ* 60 (October 1986): 463–71.

17. Roland, *Johnston*, 287–97, quoted on 297; Lowell H. Harrison, "George W. Johnson and Richard Hawes: The Governors of Confederate Kentucky," 79 (winter 1981): 3–29. Benjamin Franklin Cooling, *Forts Henry and Donelson: The Key to the Confederate Heartland* (1987), and Benjamin Franklin Cooling, *Fort Donelson's Legacy: War and Society in Kentucky and Tennessee, 1862–1863* (1997), are detailed studies of the campaign and its aftermath.

18. Roland, *Johnston*, 289–97; Arndt M. Stickles, *Simon Bolivar Buckner: Borderland Knight* (1940), 125–61.

19. Lincoln to Halleck, February 16, 1862, *Collected Works*, 5:135; Lincoln to Stanton, March 3, 1862, *Collected Works*, 5:142; Lincoln to Buell, March 10, 1862, *Collected Works*, 5:153; "Proclamation of Thanksgiving for Victories," April 10, 1862, *Collected Works*, 5:185–86.

20. James A. Ramage, *Rebel Raider: The Life of John Hunt Morgan* (1986), is the best study of that glamorous figure. For his first Kentucky raid, see 91–106. "Report of George A. Ellsworth, Telegraph Operator, Morgan's Command," *OR*, ser. 1, vol. 16, pt. 1, pp. 774–81. The telegraph to "Jerry" is on p. 780. Another telegram went to editor Prentice on July 22, 1862. "I expect in a short time to pay you a visit and wish to know if you will be at home. All well in Dixie" (780).

21. Lincoln to Boyle, July 13, 1862, *Collected Works*, 5:321 (two messages that day); Lincoln to Halleck, July 13, 1862, *Collected Works*, 5:322; Halleck to Buell, July 14, 1862, *OR*, ser. 1, vol. 16, pt. 2, p. 143.

22. Morgan to Kirby Smith, July 16, 1862, *OR*, ser. 1, vol. 16, pt. 2, pp. 733–34.

23. Smith to Bragg, August 20, 1862, *OR*, ser. 1, vol. 16, pt. 2, p. 766. Two of the best accounts of this campaign are Thomas Lawrence Connelly, *Army of the Heartland: The Army of Tennessee, 1861–1862* (1967), esp. 187–280; and James L. McDonough, *War in Kentucky: From Shiloh to Perryville* (1994). *OR* has many references to this campaign. See also Collins and Collins, *History of Kentucky*, 1:110–15.

24. D. Warren Lambert, *When the Ripe Pears Fell: The Battle of Richmond, Kentucky* (1995), is the best account of this battle. Nelson is quoted on 144.

25. Lincoln to Boyle, August 31, 1862, *Collected Works*, 5:401; Horatio G. Wright to Halleck, August 31, 1862, *OR*, ser. 1, vol. 16, pt. 2, p. 464; Boyle to Lincoln, August 31, 1862, Robert Todd Lincoln Papers.

26. Lincoln to Boyle, September 7, 1862, *Collected Works*, 5:408; Boyle to Lincoln, September 7, 8, 1862, *OR*, ser. 1, vol. 16, pt. 2, pp. 495, 496; Lincoln to Buell, September 7, 1862, *Collected Works*, 5:409; Buell to Lincoln, September 10, 1862, *OR*, ser. 1, vol. 16, pt. 2, p. 500.

27. Collins and Collins, *History of Kentucky*, 1:110–11. The General Assembly met in Louisville on September 3.

28. Boyle to Lincoln, September 11, 1862, Robert Todd Lincoln Papers; Lincoln to Boyle, September 12, 1862, *Collected Works*, 5:416; Boyle to Lincoln, September 12, 1862, Robert Todd Lincoln Papers; Lincoln to Wright, September 12, 1862, *Collected Works*, 5:419; Wright to Lincoln, September 13, 1862, OR, ser. 1, vol. 16, pt. 2, p. 513.

29. Thomas H. Clay to Lincoln, October 8, 1862, OR, ser. 1, vol. 16, pt. 2, p. 589; Lincoln to Clay, October 8, 1862, *Collected Works*, 5:452.

30. Lincoln to Boyle, October 11, 12, 1862, *Collected Works*, 5:457, 458; Boyle to Halleck, October 10, 1862, OR, ser. 1, vol. 16, pt. 2, p. 602; Boyle to Lincoln, October 12, 1862, OR, ser. 1, vol. 16, pt. 2, p. 609.

31. Kenneth A. Hafendorfer, *Perryville: Battle for Kentucky* (1991), is the best account of this battle and its part in the 1862 campaign.

32. Harrison, "Governors of Confederate Kentucky," 28–39. Hawes was sworn in as governor of Confederate Kentucky on May 31, 1862, in Corinth, Mississippi, when he caught up with the council after receiving word of his election. Richard Hawes Collection, Special Collections, Univ. of Kentucky. He was being *installed* in Frankfort on October 4.

33. Halleck to Buell, October 19, 1862, OR, ser. 1, vol. 16, pt. 2, pp. 626–27; J.R. Chumney Jr., "Don Carlos Buell, Gentleman General," Ph.D. diss., Rice Univ., 1964, 182–83; Amos Fleger to his parents, October 19, 1862, Fleger Letters, Special Collections, Univ. of Kentucky; James Lee McDonough, "Don Carlos Buell," in Hubbell and Geary, *Biographical Dictionary of the Union*, 68–69. The Buell Commission Report is in OR, ser. 1, vol. 16, pt. 1, pp. 7–726.

34. Ramage, *Rebel Raider*, 135–47.

35. Ibid., 158–82.

36. Lincoln to Burnside, July 24, 1863, *Collected Works*, 6:346; Burnside to Halleck, July 24, 1863, OR, ser. 1, vol. 23, pt. 2, p. 553.

37. Ramage, *Rebel Raider*, 183–244; Lincoln to Stephen G. Burbridge, June 14, 1862, *Collected Works*, 7:391, 391 n; Michael Burlingame, *The Inner World of Abraham Lincoln* (1994), 24; Lincoln quoted in Gross, *Wit and Wisdom of Lincoln*, 187.

38. Steelwills, *A Battle from the Start*, 176–79; "Report of Col. S.S. Hicks," April 20, 1864, OR, ser. 1, vol. 32, pt. 1, pp. 547–49.

39. Lincoln to McClellan, October 25, 1862, *Collected Works*, 5:474; Lincoln quoted in Oates, *With Malice toward None*, 385.

11. Wartime Politics in Kentucky

1. Collins and Collins, *History of Kentucky*, 1:119.

2. Ibid.; Coulter, *Civil War and Readjustment*, 171; *Cincinnati Gazette*, February 18, 1863; quotations from Collins and Collins, *History of Kentucky*, 1:119.

3. Collins and Collins, *History of Kentucky*, 1:119–20; Gillmore quoted in Coulter, *Civil War and Readjustment*, 171–72; *Frankfort Tri-Weekly Commonwealth*, March 20, 1863.

4. Cravens quoted in Collins and Collins, *History of Kentucky*, 1:121. Lincoln to Green Adams, March 4, 1862, *Collected Works*, 5:142 n; Ross A. Webb, "Thomas Elliott Bramlette," in Harrison, *Kentucky's Governors*, 77–81; Lincoln to Edward Bates, May 8, 1863, *Collected Works*, 6:202.

5. J.W. Kincheloe to Lincoln, January 18, 1865, in Coulter, *Civil War and Readjustment*, 173.

6. Ibid., 174–75.

7. Mary Clay Berry, *Voices from the Century Before: The Odyssey of a Nineteenth Century Kentucky Family* (1997), 324–30, Brutus quoted on 325-26. This account of the Clay family is the best source on Brutus Clay.

8. Collins and Collins, *History of Kentucky*, 1:127; J.G. Randall, *Lincoln the President* (1952), 3:246–47; oath quoted in Coulter, *Civil War and Readjustment*, 177–78; William Marvel, *Burnside* (1991), 265.

9. Randall, *Lincoln the President*, 3:246; Lincoln to Mary Lincoln, August 8, 1863, *Collected Works*, 6:372; Lincoln to Green Adams, August 22, 1863, *Collected Works*, 6:401–2; Collins and Collins, *History of Kentucky*, 1:127; Thomas D. Clark, *History of Kentucky* (1950), 341–42.

10. *Kentucky Senate Journal*, December 7, 1863, 11–22.

11. Bramlette to Lincoln, January 5, 1864, Robert Todd Lincoln Papers; Lincoln to Bramlette, January 6, 1864, *Collected Works*, 7:109; Bramlette to Lincoln, January 8, 1864, Robert Todd Lincoln Papers; Lincoln to Bramlette, January 17, 1864, *Collected Works*, 7:134.

12. Boyle to Fry, June 25, 1863, *OR*, ser. 3, 3:416; Fry's order quoted in Collins and Collins, *History of Kentucky*, 1:132; Marion B. Lucas, *A History of Blacks in Kentucky: From Slavery to Segregation, 1760–1891* (1992), 152–53; Jacob to Lincoln, March 13, 1864, *OR*, ser. 3, 4:175–76.

13. Hambleton Tapp, "Incidents in the Life of Frank Wolford, Colonel of the First Kentucky Union Cavalry," *FCHQ* 10 (April 1936): 82–100; Eastham Tarrant, *The Wild Riders of the First Kentucky Cavalry* (1894), 304–7; Coulter, *Civil War and Readjustment*, 200–203; "Message of the President of the United States, Papers Covering Arrests of Colonel Richard T. Jacobs, lieutenant governor of the State of Kentucky, and Colonel Frank Wolford, one of the presidential electors of that State," January 31, 1865, *Senate Executive Document* no. 16, 33d Cong., 2d sess., 1–25.

14. Coulter, *Civil War and Readjustment*, 200–203, telegram to provost marshal quoted on 200, message to Breckinridge quoted on 200, uprising proposal quoted on 201, March 15 proclamation quoted on 200–201; proposed uprising quoted in OR, ser. 3, 4:176; Jacob to Lincoln, March 13, 1864, *OR*, ser. 3, 4:175–79; James C. Klotter, *The Breckinridges of Kentucky* (1986), 84–85; Collins and Collins, *History of Kentucky*, 1:132.

The personality of Robert J. Breckinridge is well described in Hambleton Tapp, "Robert J. Breckinridge during the Civil War," *FCHQ* 11 (April 1937): 120–44.

15. *Louisville Journal,* March 22, 1864; Lincoln to Stanton, March 28, 1864, *Collected Works,* 7:272; Howard K. Beale, ed., *The Diary of Edward Bates, 1859–1866,* vol. 4 of *Annual Report of the American Historical Association for the Year 1930* (U.S. Government Printing Office, 1933), "March 23, 1864," 352.

16. B.H. Bristow and others to E.M. Stanton, December 19, 1863, *OR,* ser. 3, 3:1174–75; E.D. Townsend, assistant adjutant general, "Order on Slave Recruitment," December 21, 1863, *OR,* ser. 3, 3:1178–79; "General Orders 34, headquarters of Kentucky, regulations for drafting blacks, slave and free," *OR,* ser. 3, 4:233–34; assistant adjutant general to Burbridge, April 28, 1864, *OR,* ser. 3, 4:248–49; John Blassingame, "The Recruitment of Colored Troops in Kentucky, Maryland and Missouri, 1863–1865," *Historian* 29 (August 1967): 542–43; Lucas, *Blacks in Kentucky,* 153–66; Collins and Collins, *History of Kentucky,* 1:132–35; May 12 quotation on 1:133; June 18 quotation on 1:135.

17. Coulter, *Civil War and Readjustment,* 205–8; "Parole for Frank L. Wolford from Lincoln," July 7, 1864; "Pardon and Discharge for Wolford," July 17, 1864, both in *Collected Works,* 7:430–31, 446; Lincoln to James Speed, July 17, 1864, *Collected Works,* 7:446; Lincoln to Wolford, July 17, 1864, *Collected Works,* 7:447; Wolford quoted in Collins and Collins, *History of Kentucky,* 1:141; see *Senate Document* no. 16, cited in note 13 above.

18. Lincoln to Wolford, August 4, 1864, *Collected Works,* 7:480; Tapp, "Life of Frank Wolford," 94–95; Burbridge to Col. Norton P. Chipman, November 23, 1864, *OR,* ser. 1, vol. 45, pt. 1, p. 1010.

19. Bramlette quoted in Bramlette to Lincoln, November 22, 1864, *OR,* ser. 1, vol. 45, pt. 1, p. 994; Burbridge to Stanton, January 16, 1865, in *U.S. Senate Executive Document* 16, 38th Congress, 2nd Session; Jacob to Lincoln, December 26, 1864, in *Collected Works,* 8:182–83 n.; Lincoln to J. Bates Dickson, December 27, 1864, in *Collected Works,* 8:182–83; Dickson to Lincoln, December 28, 1864, *OR,* ser. 1, vol. 45, pt. 2, p. 402; Lincoln to Grant, January 5, 1865, *Collected Works,* 8:198; Lincoln to Jacob, January 18, 1865, *Collected Works,* 8:222; Bramlette quoted in Collins and Collins, *History of Kentucky,* 1:148–49.

20. Coulter, *Civil War and Readjustment,* 212–14; *Louisville Journal,* February 10, 1865.

21. Donald, *Lincoln,* 502–7, Breckinridge quoted on 504; Tapp, "Robert J. Breckinridge during the Civil War," 140–42; Collins and Collins, *History of Kentucky,* 1:136.

22. Donald, *Lincoln,* 518–30; Lincoln, "Memorandum concerning His Probable Failure of Re-election," August 23, 1864, *Collected Works,* 7:514. John Hay said that Lincoln read the document to the cabinet

members on November 11, 1864, after his landslide victory. See also Henry J. Raymond to Lincoln, August 22, 1864, Robert Todd Lincoln Papers; and Lincoln to Raymond, August 24, 1864, *Collected Works,* 7:517–18.

23. Collins and Collins, *History of Kentucky,* 1:137–39, Wickliffe quoted on 1:139; Coulter, *Civil War and Readjustment,* 184–87. The best general account of the 1864 election is John W. Waugh, *Reelecting Lincoln: The Battle for the 1864 Presidency* (1997), but it contains little information on the Kentucky campaign.

24. Coulter, *Civil War and Readjustment,* 184–85, Burbridge quoted on 185; Collins and Collins, *History of Kentucky,* 1:137–38; *OR,* ser. 1, vol. 39, pt. 3, pp. 321–22; Bramlette to Lincoln, September 3, 1864, *OR,* ser. 3, 4:688–90.

25. *OR,* ser. 3, 4:688–90; Collins and Collins, *History of Kentucky,* 1:143–44, Wolford quoted on 1:144; Coulter, *Civil War and Readjustment,* 186–87, Bramlette's proclamation quoted on 187.

26. Coulter, *Civil War and Readjustment,* 187–88; Collins and Collins, *History of Kentucky,* 1:146.

27. Donald, *Lincoln,* 543–44; Oates, *With Malice toward None,* 400–401; Thomas, *Lincoln,* 452–53.

28. Bramlette's message to the General Assembly, January 6, 1865, Governor Bramlette's Papers, Kentucky State Library and Archives.

29. Bramlette to Lincoln, November 9, 1864, Robert Todd Lincoln Papers; Lincoln to Bramlette, November 10, 1864, *Collected Works,* 8:98–99; Lincoln to Burbridge, November 10, 1864, *Collected Works,* 8:99; Burbridge to Lincoln, November 11, 1864, Robert Todd Lincoln Papers; Bramlette's response to Burbridge quoted in Collins and Collins, *History of Kentucky,* 1:146–47; *Kentucky Senate Journal,* 1865, 41.

12. Lincoln and Wartime Issues in Kentucky

1. Ross A. Webb, "Jeremiah T. Boyle," in Kleber, *Kentucky Encyclopedia,* 109; Lowell H. Harrison, "Jeremiah Tilford Boyle," in Hubbell and Geary, *Biographical Dictionary of the Union,* 50–51.

2. Collins and Collins, *History of Kentucky,* 1:102.

3. Ibid., 103, 115, 116, 123, 136, Henderson quoted on 103; Coulter, *Civil War and Readjustment,* 151–53; Collins and Collins, *History of Kentucky,* 1:103.

4. J.B. Temple to Lincoln, August 12, 1862, *OR,* ser. 2, 4:378; Stanton to Boyle, August 13, 1862, *OR,* ser. 2, 4:380; Stanton to Temple, August 13, 1862, *OR,* ser. 2, 4:381; Robinson to Lincoln, September 15, 1862, OR, ser. 1, vol. 16, pt. 2, p. 519; J.F. Speed to Lincoln, September 15, 1862, *OR,* ser. 1, vol. 16, pt. 2, p. 519; Coulter, *Civil War and Readjustment,* 152–53.

5. *Congressional Globe,* 37th Cong., 3d sess., part 1, 186.

6. Lincoln to Stanton, July 19, 1862; Boyle telegram of July 18, 1862, in note, both in *Collected Works*, 5:334; Boyle to Stanton, August 21, 1862 (two letters), *OR*, ser. 3, 2:431; Collins and Collins, *History of Kentucky*, 1:115, 116.

7. Collins and Collins, *History of Kentucky*, 1:122.

8. Buell to Boyle, July 24, 1862, *OR*, ser. 1, vol. 16, pt. 1, p. 751; Lincoln, "Memorandum concerning Fines Collected from Kentuckians," January 31, 1863, *Collected Works*, 6:85–86; Lincoln to Boyle, February 1, 1863, *Collected Works*, 6:87.

9. Collins and Collins, *History of Kentucky*, 1:101, 123, 124, 127, 130, 140, Richardson quoted on 1:124, Expatriation Act quoted on 1:101, July 24 order quoted on 1:127; Lincoln to Stanton, June 4, 1863, *OR*, ser. 3, 3:252; "General Order No. 91," *OR*, ser. 2, 5:741; Lincoln to Isaac N. Arnold, May 25, 27, 1864, *Collected Works*, 7:361, 363–64.

10. Boyle to Lincoln, January 10, 1864; Lincoln to Stanton, January 11, 1846, both in *Collected Works*, 7:121–22; Lincoln to Bramlette, January 31, 1864, *Collected Works*, 7:163; Webb, "Boyle," 109. Boyle became president of the Louisville City Railway Company (1864–66), then was president of the Evansville, Henderson & Nashville Railroad Company.

11. Louis DeFalaise, "Gen. Stephen Gano Burbridge's Command in Kentucky," *Register* 69 (April 1971): 101–4; Aloma Williams Dew, "Stephen Gano Burbridge," in Kleber, *Kentucky Encyclopedia*, 142; "Report of Brigadier General Stephen G. Burbridge," August 1, 1864, *OR*, ser. 1, vol. 39, pt. 1, pp. 22–26.

12. Champ Clark, *My Quarter Century of American Politics*, 2 vols. (1920), 1:79; Nathaniel Southgate Shaler, *Kentucky: A Pioneer Commonwealth* (1884), 345; Richard L. Troutman, ed., *The Heavens Are Weeping: The Diaries of George Richard Browder, 1852–1886* (1987), 183–84; W.F. Wickersham to his family, July 7, 1862, Wickersham Family Papers, Library Special Collections, Western Kentucky Univ. Browder used "country" to mean the local area or county.

13. Sherman to Burbridge, June 21, 1864, *OR*, ser. 1, vol. 39, pt. 2, pp. 135–36; Sherman to Gen. Leslie Coombs, August 11, 1864, *OR*, ser. 1, vol. 39, pt. 2, pp. 240–41; Collins and Collins, *History of Kentucky*, 1:135; Coulter, *Civil War and Readjustment*, 227–30.

14. Collins and Collins, *History of Kentucky*, 1:135, 136.

15. Ibid., 137, 138; Coulter, *Civil War and Readjustment*, 184–85.

16. Collins and Collins, *History of Kentucky*, 1:138, 139.

17. Breckinridge quoted in ibid., 1:142; Klotter, *Breckinridges of Kentucky*, 80–87.

18. Burbridge quoted in Collins and Collins, *History of Kentucky*, 1:144; Basil W. Duke, *A History of Morgan's Cavalry* (1867, 1960), 546–50; Coulter, *Civil War and Readjustment*, 232–36.

19. Bramlette to Lincoln, November 9, 1864, Robert Todd Lincoln

Papers; Lincoln on the arrest quoted in Lincoln to Bramlette, November 10, 1864, *Collected Works*, 8:98–99; Lincoln to Burbridge, November 10, 1864, *Collected Works*, 8:99; Burbridge to Lincoln, November 11, 1864, Robert Todd Lincoln Papers; Collins and Collins, *History of Kentucky*, 1:146–48, Burbridge charge of reviling quoted on 1:147, Bramlette's rejection quoted on 1:147, Bramlette on accusations quoted on 1:147; Coulter, *Civil War and Readjustment*, 188, 211–13.

20. DeFalaise, "Burbridge's Command in Kentucky," 115–16; Collins and Collins, *History of Kentucky*, 1:144–45, 151–52; Coulter, *Civil War and Readjustment*, 222–24; "Bramlette's Report to the General Assembly," *Kentucky Senate Journal*, January 6, 1865, 11–12, 42–50.

21. DeFalaise, "Burbridge's Command in Kentucky," 124–27, Burbridge quoted on 127; Collins and Collins, *History of Kentucky*, 1:151, 152, 155, 164, convention recommendation quoted on 1:151; Coulter, *Civil War and Readjustment*, 213, 214; "John McCauley Palmer," in Kleber, *Kentucky Encyclopedia*, 708–9.

22. E.B. Long, "Eleazer Arthur Paine," in Hubbell and Geary, *Biographical Dictionary of the Union*, 389; Lincoln to Paine, November 19, 1858, *Collected Works*, 3:340; Lincoln to Simon Cameron, July 15, September 2, 1861, *Collected Works*, 4:448, 504–5; Lincoln to Stanton, June 18, 1864, *Collected Works*, 7:400; Lon Carter Barton, "The Reign of Terror in Graves County," *Register* 46 (April 1948): 487–88.

23. Grant to Thomas, January 15, 1864; Thomas to Grant, January 15, 1864, both in *OR*, ser. 1, vol. 32, pt. 2, p. 103; Collins and Collins, *History of Kentucky*, 1:136; Coulter, *Civil War and Readjustment*, 221.

24. Barton, "Reign of Terror," 488–90; Coulter, *Civil War and Readjustment*, 220–22; Collins and Collins, *History of Kentucky*, 1:138, 140–41; "Report of Investigating Committee in Bramlette's Report to General Assembly," *Kentucky Senate Journal*, January 6, 1865, 24–32.

25. Barton, "Reign of Terror," 490.

26. Ibid., 491–92.

27. Ibid., 492–95; Collins and Collins, *History of Kentucky*, 1:157 (quotation), 164; Coulter, *Civil War and Readjustment*, 222; Paine relieved of command, *OR*, ser. 1, vol. 39, pt. 2, p. 349. Paine finally resigned his commission as of April 5, 1865.

28. E.B. Long, "John McCauley Palmer," in Hubbell and Geary, *Biographical Dictionary of the Union*, 391–92; "John McCauley Palmer," in *Kentucky Encyclopedia*, 708–9. *Personal Recollections of John M. Palmer: The Story of an Earnest Life* (1901) was published the year after the author's death. Lincoln to Palmer, September 7, 1854, *Collected Works*, 2:228; Lincoln to P. Quinn Harrison, November 3, 1859, *Collected Works*, 3:492–93; Lincoln to John C. Fremont, July 31, 1861, *Collected Works*, 4:465–66; Lincoln to Stanton, March 22, 1862, *Collected Works*, 5:168–69; Lincoln to Stanton, December 12, 1863, *Collected Works*, 7:61; Collins and Collins, *History of Kentucky*, 1:155. Lincoln had refused to accept

Palmer's resignation in December 1863, when he had a quarrel with some of his superiors. After the war Palmer was elected governor of Illinois in 1868 as a Republican. Because of the scandals of the U.S. Grant administration, he voted Liberal Republican in 1872, then returned to the Democratic party. Elected to the U.S. Senate in 1891, he was the 1896 presidential candidate for the Gold Democrats. Simon Bolivar Buckner was his running mate.

29. Coulter, *Civil War and Readjustment*, 213–14; Stanton to Palmer, February 8, 1865, *OR*, ser. 1, vol. 49, pt. 1, pp. 670–72; D.L. Price to Lincoln, February 11, 1865, *OR*, ser. 1, vol. 49, pt. 1, p. 698.

30. Collins and Collins, *History of Kentucky*, 1:159; Coulter, *Civil War and Readjustment*, 214.

31. J.G. Randall, *Lincoln and the South* (1940), 70; J.T. Dorris, "President Lincoln's Treatment of Kentuckians," *FCHQ* 28 (January 1954): 7–14, Lincoln's order quoted on 8; J.T. Dorris, "President Lincoln's Treatment of Confederates," *FCHQ* 33 (April 1959): 139–60; J.T. Dorris, "President Lincoln's Clemency," *Lincoln Herald* 55 (spring 1953): 2–12, 48; and J.T. Dorris's comprehensive *Pardon and Amnesty under Lincoln and Johnson* (1953).

32. Dorris, "Lincoln's Treatment of Kentuckians," 12–14; Lincoln, "Proclamation of Amnesty and Reconciliation," December 8, 1863, *Collected Works*, 7:53–56, proclamation quoted on 7:55; Lincoln, "Proclamation about Amnesty," March 26, 1864, *Collected Works*, 7:269–70.

33. Dorris, "Lincoln's Treatment of Kentuckians," 14–15; Prentice to Lincoln, April 28, 1863, *OR*, ser. 2, 5:527–28; Lincoln to Stanton, May 16, 1863, *Collected Works*, 6:219–20; "Order concerning R.H. Baptist," February 16, 1865, *Collected Works*, 8:302.

34. Palmer to Stanton, February 24, 1865, *OR*, ser. 1, vol. 49, pt. 1, p. 764; Lincoln to Palmer, February 24, 1865, *Collected Works*, 8:315; Palmer to Lincoln, February 25, 1865, *OR*, ser. 1, vol. 49, pt. 1, p. 770; Klotter, *Breckinridges of Kentucky*, 87; Collins and Collins, *History of Kentucky*, 1:149, 155; Tapp, "Robert J. Breckinridge during the Civil War," 123–27; Townsend, *Lincoln and His Wife's Home Town*, 358–60; Palmer, *Recollections*, 231–32.

35. Dorris, "Lincoln's Treatment of Kentuckians," 16–18; Lincoln to Alvin P. Hovey, November 29, 1864, *Collected Works*, 8:123; Col. Benjamin J. Sweet to James B. Fry, November 2, 1864, *OR*, ser. 1, vol. 45, pt. 1, p. 1077; John B. Castleman, *Active Duty* (1917), 176–88.

36. Humphreys quoted in Helm, *Mary, Wife of Lincoln*, 101–2; Randall, *Mary Lincoln*, 104–6, 139–40; Townsend, *Lincoln and the Bluegrass*, 124–25.

37. Townsend, *Lincoln and the Bluegrass*, 172–73, 177–83.

38. Donald, *Lincoln*, 96; Baker, *Mary Todd Lincoln*, 103; Randall, *Mary Lincoln*, 83–85.

39. Townsend, *Lincoln and the Bluegrass*, 205–8; Randall, *Mary Lin-*

coln, 142–43; Lincoln, "Answer to Petition of Edward Oldham and Thomas Hemingway," May 27, 1853, *Collected Works,* 2:195–97; Lincoln to George B. Kinkead, May 27, September 13, 30, 1853, March 31, 1854, *Collected Works,* 2:194–95, 203–4, 205, 216–17; Lincoln, "Notice to Thomas Hemingway and Edward Oldham," September 22, 1853, *Collected Works,* 2:204. William H. Townsend, *Abraham Lincoln, Defendant* (1923) is a full account of this case.

40. Randall, *Mary Lincoln,* 294–95, 309–11; Donald, *Lincoln,* 324–25; Baker, *Mary Todd Lincoln,* 222–23, Mary Lincoln quoted on 223.

41. "Benjamin Hardin Helm," in Kleber, *Kentucky Encyclopedia,* 421; Lincoln to Cameron, April 16, 1861, *Collected Works,* 4:335; Lincoln to Mary Todd Lincoln, September 24, 1863, *Collected Works,* 6:478; William C. Davis, *The Orphan Brigade: The Kentucky Confederates Who Couldn't Go Home* (1980), 34–35, 191–92; R. Gerald McMurtry, *Ben Hardin Helm, "Rebel" Brother-in-Law of Abraham Lincoln* (1943), is the most complete account of Helm. Lincoln quoted in Randall, *Mary Lincoln,* 328.

42. Baker, *Mary Todd Lincoln,* 223–26, Lincoln to perplexed officers quoted on 223; Helm, *Mary, Wife of Lincoln,* 221–27; Randall, *Mary Lincoln,* 330–36, 343–45, Sickles quoted on 334–35, Tad Lincoln quoted on 335, Emelie Helm quoted on 345–46; Lincoln, "Amnesty to Emily T. Helm," December 14, 1863; "Oath of Emily T. Helm," December 14, 1863; "Pass for Mrs. Emily T. Helm," December 14, 1863, all in *Collected Works,* 7:63–64; Lincoln to Burbridge, August 8, 1864, *Collected Works,* 7:484–85; Townsend, *Lincoln and the Bluegrass,* 313–14, 332–33, Levi Todd quoted on 330.

43. Randall, *Mary Lincoln,* 343–45; Baker, *Mary Todd Lincoln,* 226; Townsend, *Lincoln and the Bluegrass,* 314–19.

13. Lincoln, Slavery, and Kentucky

1. James M. McPherson, *Abraham Lincoln and the Second American Revolution* (1991), 29–37, quotation on page 34; Donald, *Lincoln,* 541, 633–34 n; Philip S. Foner, *Frederick Douglass* (1964), 241; Oates, *With Malice toward None,* 187, 357; Waldo W. Braden, ed., *Building the Myth: Selected Speeches Memorializing Abraham Lincoln* (1990), 99, 102.

2. Lincoln to Greeley, August 22, 1862, *Collected Works,* 5:388–89. Greeley's "Prayer of Twenty Millions" appeared in the *New York Tribune* of August 20. He replied to Lincoln's letter on August 25.

3. Oates, *With Malice toward None,* 310–12; Donald, *Lincoln,* 364–69.

4. Victor B. Howard, "Lincoln Slave Policy in Kentucky: A Study of Pragmatic Strategy," *Register* 80 (summer 1982): 281–308, is a fine analysis of Lincoln's policy toward Kentucky slavery. See also his *Black Liberation in Kentucky: Emancipation and Freedom, 1862–1884* (1983).

5. Lincoln's First Inaugural Address, March 4, 1861, *Collected Works,*

4:263. "William Mobley Report," July 1861, American Missionary Association Archives; Howard, "Lincoln Slave Policy in Kentucky," 284–85.

6. *Louisville Journal,* September 3, 1861; E.T. Bainbridge to Joseph Holt, September 10, 1861, in Coulter, *Civil War and Readjustment,* 111–12; *Louisville Courier,* September 2, 1861; Joshua Speed to Lincoln, September 1, 3, 1861, Robert Todd Lincoln Papers; James Speed to Lincoln, September 3, 1861, Robert Todd Lincoln Papers; Howard, "Lincoln Slave Policy in Kentucky," 287–89. Editor Walter N. Haldeman of the *Louisville Courier* fled to avoid arrest when Kentucky's neutrality ended. He published the *Courier* in Nashville (although a few issues carried a Bowling Green dateline) until the Confederates evacuated that city in February 1862. Haldeman reestablished the *Courier* in Louisville after the war, and in 1868 he engineered the merger of newspapers that resulted in the *Louisville Courier-Journal.* Dennis Cusick, "Walter Newman Haldeman," in Kleber, *Kentucky Encyclopedia,* 398.

7. "Fremont Proclamation," August 30, 1861, *OR,* ser. 1, 3:466–67; Lincoln to Fremont, September 2, 1861, *Collected Works,* 4:506–7.

8. Fremont to Lincoln, September 8, 1861, Robert Todd Lincoln Papers; Lincoln to Mrs. Jessica Benton Fremont, September 10, 1861, *Collected Works,* 4:515; Lincoln's refusal quoted in Donald, *Lincoln,* 315; Lincoln to Fremont, September 11, 1861, *Collected Works,* 4:517–18; Lincoln to Mrs. Fremont, September 12, 1861, *Collected Works,* 4:519; Christopher Phillips, "John Charles Fremont," in Hubbell and Geary, *Biographical Dictionary of the Union,* 187; Lincoln, "Annual Message to Congress," December 3, 1861, *Collected Works,* 5:48–49; "Drafts of a Bill for Compensated Emancipation in Delaware," November 26[?], 1861, *Collected Works,* 5:29–31; Howard, "Lincoln Slave Policy in Kentucky," 294–95.

9. Lincoln, "Message to Congress," March 6, 1862, *Collected Works,* 5:145–46; Lincoln to James A. McDougall, March 14, 1862, *Collected Works,* 5:160–61. McDougall was a Democratic senator from California.

10. *Covington Journal,* March 15, 1862; *Louisville Daily Democrat,* March 15, 1862; *Covington Journal,* March 22, 1862; *Frankfort Weekly Yeoman,* March 28, 1862; *Louisville Daily Democrat,* n.d., quoted in *Daily Nashville Patriot,* December 14, 1861.

11. Lunsford Yandell Jr. to Sally Yandell and his father, April 22, 1861, Yandell Papers, Filson Club, Louisville, Kentucky; Browder diaries, July 23, 1862; December 25, 1862; December 11, 1863, in Troutman, *The Heavens Are Weeping,* 119, 141, 171; Alfred Pirtle to his sister, August 3, September 8, 1863, Pirtle Papers, Filson Club; Benjamin Jones to Lemuel Jones, March 9, 1864, Miscellaneous Civil War Letters, Filson Club.

12. *Congressional Globe,* 37th Cong., 2d sess., March 10, 1862, 1150; March 11, 1862, 1172–73; March 24, 1862, 1333; March 26, 1862, 1371–75; April 2, 1862, 1496.

13. Collins and Collins, *History of Kentucky*, 1:102; Howard, "Lincoln Slave Policy in Kentucky," 296 n; John Hope Franklin, *The Emancipation Proclamation* (1962), 19–20; Donald, *Lincoln*, 364–65, 380, Lincoln quoted on 365.

14. Lincoln, "Appeal to Border States Representatives to Favor Compensated Emancipation," July 12, 1862, *Collected Works*, 5:317–19.

15. Ibid., 319 n.

16. Howard, "Lincoln Slave Policy in Kentucky," 297–98.

17. B.F. Buckner to Helen M. Martin, November 5, 1862, Buckner Collection, Special Collections, Univ. of Kentucky; *Frankfort Tri-Weekly Commonwealth*, November 19, 1862; *Louisville Daily Democrat*, February 11, 1864.

18. Utley to Lincoln, November 17, 1862, Robert Todd Lincoln Papers; Townsend, *Lincoln and the Bluegrass*, 299–304.

19. Utley to Alexander W. Randall, November 17, 1862, Robert Todd Lincoln Papers; Robertson to Lincoln, November 19, 1862, Robert Todd Lincoln Papers; Lincoln to Robertson, November 20 (not sent), 26, 1862, *Collected Works*, 5:502–3, 512–14; Robertson to Lincoln, December 1, 1862, Robert Todd Lincoln Papers. Lucas, *Blacks in Kentucky*, 147–50, discusses the problem of blacks fleeing to Union military lines. Howard, "Lincoln Slave Policy in Kentucky," 300 n, mentions two other cases that attracted considerable attention in the state.

20. Collins and Collins, *History of Kentucky*, 1:128, 129; Lucas, *Blacks in Kentucky*, 147–50; Coulter, *Civil War and Readjustment*, 156–58.

21. Donald, *Lincoln*, 429–31, Lincoln's Mississippi quotation is on page 431; Howard C. Westwood, "Lincoln's Position on Black Enlistments," *Lincoln Herald* 86 (summer 1984): 101–12.

22. Coulter, *Civil War and Readjustment*, 197–204, Bramlette quoted on 198; Lucas, *Blacks in Kentucky*, 151–58; *Louisville Journal*, January 19, 1864.

23. See chap 11., the paragraphs relating to notes 12–17. Lincoln to Stanton, March 28, 1864, *Collected Works*, 7:272; Howard, "Lincoln Slave Policy in Kentucky," 301. An excellent study of the problem is John David Smith, "The Recruitment of Negro Soldiers in Kentucky, 1863–1865," *Register* 72 (October 1974): 364–90.

24. *The Diary of Orville H. Browning*, ed. Theodore Calvin Pease and J.G. Randall, 2 vols. (1925), April 3, 1864, 1:665; Lincoln to Hodges, April 4, 1864, *Collected Works*, 7:281–83.

25. Hodges to Lincoln, April 22, 1864, Robert Todd Lincoln Papers.

26. Lucas, *Blacks in Kentucky*, 152–60; Prentice in *Cincinnati Gazette*, March 6, 1865, quoted in Coulter, *Civil War and Readjustment*, 260.

27. Lucas, *Blacks in Kentucky*, 165–66; John David Smith, "Kentucky Civil War Recruiting; A Medical Profile," *Medical History* 24 (April 1980), 185–96.

28. Lincoln, "Annual Message to Congress," December 1, 1862, *Collected Works*, 5:530–37, amendment proposals quoted on 5:530; Lincoln to John D. Defrees, February 8, 1864, *Collected Works*, 7:172–73 n; "Reply to Committee Notifying Lincoln of His Renomination," June 9, 1864, *Collected Works*, 7:380–83; Oates, *With Malice toward None*, 388–89; Collins and Collins, *History of Kentucky*, 1:154–55, Judiciary Committee minority report quoted on 1:155; Coulter, *Civil War and Readjustment*, 259–60; *Congressional Globe*, 38th Cong., 2d sess., January 31, 1865, 523–31; "Bramlette Message to the General Assembly," *Senate Journal*, February 7, 1865: 274–77.

29. Collins and Collins, *History of Kentucky*, 1:154–55; Coulter, *Civil War and Readjustment*, 260–61; "Bramlette Message," March 1, 1865.

30. Prentice quoted in *Cincinnati Gazette*, February 11, 6, 1865. In 1976 the General Assembly, admitting that "this Bicentennial year is an appropriate time to erase the shadow on Kentucky's history," ratified the Thirteenth, Fourteenth, and Fifteenth Amendments to the federal Constitution. Coulter, *Civil War and Readjustment*, 260–62; Harrison and Klotter, *A New History*, 180 n.

31. Lincoln, "To the Senate and House of Representatives," February 5, 1865, *Collected Works*, 8:260–61; Donald, *Lincoln*, 560–61.

32. Donald, *Lincoln*, 576–79.

Bibliographical Essay

Of the many Lincoln biographies, the best one-volume study is David Herbert Donald, *Lincoln* (1995). Extensively researched and clearly written by a longtime Lincoln scholar, it should be the standard account for years to come. Other good modern one-volume biographies are Benjamin P. Thomas, *Abraham Lincoln, A Biography* (1952), Stephen B. Oates, *With Malice toward None: The Life of Abraham Lincoln* (1977), and Reinhard H. Luthin, *The Real Abraham Lincoln* (1960). Among the multivolume biographies, two important ones were published before the twentieth century. John G. Nicolay and John Hay, Lincoln's devoted secretaries, published *Abraham Lincoln: A History*, 10 vols. (1890). William H. Herndon, Lincoln's last law partner, collected materials assiduously and had the advantage of having worked closely with Lincoln before 1861. The result was William H. Herndon and Jesse W. Weik, *Herndon's Lincoln: The True Story of a Great Life*, 3 vols. (1889). All later studies have drawn heavily upon these two works. Ward H. Lamon, *Life of Abraham Lincoln: From His Birth to His Inauguration as President* (1872), was one of the first important biographies. It relied heavily on Herndon's collection of sources and was ghost-written by Chaunley F. Black. Ida Tarbell, *The Life of Abraham Lincoln*, 2 vols. (1900), reads well even after a century. Especially good on the early years is Albert J. Beveridge, *Abraham Lincoln, 1809–1858*, 2 vols. (1928). Most poetic of the biographers is Carl Sandburg, *Abraham Lincoln: The Prairie Years*, 2 vols. (1926) and *Abraham Lincoln: The War Years*, 4 vols. (1939). Sandburg too often accepted legend as fact. J.G. Randall, *Lincoln the President*, 4 vols. (1945–

55) is the fullest account of the presidency. The fourth volume
was completed by Richard N. Current. A good recent history
of the presidency is Phillip S. Paludan, *The Presidency of
Abraham Lincoln* (1994). John C. Waugh, *Reelecting Lincoln: The
Battle for the 1864 Presidency* (1997), tells the story of the campaign that Lincoln thought for a time he would lose. Benjamin
P. Thomas, *Portrait for Posterity: Lincoln and His Biographers*
(1947), is an interesting study of the biographers prior to World
War II. Joseph E. Suppiger did an extended study in the early
1980s for the *Lincoln Herald*. Called "The Intimate Lincoln,"
it ran for twelve issues, from "The Boy," 83 (spring 1981), to
"The Sixteenth President, 1864–1865," 85 (winter 1983).

Anyone studying Lincoln will find Mark E. Neeley Jr., *The
Abraham Lincoln Encyclopedia* (1982), invaluable, and Earl S.
Miers and others, *Lincoln Day by Day: A Chronology, 1809–
1865*, 3 vols. (1960), answers many questions. Merrill D.
Petersen, *Lincoln in American Memory* (1994), is a fine account
of the ways Americans have viewed Lincoln. It also discusses
the ways in which some of his biographers have viewed their
subject. James M. McPherson, *Abraham Lincoln and the Second
American Revolution* (1991), is an important study of the
president's revolutionary accomplishments. Helpful for an over-
all view of events during the last eighteen years of Lincoln's life
is Allan Nevins, *The Ordeal of the Union*, 4 vols. (1947–50) and
War for the Union, 4 vols. (1958–71). John E. Kleber, ed., *The
Kentucky Encyclopedia* (1992), is an indispensable reference for
anyone doing work on Kentucky.

Jay Monaghan, *Lincoln Bibliography, 1839–1939*, 2 vols.
(1943), cited 3,958 books and pamphlets on Lincoln. As of July
1998 the Library of Congress listed 4,199 books about him,
while acknowledging that the list is not complete. Richard
Booker, *Abraham Lincoln in Periodical Literature, 1860–1940*
(1941), is still helpful although badly dated. Since April 1929
Lincoln Lore, published by the Lincoln National Life Insurance
Company, Fort Wayne, Indiana, has published thousands of
short articles about many aspects of Lincoln's life and career.
Longer articles appear in such specialized publications as the

Lincoln Herald (1898–) and the *Journal of the Abraham Lincoln Association* (1979–). Occasional articles on Lincoln have appeared in numerous periodicals. Especially important for his Kentucky connections are the *Register of the Kentucky Historical Society* (1903–) and the *Filson Club History Quarterly* (1926–).

Students of Lincoln are not overwhelmed by the mass of manuscripts generated by such other presidents as Thomas Jefferson and Woodrow Wilson. Roy P. Basler and others edited *The Collected Works of Abraham Lincoln,* 8 vols. (1953). An index was added in 1955 and two supplementary volumes in 1974 and 1990 as other Lincoln papers surfaced. David H. Donald evaluated the first volumes in the *American Historical Review* 59 (October 1954): 142–49. The copious notes provide a wealth of information and often quote extensively from Lincoln's correspondents. Largely unpublished are the Lincoln Papers in the Library of Congress, often referred to as the Robert Todd Lincoln Collection of Abraham Lincoln Papers. David C. Mearns described this collection, which was closed until 1947, and edited a sampling of its contents prior to July 4, 1861, in *The Lincoln Papers,* 2 vols. (1948). Available on ninety-seven reels of microfilm, the Robert Todd Lincoln Collection was especially important for this study because it includes most of President Lincoln's incoming letters, including a number from Kentuckians. Another valuable but smaller collection in the Library of Congress is the Herndon-Weik Collection. Consisting mainly of the materials Herndon collected for his proposed biography, it is available on fifteen reels of microfilm.

A number of other manuscript collections, identified in the notes, have been used to show the attitudes of Kentuckians toward Lincoln. A great deal of information about the war and conditions in Kentucky is found in *The War of the Rebellion: A Compilation of the Official Records of the Union and Confederate Armies,* 128 vols. (1880–1901). Some thirty volumes contain Kentucky materials. Robert Underwood Johnson and Clarence Clough Buel, eds., *Battles and Leaders of the Civil War,* 4 vols.

(1887, 1956), have considerable Kentucky information, especially in volumes 1 and 3. Also helpful is Frank Moore, ed., *The Rebellion Record: A Diary of American Events . . .* , 11 vols. (1861–69). The "Annals of Kentucky" in Lewis Collins and Richard H. Collins, *History of Kentucky,* 2 vols, (1874), is a fascinating mass of undigested facts. Especially useful are the ones for the Civil War years. Also useful are the *Journals* for the Kentucky House and Senate. Although they do not report debates, the *Journals* included the messages of the governors and trace the progress of bills and resolutions.

As a result of the Kentucky Newspaper Project, which amassed all known state newspapers and put them on microfilm, the best collection of Kentucky newspapers is in Special Collections of the University of Kentucky, although most major libraries in the state have at least some papers of the war period. Willard Rouse Jillson, *Lincoln Back Home* (1932), contains a number of accounts from state papers from 1860 through 1865. David L. Porter found little support for Lincoln in his examination of "The Kentucky Press and the Election of 1860," *FCHQ* 46 (January 1972): 49–52.

Despite its age, the best study of economic and political conditions in Kentucky during the Civil War is E. Merton Coulter, *The Civil War and Readjustment in Kentucky* (1926, 1966). It was ably critiqued by John David Smith, "E. Merton Coulter, the 'Dunning School,' and *The Civil War and Readjustment in Kentucky,"* *Register* 86 (winter 1988): 52–69. Coulter almost ignored the military aspects of the war. An introduction to the war in the state is Lowell H. Harrison, *The Civil War in Kentucky* (1975, 1988), but it was restricted in scope by the format of the *Bicentennial Bookshelf,* of which it was a part. A selected Civil War bibliography is found in Harrison and James C. Klotter, *A New History of Kentucky* (1997), 476–78. General accounts of some of the major campaigns in Kentucky are given in Thomas Lawrence Connelly, *Army of the Heartland: The Army of Tennessee, 1861–1862* (1967), and James L. McDonough, *War in Kentucky: From Shiloh to Perrysville* (1994). The highly partisan Thomas Speed, *The Union Cause in Ken-*

tucky, 1860–1865 (1907), should be balanced with J. Stoddard Johnston, *Kentucky,* vol. 9 of Clement A. Evans, ed., *Confederate Military History* (1899). The state's major battles have all received individual studies. Forts Henry and Donelson were south of the Kentucky border, but their surrender forced the Confederates to withdraw from the state in early 1862. Benjamin Franklin Cooling, *Forts Henry and Donelson: The Key to the Confederate Heartland* (1987), is a detailed study of that campaign. Cooling's *Fort Donelson's Legacy: War and Society in Kentucky and Tennessee, 1862–1863* (1997) describes life in Kentucky under wartime conditions. Raymond E. Myers, *The Zollie Tree* (1964, 1998), describes the first major battle of the war in Kentucky at Mill Springs. Lowell H. Harrison, "'Should I Surrender?': A Civil War Incident," *FCHQ* 40 (October 1966): 297–306, discusses the unusual Union surrender at Munfordville. The two most important battles during the summer 1862 Confederate invasion of Kentucky are well described in Kenneth A. Hafendorfer, *Perryville: Battle for Kentucky* (1991), and D. Warren Lambert, *When the Ripe Pears Fell: The Battle of Richmond, Kentucky* (1995).

Brief biographies of the generals who were active in Kentucky during the war are available in John T. Hubbell and James W. Geary, eds., *Biographical Dictionary of the Union: Northern Leaders of the Civil War* (1995), and William C. Davis, ed., *The Confederate General,* 6 vols. (1991). Full biographies are available for most of the generals who led troops in the state during the war years. Among the best for the Confederate leaders are Charles P. Roland, *Albert Sidney Johnston: Soldier of Three Republics* (1964); William Preston Johnston, *The Life of General Albert Sidney Johnston* (1878); Arndt M. Stickles, *Simon Bolivar Buckner: Borderland Knight* (1940); William C. Davis, *Breckinridge: Statesman, Soldier, Symbol* (1974); Frank H. Heck, *Proud Kentuckian: John C. Breckinridge, 1821–1875* (1976); Grady C. McWhiney, *Braxton Bragg and Confederate Defeat* (1969); Don C. Seitz, *Braxton Bragg, General of the Confederacy* (1924); Joseph H. Parks, *General E. Kirby Smith, C.S.A.* (1954); James A. Ramage, *Rebel Raider: The Life of John Hunt Morgan*

(1986); and R. Gerald McMurtry, *Ben Hardin Helm, "Rebel" Brother-in-Law of Abraham Lincoln* (1943).

President Lincoln had to deal more directly with the Union generals who were involved in Kentucky. James Barnet Fry, *Operations of the Army under Buell from June 10th to October 30th, 1862, and the "Buell Commission"* (1884), is a detailed account of this unfortunate general's 1862 campaign and the testimony before the commission that studied his leadership. A more modern study is James Robert Chumney Jr., "Don Carlos Buell, Gentleman General," Ph.D. diss., Rice Univ., 1964. Other Union biographies include William Marvel, *Burnside* (1991); William T. Sherman, *Memoirs of General William T. Sherman* (1875, 1997); Lloyd Lewis, *Sherman, Fighting Prophet* (1932); John F. Marszalek, *Sherman: A Soldier's Passion for Order* (1993); Freeman Cleaves, *Rock of Chickamauga: The Life of General George H. Thomas* (1948); Francis F. McKinney, *Education in Violence: The Life of George H. Thomas and the History of the Army of the Cumberland* (1961); and John M. Palmer, *Personal Recollections of John M. Palmer: The Story of an Earnest Life* (1901).

Among the many articles that have been written about the Civil War in Kentucky, these are of particular interest: Daniel Stevenson, "General Nelson, Kentucky, and the Lincoln Guns," *Magazine of American History* 10 (August 1883): 115–39; Hambleton Tapp, "Incidents in the Life of Frank Wolford, Colonel of the First Kentucky Union Cavalry," *FCHQ* 10 (April 1936): 82–100; Hambleton Tapp, "Robert J. Breckinridge during the Civil War," *FCHQ* 11 (April 1937): 120–44; Louis DeFalaise, "Gen. Stephen Gano Burbridge's Command in Kentucky," *Register* 69 (April 1971): 101–27; and Lon Carter Barton, "The Reign of Terror in Graves County," *Register* 46 (April 1948): 484–95.

Lincoln's problems in finding generals who would fight as he wanted them to do have been carefully studied in Kenneth P. Williams, *Lincoln Finds a General*, 5 vols. (1949–59), and T. Harry Williams, *Lincoln and His Generals*, 2 vols. (1952).

Much has been written about Lincoln's views on slavery and his efforts to end it. A good brief introduction is Robert W.

Bibliographical Essay

Johannsen, *Lincoln, the South, and Slavery: The Political Dimension* (1991). All the full biographies deal with slavery in some detail. A useful guide to slavery and antislavery issues in Kentucky is Marion B. Lucas, *A History of Blacks in Kentucky: From Slavery to Segregation, 1760–1891* (1992). His is the best account of slavery in Kentucky, but see also J. Winston Coleman Jr., *Slavery Times in Kentucky* (1940). The state opposition to slavery is discussed in Lowell H. Harrison, *The Antislavery Movement in Kentucky* (1978), and Victor B. Howard, *Black Liberation in Kentucky: Emancipation and Freedom, 1862–1884* (1983). As the title indicates, slavery during the Civil War in Kentucky received detailed attention from William H. Townsend, *Lincoln and the Bluegrass: Slavery and the Civil War in Kentucky* (1955, 1988). Cassius M. Clay exaggerated his antislavery role in his *Life of Cassius Marcellus Clay: Memoirs, Writings, and Speeches* (1886). He received scholarly treatment in David L. Smiley, *Lion of White Hall: The Life of Cassius M. Clay* (1962), and H. Edward Richardson, *Cassius Marcellus Clay: Firebrand of Freedom* (1976). The unusual C.M. Clay–John G. Fee relationship is examined in Richard Sears, *The Kentucky Abolitionists in the Midst of Slavery, 1854–1864: Exiles for Freedom* (1993). Smiley showed Lincoln's skill in dealing with a difficult problem in "Abraham Lincoln deals with Cassius M. Clay," *Lincoln Herald* 55 (winter 1953): 15–23. Lowell H. Harrison examined Lincoln's failure to secure voluntary emancipation in Kentucky in "Lincoln and Compensated Emancipation in Kentucky," *Lincoln Herald* 84 (spring 1982): 11–17. George M. Fredrickson analyzed Lincoln's racial attitudes in "A Man but Not a Brother: Abraham Lincoln and Racial Equality," *Journal of Southern History* 41 (February 1975): 39–58. Michael Vorenberg, "Abraham Lincoln and the Politics of Black Colonization," *Journal of the Abraham Lincoln Association* 14 (summer 1993): 23–45, explains why Lincoln clung so long to the idea of colonization. The controversial issue of using black soldiers is examined in John W. Blassingame, "The Recruitment of Colored Troops in Kentucky, Maryland and Missouri, 1863–1865," *Historian* 29 (August 1967): 533–45, and

John David Smith, "The Recruitment of Negro Soldiers in Kentucky, 1863–1865," *Register* 72 (October 1974): 364–90.

All biographies deal with Lincoln's family to some degree, but a good comprehensive account is Louis A. Warren, *Lincoln's Parentage and Childhood* (1926). The Beveridge study, cited above, is also good on Lincoln's early years but is unfair to Thomas Lincoln and the Hanks family. Louis A. Warren, "Abraham Lincoln, Senior, Grandfather of the President," *FCHQ* 5 (July 1931): 136–52, reveals a prosperous ancestor. The troubled relationship between Lincoln and his father is carefully studied in John Y. Simon, *House Divided: Lincoln and His Father* (1987). The best studies of Mary Todd Lincoln are Jean H. Baker, *Mary Todd Lincoln* (1987), Ruth Painter Randall, *Mary Lincoln: Biography of a Marriage* (1953), and Justin G. Turner and Linda Levitt Turner, *Mary Todd Lincoln: Her Life and Letters* (1987). Also useful are Katherine Helm (a niece of Mary Todd Lincoln), *True Story of Mary, Wife of Lincoln* (1928), and William E. Barton, *The Women Lincoln Loved* (1927). C.W. Hackensmith, "Family Background and Education of Mary Todd," *Register* 69 (July 1971): 187–96 is good on her early years, as is William H. Townsend, *Lincoln and His Wife's Home Town* (1929), and its revision, *Lincoln and the Bluegrass: Slavery and Civil War in Kentucky (1955, 1988)*. Douglas L. Wilson has carefully studied Lincoln's love for Ann Rutledge and his broken engagement with Mary Todd in "Abraham Lincoln, Ann Rutledge, and the Evidence of Herndon's Informants," *Civil War History* 36 (December 1990): 301–24, and "Abraham Lincoln and 'That Fatal First of January,'" *Civil War History* 38 (June 1992): 101–30. His *Honor's Voice: The Transformation of Abraham Lincoln* (1998) is a perceptive study of what he concludes were the most important years in Lincoln's amazing development. Don E. Fehrenbacher and Virginia Fehrenbacher, comps., *Recollected Words of Abraham Lincoln* (1996), confirms Wilson's acceptance of the Ann Rutledge romance.

Lincoln's limited schooling is described in C.W. Hackensmith, "Lincoln's Family and His Teachers, *Register* 67 (October 1969): 317–34, and in a number of short items in *Lincoln Lore*.

Lincoln's one political speech in Kentucky is described in George B. Simpson, "Abe Lincoln's 1840 Kentucky Political Speech and the Whig Presidential Campaign of 1840 in Southern Illinois," 1989 typescript in the Kentucky Library, Western Kentucky University, and in Louis A. Warren, "Lincoln Stumps Kentucky," *Register* 27 (May 1929): 545–47.

Samples of Lincoln's humor, often self-depreciative, may be found in Anthony Gross, *Lincoln's Own Stories* (1912, 1994); James C. Humes, ed. *Wit & Wisdom of Abraham Lincoln* (1996); and Keith W. Jennison, *The Humorous Mr. Lincoln* (1965).

J.T. Dorris made intensive studies of Lincoln's attitude toward those who opposed him and his union policies. His conclusions appear as "President Lincoln's Clemency," *Lincoln Herald* 55 (spring 1953): 2–12; "President Lincoln's Treatment of Kentuckians," *FCHQ* 28 (January 1954): 3–20; "President Lincoln's Treatment of Confederates," *FCHQ* 33 (April 1959): 139–60; and his standard study, *Pardon and Amnesty under Lincoln and Johnson* (1953).

As an adult Lincoln had contacts with a number of Kentuckians whose lives have been recorded. Robert V. Remini, *Henry Clay: Statesman for the Union* (1991), is the most complete biography of Lincoln's political idol; George R. Poage, *Clay and the Whig Party* (1936), discusses the principles that so appealed to Lincoln. *The Papers of Henry Clay*, 11 vols. (1959–92), were ably edited by James F. Hopkins, Mary W.M. Hargreaves, Robert Seager III, Melba Porter Hay, and others. Albert D. Kirwan, *John J. Crittenden: The Struggle for the Union* (1962), is the best biography of the man who tried to find last-minute compromises to prevent the war, but also useful is the work by his daughter, Mrs. Chapman Coleman, *The Life of John J. Crittenden*, 2 vols. (1871, 1970). Robert J. Breckinridge still lacks a biography, probably because he lived so long and was so much involved in different fields. His wartime activities are discussed in James C. Klotter, *The Breckinridges of Kentucky* (1986); Hambleton Tapp, "Robert J. Breckinridge during the Civil War," *FCHQ* 11 (April 1937): 120–44; and Ruth Eleanor Kelley, "Robert Jefferson Breckinridge: His Political Influence and Leadership during 1849 and the Civil War," master's thesis, Univ. of Kentucky, 1948. Especially helpful is Robert L. Kincaid, "Joshua Fry Speed, 1814–1882: Abraham Lincoln's Most Intimate Friend," *FCHQ* 17 (April 1943): 63–123. Betty Carolyn Congleton, "George D. Prentice: Nineteenth Century Southern Editor," *Register* 65 (April 1967): 94–119, contains considerable information on the editor's relationship with Lincoln and his influence in Kentucky. Most of Lincoln's contacts with Governor Magoffin occurred in 1860–62, and they were usually acrimonious. They are related in Michael T. Dues, "Governor Beriah Magoffin of Kentucky," *FCHQ* 40 (January 1966): 22–28, and Lowell H. Harrison, "Governor Magoffin and the Secession Crisis," *Register* 72 (April 1974): 91–110. Louis A. Warren, "Lincoln's Contacts with Kentuckians," *Kentucky School Journal* 9 (February 1931): 32–33, only suggests the scope of such contacts.

Lincoln won support for his two major objectives—preserving the Union and ending slavery—in part by accepting the goals of other Republican leaders. The resulting program was almost revolutionary. It is well described in Leonard P. Curry, *Blueprint for Modern America: Non-Military Legislation of the First Civil War Congress* (1968), and Heather Cox Richardson, *The Greatest Nation of the Earth: Republican Economic Policies during the Civil War* (1997).

Lincoln's tragic death has received coverage in all the general biographies and in a number of specialized studies. Among the more interesting of the latter are Jim Bishop, *The Day Lincoln Was Shot* (1955); Ralph Borreson, *When Lincoln Died* (1965); and W. Emerson Reck, *A. Lincoln: His Last 24 Hours* (1987). Timothy S. Good presented eye-witness accounts by persons who were in Ford's Theatre that fateful evening in *We Saw Lincoln Shot: One Hundred Eye Witness Accounts* (1995). One account was taken as late as 1954!

The notes will direct interested readers to other sources not cited here, but they represent only a fraction of the sources that were consulted.

Index

Index